Eat (Less) Pray (More) Love (Christ)

Eat (Less) Pray (More) Love (Christ)

Reflections from an Orthodox Prodigal

EIRENÉ ARCHOLEKAS

RESOURCE *Publications* • Eugene, Oregon

EAT (LESS) PRAY (MORE) LOVE (CHRIST)
Reflections from an Orthodox Prodigal

Resource Publications
An Imprint of Wipf and Stock Publishers
199 W. 8th Ave., Suite 3
Eugene, OR 97401

www.wipfandstock.com

PAPERBACK ISBN: 978-1-6667-5261-8
HARDCOVER ISBN: 978-1-6667-5262-5
EBOOK ISBN: 978-1-6667-5263-2

Contents

Prologue

I AM WRITING THIS vain attempt at a spiritual memoir under the shadow of the COVID-19 pandemic. The dark face of the virus, like some medieval plague doctor costume with a menacing crow, is staring from the other side of the pane. The pandemic has pushed me into writing this with the urgency one gets from a death sentence, "You have two more months to live." If I only have these next two months to live, so help me God, this is the one book I would need to write. The fear of death spurs the creation of art. The need for transcendence transforms the mundane and quotidian into sublime carriages of the eternal.

For decades, I have been deluding myself with the idea that I am an artist and a writer. But I have conveniently made it impossible for me to write. I have worked two jobs, raised two daughters as a single mom, run around like a chicken without a head, managing the minutia of duties, errands, scratching off TO-DO lists. I have lived the life of a harried housewife/working woman in the most stressful city in the US—NYC. Yet the thing that is the most necessary—to pray, to be in stillness, to write—I have avoided like some plague. But now, the plague has found me, and the world entire. I have no more excuses. Schools are closed; I am working from home without the madness of morning traffic. I have escaped the city to the serenity of the woods in upstate NY close to the monasteries of Jordanville, the Holy Myrrh-bearers, and Holy Veil of our Lord. For the first time in my life, I have the time and the stillness to write.

But beyond the physical stillness, I have arrived at the spiritual stillness now in my late 40s to be able to plomb the depths of my soul with a steady hand. I have always been convinced that an artist's life is linked with his or her spiritual life. To produce works of beauty, redemption, and healing requires Grace. One cannot create in a state of disarray, distraction, and disillusion. As St Isaac the Syrian has said, "Just as the dolphin stirs and swims about when the visible sea is still and calm, so also, when the sea of the heart is tranquil and still from wrath and anger, mysteries and divine revelations are stirred in her at all times to delight her."[1] I believe I have managed just *a little bit* to become more Christ-centered; I have started turning away from the visible to the invisible. I have begun to put a prayer rule in practice, to breathe the Jesus Prayer. I am still a wretch and full of passions, but at this point, I have discovered how to prepare the table. More appropriately for me, I have begun to *clear* the table. To declutter all the unnecessary junk that I burden myself with in my attempts to save the world and be this wonder woman, this larger-than-life heroine who accomplishes so much. Well, I am here to let everyone know who dares to read this volume that I am anything but. As you will discover from the sad unfolding of the events and insights from my sinful life, I am a wretch, writhing with infernal passions that have threatened to drive me into the abyss.

As I am truly afraid that I might die before I can receive confession, I am writing this memoir to serve as an actual confession, to serve as an apologia *pro vita sua* of sorts. But unlike the other spiritual memoirs you might have read, like the one from whose title I have borrowed, this confession bows under the *epitrachelion* of Orthodox Christianity. I have attempted to write my life as a case study for how the truth of Orthodoxy in its keen insight into the movements of the soul shows through an everyday person's struggle. Another difference—it is told from a woman living in the 21st century. The struggles may be a bit different from those experienced in the Middle Ages and from a gender that is foreign to the patristic tradition. Far from the "chic lit" but far also from the gravity of the writings of women mystics, this spiritual memoir is told in the candid style of a modern woman who has struggled to find meaning through her search for God and all the twisted and crooked paths that search has taken.

The memoir is presented as collage—a post-modern form—that stitches together journal entries, meditative essays, prayers set as poems, excerpts from the Desert Mothers and Fathers, and saint's lives, held up on a clothesline of narrative plot that traces the life of this sinful woman. It also tells the tale of trauma. They say to pass to heaven you must first bathe in the River of Forgetfulness. This is so that every trauma, every painful memory can be erased so it will not ruin the joy that awaits you

1. St Isaac the Syrian, *Ascetical Homilies*, 204.

on the other side. You can't ever be happy till you forget the misery of your earthly existence. Paradoxically, it is by remembering the pain that you can finally get rid of it. This confession is my attempt to erase the sorrow of my childhood. The written pages become my river of Lethe. Researchers have shown that trauma wrenches deep within the psyche, so deep that it wreathes into the building blocks of its very DNA, twisting around the double helix like a killer vine, extra tightly. To release it is painful; it's like ripping your guts out, like un-wreathing the sinews of your heart to shape a different beating thing. The patterns imprinted from that primordial phase of our existence throw shadows on our souls that creep so subtly in our subconscious we cannot recognize their workings. The act of writing is itself an act of confession, of calling the dark into the light, and exorcizing it. The act of writing has been for many a way to plomb the abyss, the Ariadne's thread out of the labyrinth. Had I not lived through a childhood of loss and trauma, I would not be here writing about it. I would have become a scientist or researcher. Pain has made me into a poet. My hope is that this testimony stands as a marker for the broken, the lost. It is proof that I have traversed the valley of tears and have lived to tell the tale.

I apologize beforehand if the scenes and events offend you. Sin stinks. But it is the only way to get clean of it—to put it blankly front and dead center for all to look at and be horrified. This is what confession is supposed to do. But take heart, my sin is a reflection of your own. Even if a man lived but one day, the fathers say, he would sin. We sin constantly. Grace and the loving kindness of our Lord forgives our sins and loves us despite them. If I get something wrong theologically, don't hang me, please. I am not a theologian. If I do a sloppy job of translating the Greek or the Slavonic, or some other klutzy thing, don't drop the book. Keep reading because God's truth is written in crooked lines. It is my intention that these crooked lines point you to your own straight and narrow path. This is my petty attempt to express the Truth with a capital T through my personal truth. Lord have mercy on me.

Sunday of the Paralytic
May 10, 2020

SECTION 1

Essays on Hope, Faith, and COVID

Author's daughter lighting a candle in a chapel on the grounds of Holy Protection Monastery, White Haven, PA

Choose Your own Adventure

On the apex of Volcano Pacaya on a mission trip to the Monastery of Holy Trinity-Mambre Lavra, Lake Amatitlan, Guatemala

IT IS THE WEEK before Christmas. The wind chill registers at -5 F. Surprisingly, in the midst of the cold and the darkness, I am happy. Ironically, it is in the thick of the battle with the pure fury of total annihilation that I feel alive. Or maybe it's just the cold.

It is a weird quality of the soul, I guess. It is probably a survival mechanism. Call it hope or resilience or plain stubbornness. Under the weight of real struggle—

- the ever-encroaching possibility that my elderly mother will die of her cancer

- mushroom cloud realization that my daughter will never talk to me again
- the deep-driving fury and resentment at myself for my co-dependency
- the loneliness and disappointment of so-called friends who are non-existent or so engrossed with their own lives to offer any support or so far away to make any relationship moot
- the daily drudgery of dealing with deranged coworkers who do not even say hello because of their masculine superiority /inferiority and the daily exhaustion of dysfunctional teens whose parents explode and scapegoat me for their problems.

Even with the soul-harrowing, knifing despair that maybe there is no reason to life, that the randomness of disaster and the banality of evil exist everywhere, that life is but a passing shadow that offers only a filthy rag to wipe away the blood.

Even with the full knowledge that mankind is a bloodthirsty greedy irrational perverted mass whose only goal is to pivot its own power and needs over others. Even if it's a dog-eat-dog world with only tiny glimpses of beauty. Even with the fear and the trembling and the shit-in-your pants terror that maybe it is all a bunch of atoms tied together and we are nothing but recycled parts, consciousness a mixed blessing and a mere after-effect of a brain with 80 billion nerve cells, even with the coming of the deep dank dark of the grave—even with all that—I can hope against hope that there is meaning to all this.

It is the most strange thing really. Sort of like diving into the pit of Mordor, diving into the abyss, and in the deepest darkest bottom, recovering the ring. You can't be a hero of your own life without plunging into the depths. It is the darkness, the deepest ring of hell that enfolds the gold; it is in the belly of despair that the light shines out. The treasure that takes you aback. The diamond is in the belly of the beast. It is the struggle that gives the meaning to the whole battle, even when on its face it seems meaningless. The struggle to find meaning and keep it is what gives significance to this thing, this whole gory filthy disappointing thing we live with every day.

That thing that keeps you alive in the thick of the battle is faith or hope or resilience. It is the very mechanism for meaning making and it works in mysterious ways. I cannot really describe how it works except through Hollywood examples. Indiana Jones in *Raiders of the Lost Ark* is one. Remember in the climax? He must walk through the chasm to get to the clock. It seems that if he takes a step he will plunge to certain death. He holds his heart against his better logic; he closes his eyes and takes a leap of faith into the abyss. And lo and behold, a foothold appears. He takes another step and whoa! another step revealed. Those stone pinions that provided the steppingstones to his crossing the abyss instead of vaulting into it—*that* is what faith is. And this is not to simplify or reduce the thing to a mere wish-fulfilling fantasy.

Or how about the scene in *Labyrinth* when Sarah is falling through the bottomless well and falling fast. When from the walls of the black well, a thousand white gloved hands ("the helping hands") appear, grab her, and stop her fall. "Which way?" the helping hands ask impolitely. "Up or down? C'mon c'mon, we haven't got all day. Where's your big decision? Which way do you want to go?"[1] She chooses down as that is the way she is pointing anyway. They proceed to pass her limb by limb in the opposite direction until she climbs out of the whole thing. There is something in that scene that speaks to the choice of the human will to decide the path for itself. That perhaps we have more choice in the way our destiny plays out or rather we create our own destiny by the way we choose to write it.

Then again, I remember when I was in 2nd or 3rd grade. There were these series of books titled *Choose Your Own Adventure.* The premise was you would read a chapter and at the end of it, you would have to make a choice. If you chose one way to handle the problem, you would be directed to head to another page, sometimes further, sometimes back, in the book; if you chose a different route, you would be directed to read another. For every chapter, you had to make a choice. The ending of the book depended on the sum of the choices you took to get there.

In some books, the endings were so very far apart that you might wind up dead if you took one course, or alive and happy, if you took another. Faith and the mindful deliberate living of life as if it does have meaning function like the plot mechanisms in the *Choose Your Own Adventure* books. It was the sum total of those choices, one choice led to another and then another, and then another, that creates a life worth living.

Take another metaphorical example: Schrödinger's cat. This is a thought experiment (no cats were harmed in this experiment, not to

1. Henson, *Labyrinth*, 00h 29m 02s.

worry). A cat, a flask of poison, and a radioactive source are placed in a sealed box. If an internal monitor (e.g. Geiger counter) detects radioactivity (i.e. a single atom decaying), the flask is shattered, releasing the poison, which kills the cat. For the cat to stay alive, no radioactivity must be present. Otherwise, it sets off a chain of events that leads to the cat's death.[2] But if there is, then the cat is as good as dead. The conundrum is that the device has a 50 percent chance of killing the cat in an hour. We can't predict the outcome of the experiment without getting involved with it and killing the cat. But how can we tell if the cat is alive or dead without the experiment? Until we open the box, we cannot tell if the cat is one way or another; it can be both states or half-dead/half-alive. The interpretation that quantum mechanics supplies is that after a while, the cat can simultaneously be alive and dead. This is due to superposition, the dual quality of matter to be both wave and particle at once. It does not make logical sense: when one looks in the box, one sees the cat either alive or dead, not both alive and dead. But they are both wrapped up in each other. The choice in how you conduct the experiment creates the outcome: dead cat, living cat. And both outcomes are possible at the same time.

The complex interplay of the gazillions of choices compounded over millennia on the surface can erase the importance of your own personal choice, the iota of will that is yours. It seems as if the game is rigged no matter what card you are dealt. But the way you play your card has a bearing on the game. It swerves the outcome in a twisty-turny domino cascade of events. It is impossible to say that your existence does not matter one way or another; the fact that you are, that you exist, has introduced another vector, another variable, another curve in the way the universe moves. It is hard to know the effect that your not existing would have had on the universe, but the very fact that you exist, has altered the equation forever. That was the point in that classic Christmas flick, *It's a Wonderful Life*. For better or for worse, the unraveling of the events in the universe could not be as they are without the simple fact of your being here.

In contrast to the nihilism and transitory contentment of my contemporaries, I am pinioned with the hope that true faith brings. It is this hope—that my life is not meaningless, not just that it has meaning despite the darkness, death, and worse of all, the abyss, but precisely *because of* the death and darkness and the abyss. It is the very wrestling with

2. Baggot, "Cat That Wouldn't Die."

the dark that weaves the light. I feel like that. A fisher of the depths ungrounding nuggets of gold to bring to the surface. I have more power than I know *because I have the will to change the ending of the story.* I can live to write a happy ending just by the power of my choosing to live it so. That's the meaning behind Christmas; that's the meaning of life itself. The gift box is empty until you put the gift inside.

The power of choice to fabricate meaning, miraculously like pulling yourself up from your bootstraps during a free fall or creating the planks for the bridge between the abyss as you walk it, that gives me hope this Christmas season. I do not think I can separate my idea of hope and resilience from the Person of Christ. For me, He is the Highest Poet, the meaning maker, the *resilienceur* par excellence. And if I believe in the mechanism of the Holy Spirit, I have to give credit where credit is due--- that this thing of feathers called Hope, it must come from that Dove. I can't put my finger on it. But it never ceases to surprise me that in the times I struggle to subdue my passions and stay obedient to the strict fast that as a form of sacrifice and willing submission to the laws of a higher power, that I am rewarded with the buoyancy of faith.

Christ is both the Gift and the Gift-Giver. He chose to enter temporality as a gift and sacrifice for mankind. His choice (and, of course, the choice of Mary, the handmaiden of the Lord who uttered "Thy will be done") allowed for another ending to the story, a triumphantly joyous one to be not only a possibility but an inevitability for those who choose to love and believe in Him.

Christ is born! Glorify Him.

Carpe Diem via Ground Hog Day

Random graffiti on a building in Prague, Czech Republic

In the film, *Ground Hog Day*, the protagonist Bill Murray is an arrogant forecaster who is forced to cover the annual event of Groundhog Day in Punxsutawney, PA, where the citizens await the appearance of Punxsutawney Phil, the groundhog that lets them know whether they will have six more weeks of winter or an early spring. By outward appearances to see Phil on the screen prognosticating the weather with witty remarks thrown in, you would not know what an arrogant s.o.b. he really is. He treats his co-workers with disdain, especially Andy MacDowald, his producer; he is bitter that he is only working at a local TV station as his ambition and grandiosity propel him to seek national news stardom. It is while covering Groundhog Day in the little village of Pennsylvania that a freak snowstorm strands him there. From then, something strange happens. After the first night of the snowstorm, Phil wakes up to the same day in a sort of psychedelic de je vu. He is forced to live the same day repeatedly. No matter what he does he is stuck in Ground Hog Day February 2nd.

Yet, because Phil is doomed to repeat the same day over and over, something happens to him on the inside. He becomes more sensitive to people's reactions; he starts caring about those around him because he knows how the script will go. When he gets himself out of the script, he can come out of himself to care about the homeless man that appears on the corner day after day. Because he is forced to repeat the same day, he realizes that his actions have no real long-term consequences. He has the foreknowledge of what people will say so he starts tailoring his actions to them. Ironically, it is the act of living the same day again and again that makes him get it right. It is the opportunity he gets to change his day on the inside that matters. When he keeps the external circumstances constant, only then does he have the time and focus to look into his soul, his outlook, and his reactions. He eventually falls in love with Rita, his producer, and that itself changes the day for him.

The thesis behind Ground Hog Day is a twist on the *carpe diem* theme. Yes, we have to treasure the day because it is the only one we have. But in our lives, especially if you are like me about to enter middle-agedom, we have lived so many countless days they might as well have collapsed into one long one. All my years have become one long day. It's the same script day in, dayout: get up 6-6:30, get ready, go to work, come back from work, make dinner preparations, help kids with homework, go to bed. My mood, my stance, my general conduct in major lines remain the same day in, day out. The great Sisyphean struggle of living the same day, week after week, year after year, with full knowledge that our destinies won't matter in the great scheme of things; that what we do in our daily lives, even what in our heads might appear as "great," will be of little to no significance with the shifts of time–this is the thesis that this film wears inside out. If you could live the same day every day for the rest of your life (more or less this is what you do), maybe you could be forced to "get it right"; you could be forced to find the beauty and the meaning in its nuanced slopes even in the face of its fleetingness.

Meaning is made by the repetition of meaningless acts. Like that 3rd century monk who spent an entire year making straw baskets; Not counting the ones he could sell in the market, he would proceed to burn in a bonfire when his cave became too cramped to keep them in. He kept at his work, painstakingly threading straw into baskets knowing that in the end they would end in a bonfire of vanities. This is what is required. Like an old strict schoolmaster, life forces us to do the daily drills of verbal declensions to the point of nauseum. This is all you get–puella, puellae, puellum, puella–ad infinitum until you make it meaningful. Boredom and monotony have a purpose–to teach us: the beauty is in the process, not the product. The beauty lies in the caress of the straw strands through the fingers drawn tight over the hubs of the basket; the creasing of the clothes disappearing under the smoky iron's plate; the simmering of the tea cup just at the brink of boiling.

I think God gives us the same day, the same prayer, the same-old same-old to force us to pay attention to it. You cannot learn without a lot of repetition and human beings more than some other mammals (say dolphins or chimps, for example) need much more of it. We are forced into the monotony of everyday existence to savor the day. To have the opportunity like the actors who practice the same script over and over, to get it right. To tweak our lines, to change our tone, to learn something about ourselves and others. The twist on the theme of "seize the day" is not that it will go away and that it is short, but that in the reality of modern life with all its drudgery and mind-numbing sameness, it will be the same day, for the same kind of person, for so many centuries. This day–there is no other–there will be no other type of day either. It's the same slop of Irish oatmeal in the morning. And you will be required to eat it and like it and be grateful for it on top of that too. To appreciate the day for what it is–not what it could have been or could be–or the dream of a day we might have in the future, but to look at the day squarely in the face with all its pimples, pock marks, creases, and say, "Thank you God for this day. It's you again." Look into the wrinkled forehead and dark circles–dealing with the disappointment of not having the day we think we deserve. I didn't have lunch with the blonde starlet but the annoying busybody Mrs. Oakfield down the block. Not so glamorous but is kind and can make a killer corn bread.

And maybe it's not the day itself that matters. It can be the same as it ever was. But what matters is *you*. How you change in relation to it. It was not that Phil's day changed in the movie, but his attitude to it did. This is what we are supposed to do--to become the people we were meant to be in it: patient, kind, caring, responsible, grateful, humble. As Aristotle is believed to have said, "Perfection is the sum of habitual actions practiced every day." May this same boring day be the practice for our spiritual perfection.

Lessons about Sitting Still Or What the PAUSE taught me

Metal gate on a local beauty salon, Crush Studio, during COVID

My flight to Europe was canceled—twice. No flights allowed from the US to Canada. The sweet lady from PA whose house I wanted to rent for two months called and apologized, "So sorry, ma'm. Our governor does not want us to rent to New Yorkers for fear of the pandemic. I have to cancel your reservation." The beautiful resort in Vermont said in order to come I would have to show a negative COVID result, but if I did return to NY, I would most probably have to go through a 14 day at-home quarantine. What's the point? Two weeks shut in for two days of escape?

I am officially on house arrest. For someone with ADD and a concomitant wanderlust, staying put has been anathema. Since the beginning of the lockdown in mid-March, my struggle to stay sane in the same place while still making motions has been akin to Sisyphus pushing up his stone while sitting on it.

OK. So I'll take this time to be more "contemplative." The situation brings up an anecdote from the early Desert Fathers. When a young novice got antsy and ran to Abba Moses asking for permission to go to the city for some shopping or to go get water from the well, Abba Moses famously remarked, "Go, sit in your cell, and your cell will teach you everything." Other Desert fathers coined lines like: "Go, eat, drink, sleep, do no work, only do not leave your cell." Or "Don't pray at all, just stay in your cell." Thomas a Kempis, in *The Imitation of Christ*, famously wrote: "Every time you leave your cell, you come back less a man."[1]

I feel for that novice monk right about now. I would do anything to escape home, what has become a prison cell. I am going to implode and explode at the same time. I do not do well with routine and monotony. It crushes my creativity. Like a cornered rat I am scratching for any way possible to escape. It is an agonizing punishment. It corresponds to a vision of hell, the lone soul separated from God and his fellow creatures. To be in hell is to be in solitary confinement.

What to do now? How many times can you go to the corner grocery? How many times can I check email? How many times can I call the same friends?

Try as I might, what I am scrambling to escape most is myself. With all my insecurities, my hang-ups, my passions. I am sucked into the vortex of memories, roads not taken so that I spiral around the sewer drain of eternal regret and despair. Why did I marry that boy? Why did I not take that opportunity? I shouldn't have moved here, or I should have gone there.

Confinement for such a long period of time summons lots of soul searching in everyone and its corresponding resistance. It reminds me of detention in high school. When you are sitting shiva with yourself, the demons that camouflage in the crevices of full schedules and deep sleep rise up to stare you in the face. You can't escape.

One of my demons is exactly that— my inability to sit still, my inability to just be. Always traveling, always searching, always doing

1. A Kempis, *Imitations of Christ*, 22.

something. I have a lot of potential energy; my mind races. Sitting still is insufferable. But there is nowhere to go, there is nothing to do. Even the garage has been cleaned out and the sock drawers organized. When you switch from operating at 150 mph on any given day to 15, the engine startles.

What to do? What to do? Where to go? My mind spins wheels like a frenetic hamster. I went out of my way to distract myself with tasks and projects until it was useless. I was left to the void. The silence. The nothingness.

I sat with the nothingness long enough to feel the vanity of existence. My guts churned with the soul crushing sadness of my own nothingness. My own mistakes and weaknesses. This tendency to do, to do, to do is a reaction to the overwhelming oppression of silence. The unbearable heaviness of being; a way to fill the void. In the modern world, I have become so used to noise, to chatter, to running around doing this and that, that I do not know how to handle the opposite–the silence, the absence of motion, so much empty space. These things make me depressed. To silence the clutter is to pay attention to the deep nothingness that lies on the fringes of life, that might, *gulp*, be at the center of life itself. It might be that I am so afraid of this existential angst of confronting the void, that I create all kinds of artificial and distracting environments to stray my attention away from it.

What has happened during the PAUSE is all these distractions have been put away. So the dread emerges, that existential dread of nothingness, in those listless blue hours when no one is at home. It attacks me like a wild panther on an open plane with no cover or underbrush to hide in. When I feel exposed and vulnerable, that void which I fear is at the center of life emerges to scare the daylights out of me. Pre-PAUSE I would have filled my world with easy distractions–a money-making career, cell phones, Macy's sale days, cameras, Facebook, contacts, BMWs, socially scripted ways of climbing up the social ladder, a Nobel Prize even, a husband and two kids in a colonial in the suburbs. I would even distract myself with myself.

But no more—Whoosh! All gone. Nothing but me and the void.

And slowly it happened. The nothingness and the sitting still forced me to do battle with my demon-- to perform, to achieve, to do, to do, to do. I surrendered to the silence and the stillness and became silent and still. I sat and sat and sat through the stillness. I could not run away from myself anymore because there I was, there I always was. I was locked in my cell, day after day. Nothing to do and nowhere to go. There you are—here. Deal with it.

In that stillness I heard the susurration of God: "You do not need to be in motion to move mountains. You do not need to accomplish it in order to be validated. You do not need to be needed to exist as a being valued in and of yourself." Sitting still this long by myself had opened up the vistas of self -awareness, as I had been running around so many trees.

I have learned to settle in the stillness. I have learned that just being is not a waste of time. It is the grounding and the centering of self; it serves as the springboard for jettisoning into righteous action. I have slowed down long enough during this enforced confinement to sense the seconds not just the minutes passing by. Sitting still has forced me to become acutely aware of every passing moment. To live in the space of this present time. Not trying to escape it by retreating into the regrets and nostalgias of the past nor by racing to new horizons, plans and fantasies of some untenable future. Sitting in stillness has taught me the law of now, the power of the present. Sitting still is the opposite of wasting your life: it enriches it.

The good that has come out of the "Pause" is the enforced reflection period. So many of us are thrust into the dialectic of meaning/meaninglessness. We have been forced to reevaluate our life's choices and our goals. It has given us space and time to put the meanings in the centerpiece of our lives. When I consider how much fluff and nonsense, the minutiae and non-essentials that take up precious moments of every living day, I could scream. The "Pause" has allowed me to focus on the things that really matter—love, beauty, truth, creativity.

Strangely, I am starting to like the "Pause."

Surrender to the Tsunami

Wading Nymph, watercolor on paper, 2024 by the author

"Purge me with hyssop and I shall be clean.
Wash me and I shall be whiter than snow." Ps 5

WHEN I WAS ABOUT 8, my father, a native of a small Cycladic island and obsessed with the sea, would take me to Jones Beach for swimming lessons. Looking at the wild waves of the Atlantic frothing in fury, I was overwhelmed by dread. In between the lull of one white cap surging and the other, Baba forced me to float, the first step in the swimming process. But I would double up, contort and squeeze my stomach tight, which acted like a deadweight, the complete opposite of what was required to float. I was terrified of drowning—the sensation of heavy water pushing me down to the depths of which I had no control. I struggled within myself to trust the directive of my father—to relax on the water, to open my body like an open palm. The more I focused on my body and my fears of sinking, the less I was able to ride the waves. It was only when I trusted in my Baba's hand, a thick, muscular working man's hand, to a buoy me up underneath the waves; it was only when I let go of my need to control my body and became one with the sea that I was able to allow the ocean to take me where it wanted. I was only able to swim when I surrendered to the sea. Even as the rush of rushing waves returned to assault me again and again.

The Governor of New York has issued a warning that we must be ready for a tsunami. What we have lived up to now will only get worse in the next two weeks. Understandably, I have freaked out. The terror of death confounds me—tightening up every sinew into chicken wire. I have made sure my will is in order. I am scrambling to find a priest to take a virtual confession. Mindful of death in my middle age, now I walk around with the hourglass of sand trickling at its last quarter inch. I believe that every day will be my last. Like a chicken without a head, I shed the virus of fear to my family around me. "Calm down," my daughter says, "You are driving me crazy! Stop freaking out!" "Maybe you should smoke some weed," my brother says. "You are not really a Christian if you are so full of anxiety and not trust. Your religion goes out the window when you face a crisis," my older daughter digs in. "You are a hypocrite."

My normal mode of survival is "flight." To escape my prophesied fate, I rented a small apartment in the upstate NY college town of Oneonta.

I spent the day listening to the life of Saint Mary of Egypt whose memory we commemorate today, the 6th Sunday of Lent, and scrubbing, sweeping, scouring with a potent brew of cocktails of chlorine, Windex, Great Value bathroom cleaner and other disinfectants. The drive through Delaware County was deliciously beautiful. Even though the spring has not ascended yet, the birch trees huddled in their fantastic fractal frenzy against a backdrop of blue sky; cumulus clouds hovering over rolling mountains casting moving shadows over swaths of pine and fir; red barns sentinel against chestnut lines scratching in fine lines the receding majesty of green. It was utterly beautiful, not a soul was on the highway. I spent the day in silence and solitude. These wide-open spaces humble me, allow me to remember that I am nothing, and have little control in the grand scheme of things. This is where I kick myself. It doesn't really matter that I have not accomplished this or that, that I have fallen short of my dreams and grand expectations for myself. Because in the end, it wasn't much in my control anyway. My life has manifested in its own course, and I must accept it for what it is. The anxiety over life comes from our need or rather delusion that we can control it.

Funny, when I do a lot of housework, my mind roams through a backcountry that normally I do not tread, just like the drive through the mountains.

As I scrubbed deep the surfaces of the visible life, eliminating the dirt and grime and this invisible mortal enemy, I was overcome by a bittersweet peace that comes with acceptance. It feels like I am waving goodbye to my life (even though I do not know if I will survive this plague). I am so grateful for it. I have lived a long, rich life. I know many people will lose their lives today and every day after that. However frail the human condition is, we must accept it as it is. We must have the humility to accept that certain things are beyond your control. The younger you are, the more you think you can control the circumstances of your life. The older you get, the more you realize how curtailed they are.

Mopping the old carpet, another thought fluttered through my mind about the gravity of simplicity.

By paying attention to the simple act of cleaning the nooks and crannies of a grease-filled apartment, wiping away dust, bringing cleanliness to what was filthy—it is this simple act that brings meaning. Indeed, the act of cleaning and organizing relegated to women throughout the ages has become a heroic feat in this battle against the virus. What was once devalued and meaningless is elevated into the highest act of courage. The minimum-wage cleaning lady, or the harried unpaid housewife, is more important now than the 5-star decorated general or the high-powered lawyer. The simple acts of the women who have slaved at for millennia, putting things away, ordering and organizing, making sure life is livable—how infinitely powerful and valuable. In the end it's not *what* we do, but *how* we do it that really matters.

With the tsunami coming, the grim reality of hundreds of thousands of deaths imminent, I try to relinquish control. "Wash me thoroughly from my iniquity and my sin, for my sin is ever before me." I am trying to come to peace with my soul and the God in it. They say that prayer is the conscious presence of God in the deep heart, not just words rattled off the lips. Prayer is a condition of the heart. I am praying for this prayerful condition, so I can acquire it before it is my time to go.

I have always tried to escape in my life, never satisfied with what I am doing and where I am standing at the moment. I have been searching and wandering for a utopia that does not exist. I am starting to understand that what I am searching for is not some physical place, but a spiritual space. I think God has given me the wisdom to realize that right here, right now there is beauty, there is light. Heaven and hell can reside on the same pinhead. I am struggling with my fear and anxiety, asking God, to have mercy on my soul, and if it is my time to die, to give me the peace to accept it. That is all we want really, peace, isn't it?

Strange, but this is exactly what the circumstances have been pointing to. This "Pause" allows for the reflection to find our peace. I am going to be alone in this house in the mountains. Away from my family who has refused to follow me. (Sometimes it is our very families that we need to separate from to find our inner peace). I'm going to use this experience of being separated from my family, just my soul and God, to see if I could endure the solitude. In a way this is enforced monasticism.

When I first entered the dilapidated cabin, window screens punched in, storm door rusty not able to open but half way, I shook my head and said, "No I can't do this. I can't live all by myself without anyone. I am going to die all alone in the mountains." And then I entered into the space; in the solitude and silence I could hear God's whisper: "Use this time as an experiment." I will pray more here, I will struggle to be in communion with God more. I can manage the loneliness because I can be at peace with God in my heart. That's all I need—God. St Mary of Egypt kept quarantine for 47 years in the desert. She became saintly because she focused her attention on the Holy.

I will use this time to get closer to God; I will learn slowly to trust in God, really trust, not just when things go right. I will have to struggle with the dead weights of my fears and anxieties. I will have to learn to let go and trust in God, the universe, so I can float along its Will.

This is what we all must do now: surrender to the coming wave, float on the surface of the sea with our Father's hand underwater, even if it is a tsunami.

The Alchemy of Faith: Natural Law vs Divine Providence

Sketch of Saints Anargyri, Aghia Theodoti, Ios, Cyclades, 2025.

It is said that the alchemists of old worked feverishly for their one desire—to transubstantiate normal metal into gold. They wanted to turn something base, common copper or aluminum, into the most perfect of metals—AU. Alchemy, the prototype of chemistry, is science infused with faith. An alchemist takes the ordinary and makes it extraordinary. Setting aside the connections alchemy has had with the dark arts, it is the intermingling of philosophy, perseverance, and knowledge that makes alchemy the art of science. The alchemist's quest is to find just that—the mystery that turns something like urine into phosphorus (apparently that's how the flammable element was discovered, thanks to Hennig Brandt)[1], to take the shit and make it into light. The stuff of the universe, they claimed, is all the same; it's all about transforming it so that in an effort of combination, creation, transfiguration what was once ordinary becomes extraordinary.

This is a fitting metaphor for faith. Is it not a person's deep faith that transforms a dull and ordinary life into a hero story? Is not faith the stuff that can supercede the natural laws of science to defy set chemical processes? The Bible is full of stories that defy natural law: a body dead and decomposing for three days comes to life again, a weighted body floats on the surface of the water, a bushel of five loaves and three fish multiplies to feed thousands, a star appears long enough to act as a GPS for astrologers/astronomers to arrive after a two year's journey to a stable. Yes, there will be those of rational mind who shoo these myths and make them stories for strained hearts. It would seem that the more knowledge of science in the world, the less room for faith, as if the ring of knowledge has corralled the Almighty into a corner of the universe, where curious passersby can drop in and feed a carrot or some corn pellets.

Indeed, in the 21st century, it would seem it is the fool that believes in God against what King David says, "It is the fool that says in his heart there is no God" (Ps 14:1). Nature, the scientist says, is the process of the Almighty. Only man in his vanity believes he can live forever, a pastor's son told me on a lunch break. When every other creature, from amoeba to blue whale is prone to corruption and death, why does man feel he is so special? There is no after life. The stuff of life transforms from conscious to unconscious, from breath to un-breath.

Especially in the present this virus has pitted faith against reason in a most sinister way. The faithful cry that this is a consequence of humanity's apostasy, a plague brought on to punish a wayward nation by the likes of Egypt. The faithful walk by faith. They trust in God's Providence and believe that His divine energies protect their places of worship so that no plagues can enter. They continue with their traditions of kissing icons and taking Holy Communion from a communal cup. It is their faith, they say, that imbues them with life and salvation. They do not fear death because if it is part of God's plan for humanity, so be it. God

1. Hanson, "Hennig Brandt."

surpasses nature. It is an instrument of His will and under His control, not the other way around.

Yet, some pause. I have seen so much schism in congregations pitting those with radical faith against those who chose to follow reason, or at least the state authorities. Monasteries have been shut up. "We have to acknowledge that humans are made of flesh and body," a priest in Pennsylvania explained to me. "We have to protect the body as it is the temple of God and it would be a sin to subject it to disease." Some other churches see congregants taking communion from individual spoons and separate Dixie cups. Those of radical faith tear their clothes and pull their beards saying, "Anathema. Where is your faith?"

So which do we follow? Reasonable caution and respect for the safety of the body or radical faith that God's energies and Providence will protect us as His will is above natural law?

This virus has become the keenest test of faith perhaps since the beginning of Christianity. This virus forces us to look deeply into our faith to see its mettle. Do we believe wholeheartedly, even in the face of clear evidence, that this is a very contagious virus that can kill? Or do we turn lukewarm and abandon our beliefs and sacred practices, the central of which is Holy Communion, and bow to science and common sense?

A recent *NY Times article* brought the issue to a wider audience. It pointed out that criticism has come within the ranks of the Church of Greece as to how it has handled the pandemic, especially for those clerics who have not followed the rules.[2] Those same clerics who defied social distancing orders wound up contracting the virus and dying. Some clerics have called their fellows "criminals" and irresponsible for not urging congregants to stay away. So, how do we broach the clear and present danger of dying from a pandemic with our deeply seated faith that God is above all things natural? It is time for all good Orthodox to examine their souls and for each to come to their own conclusion. This watershed moment will separate the chafe from the wheat—those who believe superficially from those who have a deeper radical faith. It is a polarizing issue.

A case in point is Oberammergau. During the height of the Black Plague, this German village came together and prayed and made a vow with God that if He should deliver them from the plague they would carry on a Passion Play in which all members of the village take part

2. Kitsandonis, "Greek Orthodox Church Faces Criticism."

every ten years. From the legend based on oral history, it seems that not a single villager fell victim to the plague. (The scientific truth is different–the plague followed a natural curve and did not end abruptly.) Every decade from that time in 1634, Oberammergau puts on a play narrating the events in the life of Christ.[3] Ironically, this year 2020 was supposed to be the year of the play. The town decided to postpone it until 2022 when hopefully the virus will have died down. (Does this not break their promise to God in a way? Does their break with this tradition on this very momentous year not belie an apostasy of faith and a couching with scientific reason? Or does it present a reasoned approach to the realities of a pandemic?)

As for myself, I will take part in the Holy Mysteries and take Holy Communion, because that is at the core of my faith. I cannot call myself a Christian and not take the Holy Body and Blood of Christ at the time I most need it because I fear I might die. That would be sacrilege. But I am not going to be irresponsible and foolhardy by going around without a mask and not isolating myself in my everyday life. I do not deny that this is a natural phenomenon with dire consequences; it is common for plagues to hit humanity throughout history. I wear a mask and keep my 6 feet of distance with other faithful in the temple. Yet I do believe in God's Providence and power over nature; if God allows a virus to take thousands, it is His Will. If He wishes to protect others who seek out His mercy, He will. There have been medical miracles and other supernatural events that do defy natural law. The virus will force each person to come to measure the depths of their conviction in their faith. It will force many to examine their deep heart and come to their own conclusions in good conscience.

I guess I am a medieval alchemist at heart. I know about the processes behind the elements. I know that if you add oxygen to hydrogen you get water. I spend sleepless nights shifting through the dark matter. I feel the fire of the phosphorus against my beard. But I have faith that given the right conditions, nature can be twisted to turn iron into gold. That extraordinary things can happen. Not preposterous things, but incredible things, Things that defy the laws of nature as we far as we know it. Things that you would not believe because they defy common sense and logic.

I believe there is a deeper magic in the universe, much older and more powerful than time and reason itself. (But I am still going to keep my mask on.) Such is the alchemy of faith.

3. See their website at https://www.passionsspiele-oberammergau.de/en/home

Waxing into the Threshold: The Liminal as Spiritual Experience

Old door in one of the traditional houses in Chora of Patmos, Dodecannesse, Greece

In my old apartment building in NYC, there was a space between the wooden interior door with a glass pane and the outside heavy storm door. You would have to be sandwiched in this space cluttered with symmetrical silver mailboxes, overstuffed with bills and marketing flyers, with reams of ShopRite weekly ad circulars swiveling around your feet in the cold, while you waited for someone from the third floor to open up. This hallway space felt like a jail cell; it smelled funky. It was a waiting room to get you from the outside world to the inside one and vice versa. That experience of waiting in a tight space between two worlds is known as the liminal space.

I have been reading a lot about liminality or the liminal space (menopause does that to you). Liminality– the term comes from anthropology to describe the stage during the ritual performance where the subject cannot return to the prior state but is not yet ready to enter the next phase. Limen, Latin, literally means "threshold". It describes those phases in life where one is crossing from one stage to another. The liminal space is the time between "what was" and the next. A place of entering or exiting, a point that marks a beginning and an ending. It is a time of ambiguity, anxiety, and disorientation. Of waiting, and not knowing exactly when the door will open when you will step over the threshold into the new world.

Right now, going through a major life transition, that threshold looks more like the crazy revolving doors on some midtown office building. So many ideas, so many motions at new action, and then the taking back of those actions. I don't know how to feel—most times I feel angry, overwhelmed, sad. Sad because I have to let go of a part of my life that I will never be able to live again, with all the regrets and glories that came with it. The kind of mind I have asks a hundred questions and rebuts them with a hundred more. From each question splits two or more conflicting answers like some Hydra that then proceeds to battle with each other. I have doubts and then doubt those doubts. I feel lost in a state of perpetual indecision, insecurity. Should I stay in New York or should I move? Should I end this career and try another? But what if I can't make it? What if I am just falling victim to the grass-is-always-greener syndrome? Why can't I be happy with what I have accomplished so far? Shouldn't I be grateful that I have reached a predictable comfortable level in my career? Why give it all up for the unknown? What about my family? How will they adjust to my changes? Am I too old to start anew? What if I am not given the chance to change? Will I be wasting my time and my efforts? Is it too late to become what I always wanted? Should I listen to my gut or should I use common sense and reason?

I am warped by the madness that these changes demand of me. I am stuck in the revolving door of my mind, going around in maddening circles with no chance to go back into the building or to get a break in edgewise to step out of it. On the one hand, the way I have lived my life up to now in the steady predictable rhythms of motherhood, tending to the myriad details of household duties, dovetailing schedules, striking off To-Do lists, slowly inching up the salary step ladder, that does not do anymore. There is a discontent, a sadness mixed up with the self-knowledge that while having served others is noble and commendable, it has not served my inner need to meet my potential. I am no longer happy with being someone's mother, taking care of everyone, being needed.

On the other hand, I feel the nudge of my foot against the open door, I smell the exhilaration of a life wafting with excitement, with the potentiality of living it on my own terms, full of days in sunshine devoted to pen and easel. The new world whose bourn is fuzzy yet emanates with breezes hugging lavender from seaside gardens, and whispers of freedom buzzing underneath bluebells, luxuriates with the open palm of time. That world beckons to me even if it is unclear through the revolving door. That world, so magical in its possibilities. Its allure pulls from within the deepest part of me—calling the seed coat to stretch its hairy fingers tentatively to taste the warmth and darkness around its earth. The same force that impinges on its containment walls, those fortifications that provide the defense against its own destruction, pulls it out. It is the submerged destiny that calls, like some magic beans that sprout a green highway to the sky. Or when you read an inscription on a wall that stops you in your tracks with the revelation that that message was meant specifically for you.

Adolescence, young adulthood, menopause—it is the crossing over stages, those times of transition that can be hard to pull through. This liminal space is hard. However, it has a magical quality to it. That's because it is the one place where all transformation takes place. In that crucible, something is changing within and without.

It is in menopause, adolescence—that liminal space that you must submerge your psyche deeper under the folds of blind earth, the subconscious, remaining motionless in anticipation. Stay trapped in the folds of the earth, patiently, until a gentle nudge, without even your own sensing, will drive you through the crazy revolving door—out from the crammed hallway smelling of funk and littered with supermarket refuse—out into the brave new world. You will emerge from the dizzying revolutions of the threshold like some Clark Kent superhero poised to fly, to reveal her powers, to seize her destiny. Trust in the process. Stay put.

The ancients symbolized the liminal by the snake turning into itself or the butterfly emerging from its pupa. We have lost the power of symbolism in our very practical post-modern culture. We have lost the ability to stay silent to hear the inner workings of our psyche's seeds groaning with growth. We have lost the sacredness in mindfully acknowledging the passing of the threshold stages.

Liminal space is a sacred space. It is a sacred space where the old world is able to fall apart and a bigger new world is revealed.

Father Richard Rohr writes:

> " . . .we have to allow ourselves to be drawn into sacred space, into liminality. All transformation takes place here. We have to allow ourselves to be drawn out of "business as usual" and remain patiently on the "threshold" (limen, in Latin) where we are betwixt and between the familiar and the completely unknown. There alone is our old world left behind, while we are not yet sure of the new existence. That's a good space where genuine newness can begin. Get there often and stay as long as you can by whatever means possible. It's the realm where God can best get at us because our false certitudes are finally out of the way. This is the sacred space where the old world is able to fall apart, and a bigger world is revealed. If we don't encounter liminal space in our lives, we start idealizing normalcy. The threshold is God's waiting room. Here we are taught openness and patience as we come to expect an appointment with the divine Doctor."[1]

1. Rohr, *Everything Belongs*, 155-56.

Growing Old: The Fine Art of Learning to Lose

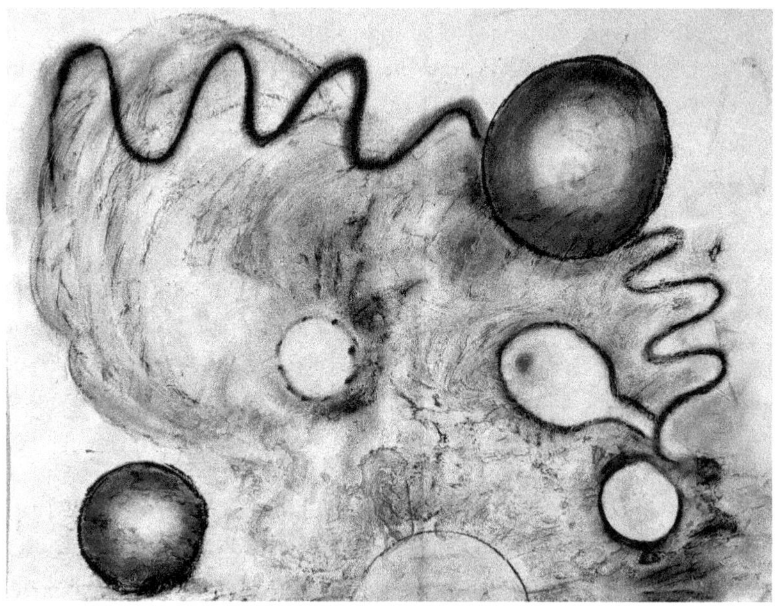

Abstraction Swivel

Have you come across this character type—the nasty old woman who barks at you when you try to help her as she is struggling to get the wheels of the shopping cart over the curb again and again? Or the reclusive miser next door who barely speaks to anyone, not even his posse of twenty mangy cats? I often cringe at images like this of old age because I fear that I, more than anyone else, will wind up a crotchety, stingy, miserable old hag. I cannot but think about the process of aging as I see so many of those around me enter the final season of their lives. In my experience I have seen two types—either the sweet, loving, patient sage who has come to terms with the vicissitudes of life (sort of like Yoda or the wise old medicine woman) or the miserable grouch like Scrooge or some of the demanding senior women who complain about everything on the early-bird menu and leave no tip. Is the path to becoming a grumpy old relic inevitable? Is there a way to think about the process of growing old in a way that does not bring with it bitterness, resentment, cynicism, and despair?

From the little I have understood about life, it seems that it does not travel in a linear path of progress and happiness. It is a fallacy that life gets better as you get older. In fact, for some of us it becomes an unlivable hell; the final chapter is the worst to read. In contrast to the many televised cases of young people falling to their doom by jumping off the Verrazano Bridge or overdosing on sleeping pills, depression and its consequence are purviews of old age. Depression and suicide are highest among the elderly in this country. As an indication of the general souring of the soul in later life, skim through *Ecclesiastes.* The last book the Wise Solomon composed at the very end of his life is the most pessimistic and hopeless of all (in fact, I believe some parts were altered or glossed over to lift its somber color). The main theme running through it is "Vanity of vanities, all is vanity." In the end, nothing matters. What you thought was so necessary, what kept you up at night, what you stressed and twisted over was not so important. With the graze of the great sickle, nothing is that important. And all is in vain.

It reminds me of a colleague who, during his farewell speech at his retirement party, raised his glass and said, "Friends, after 35 years of teaching, I have accomplished nothing. It was all in vain. It was all a waste of time." After this, he took a seat and proceeded to get drunk. At the end of your life, I believe the greatest spiritual struggle will be not to lose faith, not to fall into the spirit of despondency, and that fall into the trap of misery.

Several reasons might account for this. I think optimism and trust in the best intentions of humankind are hard to sustain with each successive year of disappointments, betrayal, heartbreaks, repeated news about the heart of darkness and the brutality in the world. It is hard to hold onto youthful enthusiasm when the trials of daily toil reduce you to a slaving, grinding automaton. By the time you are 40, you will have witnessed your fair share of horrifying acts of crime, perhaps even murders, wallowed through two or three devastating heart breaks and break ups, a few betrayals at the hands of an overly ambitious colleague, and maybe you might have experienced the worst milestone yet, the death of a beloved one. The older you get, the harder it is to keep smiling. You get tired of the whole damn thing

The path of least resistance is to retreat into yourself, become bitter and lash out at everyone. Compound this tendency with the general irritability that accompanies the breakdown of the body, the aches and pains, the strains in the back and the knees, the general increasing fatigue, and it is an hourly struggle to stay hopeful. With the changing of the seasons, the warning signs just like the turn in the oak leaf, that you too will die. You might have experienced the first scare of the "c" word and maybe you sighed with a "phew" when it was pronounced benign. The joints begin to groan with the constant to and fro. And the places you used to show off in your youth are now the ones you try to cover up.

But there is one reason that I believe can be both the cause and cure that leads to the "bitterness" in growing older. It is the realization that very few things are and have been in your control. It is the bottomless sadness that comes with the resignation that all you could have done is a kernel in the palm of what had to be. It is the wisdom gained at the hand of sweaty experience that understands that this thing called life is precious and fleeting. And it is a paradox, the grandest and greatest paradox of all– a sewer of maggots on the one side and a thimble of angels on the other. It comes with the strain in the thighs of straddling this wide paradox that this life is on one bank a tragedy and the other a farce, on one side a folly that pisses on itself and on the other a symphony of seraphim.

In order to brave this wide gap without going insane, you must, I think, relinquish control. Just allow things and people to be so that you do not grow bitter. Acceptance—this is key. Accept that human nature extends a bloody fang along with a helping arm. That you did all that you could have done. That this was the course of your life and look back and be content with it. There is a fine line between acceptance and resignation, resignation implying surrender, a certain sense of giving up while acceptance brings with it a profound peace, the peace that comes with the understanding that all is as it ever and could have been. That there are really forces outside our control, forces that we mistakenly give ourselves credit for, that govern our destinies more than we may care to think. Whoever managed at the twilight of his life to keep a positive stance on life is worthy of sainthood.

The net underneath this greater acceptance has to do with submission to God's will. Only when one submits his/her will to God's greater plan (or "the Universe" as others call the power) can he be released from the bitterness, the regret, and resentment and rage at the universe for things that did not unfold according to your plan. This leads to the serenity that accompanies old age. It is also the isotone that predicates wisdom. Once you have let go and acquired that inner stillness that transcends the throes of the subway car of life's tracks, you have already arrived at your final destination in that deep place in your soul.

This is what life may be about—learning to ride the rails and enjoy the ride as it swishes by you and not worry so much about your last stop. You cease from raging against the universe, from cursing at yourself and the should haves, could haves, would haves and just accept yourself and those around you as they are. The older one gets, the more one realizes that the things in our control are miniscule in relation to forces much larger than ourselves. To spend mental and emotional energy going against the raging current of the universe is often malproductive as it leads to stress, disappointment, exhaustion and an early death.

I remember an elderly character from an old Mexican movie. He said that when we are young, life is all about acquiring things. We work hard to gain more experiences, get more friends, make more money, more material things. But when you grow older, you realize life is about what you give up. You have to learn how to give up all those things you have acquired–friends, career, loved ones. Growing old is the fine art of learning to lose–gracefully.

Waiting for the Bridegroom

Large icon in chapel of the church of the Panagia Ekatopilliani, Paroikia, Paros, Cyclades, Greece

THE SOUL IS A lonely hunter. Its depths are so deep not even she can fathom. I do not know why some are blessed with benevolent parents, a stable home life, a genuinely supportive circle of friends, and financial security while others grovel in poverty, dodge the blows of those who are supposed to love them, alienated and isolated from the circle of human companionship. I do not know if we are cursed to pay for the sins of those who did wrong before us or if we carve our own hell through our misguided choices and our ignorance and darknesses. Perhaps the answer to the question of the problem of evil is more profound than I can fathom. This same question the disciples asked, "Master, who did sin, this man, or his parents, that he was born blind?" Jesus answered, "Neither hath this man sinned, nor his parents: but that the works of God should be made manifest in him." (John 9:2).

But even this answer does not sit right with us in our humanity. Why does God allow children, the innocent to suffer? Why couldn't He just have a rule—kids should be off limits to suffering. They could start kvetching in the hell that this life could be after they turn 12. Why do they have to be born into suffering? Children, are sacred. The creatures that need love and nurturance. Why allow them to be tortured, raped, killed, neglected, abused, traumatized? My spiritual father had a hard time answering this question for me from an emotional point of view. From a theological view, you could say that it is a consequence of free will. That those who abuse exercise their free will. Even if it is a pattern of ingrained, subconscious behavior. We live in a fallen broken world. These things happen. But this I know, that if I had not been for the genuine love of the God-Man Christ, whose love penetrated my dark recesses, my life would have had no meaning. When mother and father forsake you, when your brother is your murderer, when you have no foundation to stand on, you have the love of God. That love redeems the world and you, not in the abstract but in the personal and real. This is an age that has turned away from this love because it does not fit around the post-modern intellectual table laden with sophisticated dishes of liberalism, empiricism, moral relativism. Indeed, one needs to apologize for believing, for adhering to the traditions of "naïve" herders. As if faith is a logical faux pas. It is a thing for those who cannot withstand the complexities of life, who need clear black and white pigeonholes to order it. No intelligent educated modern denizen can believe in God. At best you are delusional, and at worst, punishingly self-righteous and monolithic. It is a fool who gives up his life for those that hate him. Who can live in a random universe governed by dumb luck and quantum layers of shady probability? From the personal encounter I have had with the Holy, I cannot go back to who I was before. While I do not discount the scientific, the logical, I also know that without the intuition, the imagination, the imaginal realm, ringed in awe and mystery, we have ceased to be human. A truly balanced colossus of modernity must plant one foot on the shore of the scientific, the logical, and the other foot on the shore of the supernatural, the imaginative, the intuitive, the awe-inspiring. The trick is to endure the contradictions in the human condition long enough, so they transform and become complements. Then, the apparent dumbness in the Christian message becomes clear: it is by losing your life that you find it; it is by loving those who hate you that you forgive yourself. By accepting your own fragility, your weaknesses can you start to change yourself. Only through self-sacrifice that you become saved; it is through the grey, the mystery, the complexity that authentic living is born. As Don Herold pointed out, "This is the greatest paradox: the emotions cannot be trusted; yet it is the emotions that tell us the greatest truths."[1]

It might sound cliched by now, but the world and the human soul cannot survive without love, kindness, and goodness. Everything else pales in magnality. The God-Man Jesus is an embodiment of this idea if you will. That love became flesh to feed, caress, and inspire the world. The magnanimity of this act of love overwhelms me so that I can only respond in kind: "My Lord and my Master." The proof of Christ's love is carved in the mercy seat of my soul; His providence manifests in the workings of my insignificant life. Even when I doubt, that love wells up engulfing my worries. Feeling is believing, social anthropologists would say. The Lord is my strength and my buckler, the shield of good hope. There is nothing greater, nothing nobler, I rest assured in His Love and His example on the Cross is proof enough. It is the suffering that provides the meaning; death that leads to life.

Christ overcomes our sins and traumas. He is hope that makes us new. As St Paul states in Corinthians 17-21:

17 Therefore, if anyone is in Christ, he is a new creation; old things have passed away; behold, all things have become new.	

1. Quotefancy, "Top 40 Don Herold Quotes."

	Now all things are of God, who has reconciled us to Himself through Jesus Christ, and has given us the ministry of reconciliation,
19	that is, that God was in Christ reconciling the world to Himself, not imputing their trespasses to them, and has committed to us the word of reconciliation.
20	Now then, we are ambassadors for Christ, as though God were pleading through us: we implore you on Christ's behalf, be reconciled to God.
21	For He made Him who knew no sin to be sin for us, that we might become the righteousness of God in Him.

Amen.

Monkey Man vs. Christ: A Crisis of Faith

(cartoon illustration of the author in spiritual crisis)

At 16, I went through my first spiritual crisis. My faith in Christ came face to face with Darwin's evolving monkeys. These two points of view clashed in what they told about who I was—an icon of the divine; a hairy primate governed by natural selection and evolutionary chance.

I had been taking AP Bio and was on track for a medical program. I had been very faithful all along the course, the vast diversity in the natural world unified in its life functions made me step back from the text and do my cross in the Orthodox way. "How magnified are Thy works oh Lord." Even while memorizing the Krebb cycle, looking at the complexity and fragility of ecological webs, these only reinforced my faith in God the

Great Poet Creator. And then we got to Unit 5, "Evolution, Natural Selection and Survival of the Fittest." Reading about the adaptations of the beaks on Darwin's finches, and how the idea dawned on him that there needn't be an external hand for the species to change. And then the text delved deeper into the actual process and how it operated on the genetic level with Dawkin's "selfish gene" theory. That's when I had to pause.

I looked around at the world with my teenaged eyes. There is no denying that there are forces at work in the way nature works: wars, the violence against one group towards another, rape, subjugation, inequality, disease, to convince me that human beings were nothing more than Stone Age barbarians. The story about Adam and Eve and the serpent in the Garden—it seemed like it had truth, but it was only a story. It could not produce the body of evidence the way science could to convince me that this was the way humanity came into the world. On the one hand I saw the clear fossil record in the photos in the thick textbook of *Homo habilis, Homo erectus, Homo neanderthalus.* I studied the forks in the evolutionary tree from one primate ancestor to the other. I peered curiously into the hairy monkey-like wax statues in the Museum of Natural History hunched over with paps hanging like deflated flapjacks. This was my grandmother going back into the Antediluvian? I saw the giant diagram on the exhibit wall; it was conceivable that the invisible, yet relentless hand of time had sculpted these anthropoid pitheci from four-legged furry balls into more erect forest dwellers, their foreheads lengthening, their eye ridges protruding less and less, their cheek bones smoothed back in the airbrush of eons.

Doubt tugged in my inward parts. Anxiety crept in at night. I spent hours agonizing on my pillow. What if there was no such thing as God? Maybe all there was was this brief moment of time tied into a body with flesh and sinews and a beating heart, flesh that would die and get sucked up into muck and mud. What if there was no eternity? No basis for good or evil? If life was utter randomness, if you only lived long enough to reproduce and die, what was it worth anyway?

Fear and trembling had beaten down with long black wings. I told my mother my doubts.

"Oh, she surmised, "you are entering the teen years. This is when the devil starts tempting young people away from the faith. Remember, sometimes your thoughts are not your own. They are put there by the evil one to lead you astray."

That was another wrench in the engine. How could I not even trust my thoughts? If I could not think, then what did I have to go on? The twitch in my toes? How would I be able to make a decision?

She had dropped out of the 4th grade, so her reassurances of the afterlife and the angels did not have much clout. She was my *mother* after all; what could she know?

So she took me to the village priest. Father Nektarios was a jolly benevolent man who looked like a shorter version of Santa in black robes. In his emphatic but sweet way he tried to explain. "Evolution is just a theory. They have not found all the pieces of the puzzle yet. There are huge gaps in the evolutionary record that they cannot account for. Scientists have yet to find the missing link."

"That being said, Father," I said, "there is an evolutionary record. You cannot deny bones that show the slow but possible change of the skeleton."

"Here," he handed me a brochure. "Go home and read this. What you see is not always what you can trust."

The brochure titled "Don't Be a Monkey's Uncle" tried to discredit evolutionary theory through extracts of critiques a famous anthropologist Steven Jay Gould had brought up. There were too many false starts and dead ends in the fossil record to accept it as the *only* way human creation could have come about. Somehow the logic of this did not assuage my fears. Just because the fossil record was not clear did not discount that it was a record. This was not the type of logical argument that helped do away with my doubt. It used faulty argumentation to make its point. Sort of like waving a bone and saying because the rest of it is missing, we can't take it as evidence.

I went home and put my Bible away. Darwin had won.

But it wasn't that easy, to let God die just like that. From nature or the Divine or personal choice, I had been born an idealist. I wanted to believe that there could be a world where love, peace, and beauty existed. I wanted to believe in the best in human nature. That we were more angel than devil; that we could be capable of acts of mercy. Like the Bard through the mouth of Hamlet had exclaimed, "What a piece of work is man, How noble in reason, how infinite in faculty, In form and moving how express and admirable, In action how like an Angel, In apprehension how like a god, The beauty of the world, The paragon of animals. And yet, to me, what is this quintessence of dust?"[1].

Whatever we were and however we arrived on the scene, we were nothing short of miraculous. A creature endowed with rational insight, imagination, the capacity to love and create—that could step outside the bounds of time and our earthly place to contemplate the stars. The fact that we as humans could ask the deep questions—of where we come from, where we are going—wasn't that proof that we were something greater than the random permutations that natural selection could concoct?

The other thing about me was that I was born with a Renaissance brain. While most students are good either in math/science or English/social studies, I was good at both. I loved science, did brilliantly in math, and I excelled in writing and languages. I got 100 on my trig Regents as well as a 96 on my English. I could not make up my mind what to major in college because if I chose the sciences, it would mean giving up my love for literature and the arts. When I thought about things, I saw issues from more than one side—the rational, the emotional, the historical. I think this had something to do with the way I saw God. If God did not truly exist, or was some impersonal watchmaker, where was the meaning in life? I was forlorn and in deep agony that I had lost God through too much textbook reading.

When I looked for answers in other churches, especially evangelical ones, the responses became even more hysterical and reactionary. Some Protestant Jesus freaky churches had blotted out any mention of evolution in the science textbooks and replaced it for the Creation story. This just added points for the Evolution scoreboard. If you react so strongly to the claim of an opponent that you just erase it, there has to be some truth to it. It seems entire factions of the country were experiencing the conflict I had going on in my head and heart.

Deep in my heart, (it was actually in my *nous* as I was to find out later), I could not give up God. I knew that it was quite possible as the experiment had shown that life could have started from the sides of a primordial soup and not from the finger of Michelangelo's Father of Ages, yet I kept looking for clues, any signs, that He could theoretically still exist. Try as I might, the problem of God did not go away. Even though in my mind God was dead, in my heart I wanted to believe. I needed to have faith in something higher than all of this—"nature red in tooth and

1. Shakespeare, "Hamlet - Act 2, Scene 2."

claw." Maybe it was what I was reading? Maybe I had to find another way to think about the problem.

When I started college, the first undergrad course I took by choice was in the Philosophy Department. It was entitled "The Philosophy of God." It explored the arguments for and against God's existence as pounded by Plato, the pre-Socratics, Socrates himself, St. Thomas Aquinas, Spinoza, Bishop Berkeley and so on and on. Here God became a concept for the syllogistic guillotine. We read Plato and his ideas of psyche; Socrates who denied the existence of gods (and paid for it by drinking poison); Thomas Aquinas and the teleological argument. I learned that I had not been the only one to ponder the question of the existence of a higher being. There had been an entire history of philosophical thought trying to deck it out. The arguments even had names: the watchmaker hypothesis, the teleological argument, the first mover argument, etc. etc.

And then came Nietzsche. Nietzsche was a juggernaut; a cerebral bulldozer that crushed the other arguments liked pulled pork. I read *Thus Spoke Zarathrustra* from cover to cover. It read like some heavy metal, spiked leather Bible from hell--"God is dead!" he pronounced. Christianity and religion are for those too weak to face the realities of life in all their gore and glory. One needed to be an *Uberman* to escape falling into delusional pits of weak argumentation. And then I read how Nietzsche had led to the Nazis and how he had died a madman shouting obscenities, syphilitic ulcers eating his insides. So much for that. His was the devil's philosophy.

I finished that course none the wiser and less the faithful. I had gone into that class with such a desire for this God problem to get sorted out. I wanted so badly to be able to come to a definitive conclusion: "Yes!" God exists or a definitive "No!"--he is only a figment of the imagination, collective delusion or subconscious, whatever your disciplinary flavor. Shucks, it just made me more confused. Thoughts and ideas split off from other thoughts and ideas, one question bred another question so that by the end of the semester my mind looked like a giant hair knot that got larger and more convoluted. I started not only to question God's existence but the entire way to know. (It turned out there was another philosophy class all about that issue, too; the foundation of how we know what we know titled Epistemology. No way was I going to get into more head games by registering for that one.)

I trudged through young adulthood with my mind empty of God, yet my heart yearning for Him. I was to take another class in the

Anthropology Department named *The Goddess: Archeology and Archetype* and that spun another spool around the already convoluted knot that was my mind. There was archeological evidence that proved a matriarchal orientation in Neolithic settlements. Those faceless figures of the earth goddesses unearthed in Çatalhöyük with bulbous boobs and belly pranced before my mind's eye. Before there was Jesus, before there was the pantheon of Olympic gods, there was the Goddess and she reigned supreme for millennia before the warrior tribes with patrilineal gods overpowered her.

That was my permission slip to become a goddess worshipper. I went to Greece and got in touch with my internal goddess. I romped around island temples, skinny dipping and setting wreaths of sage on fire in self-initiated rites to honor Artemis and Demeter. I sent in a check for a hundred dollars and became an "official" member of the cult of Isis. (Some pagans in Scotland convened in a castle in the nude and officiated over rites that reenacted the dismembering and reassembly of Osiris, her cohort.)

In Psych 101, I picked up on a name of a psychologist, pronounced Young or Yoong but spelled Jung, who had fallen out with Freud. I bought a thick book of his collected writings which I leafed through here and there. In the university library, on a shelf all the way near the ceiling, I stretched and reached for an intriguing volume bound in burgundy leather with gold lettering—*The Golden Bough.* It was by a 19th century scholar who had compiled a cross-cultural compendium of the rituals, beliefs and practices of various peoples throughout the world by the name of Sir James Frazier. "Wow!" I thought I had uncovered the secret key to the kingdom.

Here was yet another way to look at the God question. Perhaps our orientation to the Divine had to do with our collective historical and political development? Not only was God a product of the human mind, He was also a product of the collective subconscious. He/She spoke to the need of human beings to believe in a spiritual world to negotiate the mysteries of living, to assuage anxiety over death. While so many cultures, so many millennia yet the archetypes were universal: flood, virgin birth, heroes, underworlds, apotheosis. "Yes," Jung read. God(s) exist and there is truth in myth from whatever ethnicity, time and geography, but that is because of the functioning of the deep mind and the human life cycle. All gods were brought forth by the human breast.[2]

2. Jung, *The Collected Works, 176.*

While this argument did not deduce away the existence of God, it did not completely satisfy me either. The rational Enlightenment had killed off God, Jung had resurrected Him, yet that was not the kind of reasoning I was looking for either. God had to exist on His own terms, not on mine.

By that time, I had graduated from university and was living like an adult with a career, bills to pay, and love issues. I came to the conclusion that it was impossible to logically and rationally arrive at a proof for God's existence. Just as one school of thought existed to propound the fact, another bigger school would surface to chop it down. Thinking led one on an infinite loop that gave no relief. I still would chatter in cold sweat at night overwhelmed by the existential questions that pounded the walls of my heart: *Timor mortis conturbat me*, echoed the refrain of a medieval poem from the *Norton Anthology of English Literature*.[3]

Then came a life crisis. I was 23. I received an inkling that I might be harboring a fatal disease. I had to undergo a series of diagnostic medical tests. My God, I was too young to die! To make matters more complicated, I was pregnant. The night sweats intensified. In my nightmares, I saw my body corrupting into fecal matter, a swarm of flies over my open grave. The fear and the trembling so pronounced I nearly went mad from worry. It was then, at the behest of a pious English-Cypriot friend, that I walked into the only Orthodox Church in Barcelona at that time, and did the unthinkable—I prayed. I think it was the first time I really prayed in my life. Truly prayed. From the heart or *nous,* which in Orthodox theology (a subject that is never studied in the academy) is the center of the human person, not the mind. On my knees in front of the icon of the Pantocrator, I repented with tears:

> *Lord, I have driven my life to the grave. My intentions have drifted far from the mark. I am not worthy that You should hear me. Do not let my life go down to the earth. Save me from the abyss I have dug for myself. Save me and my unborn child from the mouth of Hades. Give me a new lease on life and I will walk in your commandments. I promise to serve and believe in You. If You indeed exist, not just as a concept, but as a person, as you did in your life on earth, then I will glory Your name for as long as I live. I promise to bring up the child growing in my womb in your Church. As a covenant of this promise, I will name her in your honor.*

3. Dunbar, "Lament for the Makaris."

Without knowing why, I read the Book of Psalms, 1 to 150, for an entire week before I was to be given the results of my diagnostics. (I found out later that praying the Psalms is the most powerful entreaty in times of need.) They came back negative. I had been given a new lease on life. I had wagered my whole being in the bet I made with the Unknown Watchmaker. And because He willed that I should go on living, I turned to Him. This time on His terms. I became a devout Christian. Of course, I baptized the child, Christina.

As I grew in spiritual maturity, the truth of God's existence no longer had to be proved or argued like some term paper. I came to understand that faith and reason, the underlying macro-wrestling match between evolution and creationism, speak to different parts of the human experience. Moreover, the ontological perspective one takes determines what each one is able to see. If you view the human being as originating from an ape-like ancestor, it acts like an ape. If you view the human being as originating from a divine, benevolent Creator, then it acts like a god. What you look for is what you get. (Sort of like the dual nature of light. If you are looking at it as a wave, it acts like a wave; if you are looking at it as a particle, it acts like a particle.)

Because this conundrum bothers not only creative types such as me but bona fide scientists themselves, some have proposed a middle ground approach. They named their theory "intelligent design." While they do not come out flatly to pronounce the existence of God (that would be so passe in scientific circles), they leave the possibility open. Again, it comes down to foundational perspective. If one chooses to approach the scientific world from a vantage point that allows for faith, then the evidence can be used to argue for His existence. The universe is so vast and intricate, from the tiniest particle of an atom to a giant event horizon, one stands in awe! Pure chance could not have allowed for this. But if one is skeptical from the start, well, "It is what it is," they say, "keep God out of it."

Looking back in hindsight, I can say that knowledge of the truth of God's existence comes from the baptism by fire in the crucible of the knowledge of good and evil. No one can truly know God without having the faculty of the noetic heart open. A synergy of faith and revelation work mysteriously in the deepest core of what it means to be human and from that depth calls out, "Lord, have mercy." Can I point to evidence, exhibit A, B or C that proves unquestionably that God exists? No. That would go against the tenets of faith. You believe because you know, in a way that surpasses understanding.

I came to believe in God in an experiential way, a way that defied empirical knowledge. The best way I describe it to students is by analogy. Say I love someone, say his name is Mark. I have spent much time with him and deep down I know I want to be with him for the rest of my life. I rant and rave about him. You go to meet him and come back perplexed, "What does she see in that guy anyway?" You don't love Mark; you don't know him like I do. All the words and examples of his greatness will not be enough to convince you that he is a dreamboat beyond someone's wildest dreams. You cannot deny that Mark is great, for me at least. You're not seeing him the same way makes him none the worse in my eyes.

Looking back, I can see how it would be easy for a young person to lose faith in God in school. The academy is founded on the Scientific Method. There is no room in a secular undergraduate lecture hall for theologians. Why? Because to give those voices an equal footing would be endorsing them in a way. So theological thinkers such as St Gregory Palamas and the Desert Fathers and Mothers are shunned. (St. Augustine is allowed in because he is so scholastic and rational in his approach; the same approach that led Christ to the guillotine by the Enlightened philosophes.) In America with a strict separation of Church and State, you get two different camps of thought that do not get to refute or even hear each other's discourses. Without a defender for the other side, the main front gains a victory with no contest. If I had been given a thorough Orthodox education, I might not have lost faith in my young adulthood.

As I matured both in my faith and in myself, I came to see Darwin and the Bible as two coins that flipped into different worlds. First, these worldviews differ in anthropology. The heart is the center of the human being in the Orthodox faith, not the mind, as in the academy. Saint Gregory Palamas held that man is a representation of the trinitarian mystery. Man is made of spirit, sense and *nous*. It is the nous that is the center of the soul of man; the faculty that gives him the eyes to see the spiritual world. It is his or her passions that keep him from knowing God fully. Indeed, I am starting to believe that the central engines of natural selection, greed, gluttony, concern for acquiring wealth, lust and a fixation on sex, violence, intrasexual competition, the hierarchical struggle to attain status if male (so to acquire more resources and by extension more females and have more sex and propel genes into posterity), the preoccupation with appearance and beauty if female (so to attract a powerful resource-rich male), are really passions and deadly sins. It is the struggles of the flesh that keep the human being fixated on earthly and material cares. Natural selection calls for everything that is brutish, selfish, barbaric, violent, vain, proud, and flamboyant in mankind. The mechanisms of evolution are all about the flesh and the glory of the world. But the spirit of God lies in opposition to the flesh. This is why the Gospel is foolishness to those of the world. Its tenets rest on a foundation that is other-worldly, obscure at best, and preposterous at worst. Orthodox Christian theology holds that only when one reaches *theoria*, as the saints did, can one truly grasp the Mystery of God. St. Gregory Palamas, indeed, defines *theoria* as the vision of God.[4] To see God is to have a pure and open nous. Those who see God struggle for the honor. By extension those who cannot see Him might be damned or at least so clouded by the muck and mud of physical survival they cannot raise their eyes to heaven.

The thirst for knowledge, if you accept theological dogma, can also be a consequence of the fall. (That forbidden tree was named, "the knowledge of good and evil.") There are limits to human knowledge. It is an act of pride to believe that one can understand everything. Can the watch ever truly understand the mind of the watchmaker? It would seem obstinate and disrespectful. Our minds are limited by the cage of our cranium. To think we can use only our mind, our senses to truly understand the complexities of the galaxies of knowledge is frankly adolescent. Then again, the mysteries of knowing are eclipsed by the mysteries of unknowing. What we do not know, what we do not see, what is beyond the realm of sensory or rational inquiry, might be as significant as what we do. It is the arrogance of the scientific community that insists what they say is all that needs to be known and on the terms *they* deem worthy.

Ultimately, faith becomes a choice. A choice between accepting the kind of narrative you believe human beings should come from and follow. I have met priests who are closet atheists just as I have met evolutionary biologists who do not believe in evolution. "From a speck this small they are able to construct an entire skull," Mary Thanos, a PhD in evolutionary biology explained. "When you look at the list of ten or more conditions that have to occur for a mutation to take place that leads to genetic evolution, you realize that it is very improbable. For evolution to exist, that would mean the universe runs on chance. God does not function by chance. He is the creator and allows for everything in the cosmos.

4. Gregory Palamas, *Triads*.

If there were such a thing as chance, God would be surprised. And that's not possible. God can't surprise Himself."[5] What I understood from talking to Mary was that evolutionary biologists held as much faith in science as Christians did in God. Skeptics will point out that had my prayers not been answered, I would not have been a believer. (Damned right, I would have been dead in the grave.) To that I will answer as the blind man did to the Pharisees, "Whether he be a sinner or no, I know not: one thing I know, that, whereas I was blind, now I see." (John 9:25).

In the circumstances of my life, God has made His way known. It is a question of having the eyes to see. There are 75 references in the Gospel that refer to Christ's opening the eyes. Indeed, in that same passage, He states, "For judgment I am come into this world, that they which see not might see; and that they which see might be made blind." (John 9:39).

Faith like love is a mystery. Sometimes it is a gift or a grace, a *charisma*. It is the heart that responds in awe and love at the sight of the sunrise; it is the mind through its reasoning that tries to explain how the sun rises. They are two diverse ways of knowing that should be complementary not antagonistic. Could evolution be the method God used to form the Creation even while taking a lump of clay and molding it into human form and breathing life, 'pneuma' into it giving it a soul? However mankind came about, evolution no longer pricks my faith. I can straddle two contrary shores and not get pulled in two.

5. Dr Mary Thanos, interview by author, Holy Protection Monastery Pennsylvania, November 2020.

Faith is a Many-Feathered Quetzal

Image source: Creative Commons

Several summers ago, we had the good fortune of trekking to an ecological paradise, Costa Rica. So lush and green, so verdant with life that bromeliads would sprout in mid-air from the crowded cover of other trees. Their roots would dangle freely as if suspended from the sky. Packed with explosive examples of flora in one square foot of space, Costa Rica was a mini-treasure trove of wildlife. While walking through the mossy footpaths from our lodge to the mouth of the famous cloud forest in Monteverde, the guide shouted, "Stop!" His gaze was pinned to a scramble of branches high up in a wild avocado tree. He set down his equipment, set up his tripod, adjusted his telescope binocular lens, all the while without taking his eyes off that spot in the mess of leaves and peered inside. "There it is! Qué accent magnifico!" he smiled into the lens. We scrambled to get a turn at the eyepiece and surely, one by one, each of us released a delightful sigh of wonder when we saw what had been magnified to 15X. It was a quetzal, one of the rarest, most beautiful iridescent birds of paradise in Central America. It was the mythical Quetzal that the Aztecs had hunted down for its rainbow-colored tail feathers to adorn the headdresses of their kings. The Mayans thought it was a god, who became personified in their leader and king, Quetzalcoatl. When it flew across the lush green backdrop of tropical forest, the quetzal resembled a floating rainbow.

It was magnificent! Even through the lens its radiance, the green-ebony twinkle of its eye, the iridescence of its body, speckled through. The manifold specks in its coat shimmered in the bath of sunlight over it and shot off cadences of gold, dark indigo, turquoise, red-orange flush as it shifted on the branch. Its tail plumes trailed almost three feet down from the tree. It seemed as if he did need an attendant to carry his train. To think, if it hadn't been for the keen eye of our guide, we would have missed it. We would have ignorantly walked right under it, scouring miles and miles of endless green in the forest with our binoculars to no avail. We would have gone home a week later grumbling and all disappointed about the inaccurate reports of quetzal sightings in the guidebooks, cursing our bad luck for having spent so many thousands of dollars and still not one sighting of a quetzal.

Faith is a bit like that quetzal. We go through the world with a fine magnifying glass looking for traces of God's existence to find He has eluded us.

There was a time in my life when I was so eagerly searching for God, searching for some sort of answer to the mysteries of the universe, the eternal human questions—why am I here? what is my purpose? Is there anything beyond this? I took all the classes in philosophy of religion, learned about Sophists, pre-Socratics, existentialists, phenomenologists, the argument from design, I devoured any book that dealt with the supernatural—*Thus Spoke Zarathustra*, the epic of *Gilgamesh*, *The Dancing Wu Li Masters, The Tao of Pooh, The Golden Bough.* I visited Shinto temples, synagogues, monasteries, museums, talked to rabbis, clergymen, priests and preachers, pundits and gurus. But all the while, I could not find any positive proofs of God's existence. I was more befuddled about what I had learned and less sure of what I had known before I had even started my quest to find God with my extra-sensitive, state-of-the-art binoculars on.

In the end, my metaphysical quest had led me nowhere. I went through the world with a fine magnifying glass, looking for traces of God's existence, only to find He had eluded me. All I had was a hefty magnifying glass and sore eyes for looking so long and hard. What I lacked was what our naturalist guide had—the eyes to see the signs, the sense to slow down at the slightest movement, the sensitivity that made the presence of the bird possible, the familiarity with the fabric from which the quetzal had come from, and lastly but most greatly the love of the quetzal itself. Faith is what gives us the spiritual eyes to see God's presence in the world. It's the thing that makes one person gaze into the walls of a cell in a Petri dish and understand beyond a doubt what a glorious creation God has made. No mathematical equation needed to arrive at that conclusion.

How do you get faith? Well, that is a mystery. It's a grace. It's a gift. What makes one person listen to Bach's Concerto No. 9 and hear the beating of seraphim's wings while another will only hear notes played by a violin, a cello, a flute or two? It's the sensitivity one tongue has for discerning the differences in different ages of the same wine. What is clear to one person is nonexistent for another.

And this is not to say that faith, the existence of God, is a subjective matter. The humanist argument has posed that God is a creation of the human breast, that He is a relativist construct. But that isn't the case at all. Anyone who has come in contact with the "holy" will know in a way beyond his physical senses that "something" exists and that "something" is something so strange and overwhelming, it defies our grasp of it. The same argument can be tipped on its toes—just because you have never seen the bird does not mean it doesn't exist. The quetzal is out there. You just have to be patient enough and humble enough and keen enough to catch a glimpse of it as it moves through the green clouds—resplendent, wonderful, in all its glory.

God speaks to us in subtle, mysterious ways. He leaves traces of His majesty in the robe of the poppy. God reigns in the realm of possibility—in that slim 2% chance of recovery that the surgeon circumscribes. He chisels His word on an inner-city wall when a kid is looking for confirmation as to what he will do when he grows up. When we love and become familiar enough with the way God works, He drops us clues—the fragment of Scripture that accidentally popped into your head when you were about to walk into a scene of a crime. God is out "there" in the universe, but He moves imperceptibly like a mouse. He flies around his domain equally and freely, but He alights only on those He sees fit, only those with a pure heart, with the patience to wait for His movement, with the discernment to see Him as He moves (for the bustle in the hedgerow, the stray spackling of wild avocado crumbs at the foot of the laurel tree). For now, His voice is a whisper He leaves in the falling rain, a message you hear in the hum in the heart of a flower. Make no doubt about it—His presence is there. You will know. The same way you know your lover longs for you.

But if you go out into the forest with a net, a cage, and a rifle to hunt Him down, you will be left empty-handed. If you go out into the wide universe to track down God and stuff Him as a trophy over your mantle, He will elude you like the stealthiest tiger. He will not be made into a sport for your amusement, a quarry to quench your thirst for intellectual pursuit. You will go into the jungle and come out extremely disappointed. What is more, you will miss the radiant, resplendent bird of paradise as it scintillates its robe of rainbow through the forest canopy just as you turn your shoulder.

The Importance of Being

THE ORTHODOX WAY EMPHASIZES silence. Mother Gabrielia said that in the late evening, just about the time when the sun goes down, the day winds itself into a tight spool and people gather together in clumps around sitting chairs to gossip and socialize, she would tell her companion to sit on a on the balcony of their apartment near Koliatsou Square in Athens "gia na siopasoune"[1] –that is, to silence themselves. Instead of chit-chatting as is wont around that time of day, she would embrace silence and turn her attention inward all the while reciting the Jesus Prayer in her heart.

The urge to talk, to gossip, and socialize and small talk is especially strong in women. Women tend to overuse the tongue in general; they nag, they bicker, they argue, they whisper, they gossip and spread rumors all through the work of that little organ in the mouth, the rudder that can lead the ship to capsize. It is not their fault in a way. Women have a higher verbal capacity as neuropsychologists have shown.

By practicing an order of silence, Mother Gabrielia wanted to counter this tendency in the female sex to shut up, be quiet and by focusing her attention on God using the Jesus Prayer, she would direct it away from the common backbiting gossip that spinsters are used to.

This tendency to overtalk I believe is a reaction to the overwhelming oppression of silence. The unbearable heaviness of being; a way to fill the void. In the modern world of the West, we have become so used to noise, to chatter, to running around doing this and that, that we do not know how to handle the opposite–the silence, the absence of motion, so much empty space. These things make us depressed. To silence the clutter is to pay attention to the deep nothingness that lies on the fringes of life, that might, gulp, be at the center of life itself. It might be that we are so afraid of this existential angst of confronting the void, that we create all kinds of

1. Gavrilia, *Ascetic of Love*, 45.

artificial and distracting environments to stray our attention away from it.

But it emerges that existential dread of nothingness in those listless blue hours when no one is at home. It attacks us like a wild panther on the open plane with no cover or underbrush to hide in. When we feel exposed and vulnerable, that void which we fear is at the center of life emerges to scare the daylights out of us. So, we fill our world with man-made contraptions–a money-making career, cell phones, cameras, Facebook, contacts–we distract ourselves with ourselves. We cannot sit still because stillness reminds us of death, of un-creativity, of not being productive or ambitious enough. So we create so many bells and whistles, smoke and mirrors. We dictate to ourselves the struggle for self-fulfillment through job, external accoutrement, prizes, BMWs, socially scripted ways of achievement, a Nobel Prize even, a wife and two kids in a colonial in the suburbs.

We are not content with just being–we need to do, to talk, to run, to wrestle, to get ahead. We fill the empty spaces of our lives with clutter–chatter, gadgets, painted backdrops, Macy's sale days. But there is something deep that happens when you stand still enough to feel the void. When you embrace the abyss and stare at the darkness, you get the courage to go beyond it. From the abyss you emerge a creative positive force. In that stillness you listen to the music of your own soul and feel the subtle pulse of God's wrist. It is from those empty still places that we can be free to create who we really are. It is from these lonely desert places that we can find our true voice. Our true selves–not the self dictated to us from society or who we need to be or some deluded sense of self, but who we really are, who we must be.

This is why "Being" is as important as "Doing." Meditation, prayer, stillness, listening to the sound of your own breath, "chillin'" is as important as struggling, accomplishing, creating, tinkering. How many of us can sit still under a bodhi tree and meditate for 16 hours? How many of us do not long to do this? To be instead of to do--without fidgeting or getting bored or feeling guilty.

That is the real struggle with the modern man–the struggle to be still, the struggle to pray, the yearning for silence even when he struggles by all means to avoid silence. To keep silent even when it is so easy to keep talking. To enjoy the empty spaces as the palate from which true originality and creativity spring. To look within for validation when it is so much more convenient to measure success from without. Of doing nothing. Of just being. The motto for our age should not be "Just do it" but "Just be. Just be."

"GOD" is "DOG" Spelled Backwards

Many people I know who profess to be pious and who try to follow the ways of God have expressed a universal feeling that we are living through the end times. No one knows exactly when the end is, no not even the Son knows, only the Father knows. But the Holy Scriptures have given us a hint to understand that when we see the signs, just like we can see that a fig tree is blooming with fruit, that we can assume that we are living through the end of times. Now the Good Book tells us of many signs of the end of times, but I will share with you just one that is not mentioned directly, but I believe forebodes the end most comprehensively. This sign is that the hearts of men will grow cold. One of the ways they have grown cold is that instead of administering love to their fellow man in acts of philanthropy, they have channeled it to their love of dogs.

During many an outing in my home city of Manhattan, I see women pushing baby carriages but instead of babies, they are strolling along with their pet dogs, little Chihuahuas, or terriers, shitzus and the like. They push their pooch buggies through Central Park tugging a doggie diaper bag. These strollers are specifically made for dogs, not children. In Petco and other pet stores they are displayed in the windows– in all kinds of models and colors, all for the benefit of taking their little dogs for a stroll, to spare their little paws and hearts the strain and effort of walking the pavement. Just yesterday, in the Village, I saw a "pet retreat" where they offer a spa experience to your pet, including massage, gourmet meals, including vegan ones if the owner is so inclined. Its slogan was "the most fun your pet can have without you." New York City is bursting with many dog-oriented businesses–puppy and me yoga salons, take-out restaurants that you can call in for a specially-made meal to take home for your dog, not to mention the plethora of pet grooming, pet sitting services. There are even in the far frontiers of luxury pet care dog psychics and dog psychologists. High-end services include pet hotels with heated floors, fluffy pillows, and VCRs. Other services include liposuction for dogs, animal massages, and aromatherapy treatments. Even while unemployment can fluctuate, holding steady at $90 million average, the pet industry is grossing billions per year. You should thank your dog for your job.

Luxury pet care products are popular as well. You can buy a plastic tray containing real sod. You toss it in the truck for your dog to use on long trips or take it with you to the hotel room. Other products include a treadmill for dogs, automatic timing feeders and automatic cleanup for cat litter pans. A Japanese company is selling a gadget that hangs around a dog's neck. It tells you what the dog's bark means. This item is so popular that they are making a similar product for cats. Some other products include personalized food bowls for about $22, jewelry – known as "doggy bling" – for less than $10, and $5 dog socks. I have seen plush dog beds go for close to $100, as well as seasonal pet attire that includes $27 goggles, $60 life jackets and $15 sunglasses. There are also pet beauty contests, pet wedding parlors, and pet modeling agencies where the little pups parade their couture designed doggie apparel down pooch Passarellas to the "oohs" and "ahhs" of their admiring owners. Alas, dog psychologists exist but they do not take insurance, but at least when your pooch suffers from the blues, at least you have a professional to take care of him.

While other industries suffered during the Great Recession, the pet care industry in the US is turning a high profit. Fortune Business Insights states,"The global pet food market size was valued at USD 123.86 billion in 2024. The market is projected to grow from USD 128.94 billion in 2025 to USD 179.48 billion by 2032, exhibiting a CAGR of 4.84% during the forecast period."[1] The average American spent $1,400 on their pets in 2024 and when close to 66% of all households in America own a pet, it is a highly profitable business.[2]

Now, I have a wonderful faithful dog too; he's a 135-lb lovable Golden lab. I love Titus to death. He is so patient; he instinctively knows when someone in the family is sick or depressed and so comes and sits at the edge of their bed. When my mother was recovering from surgery, he was faithfully glued to her bedside for weeks. He never talks back to me like my unruly teen; he greets me no matter how many times I leave and come back into the house with unconditional love and whimpers

1. "Pet Food Market Size, Share, Trends | Growth Analysis [2032]," n.d. https://www.fortunebusinessinsights.com/industry-reports/pet-food-market-100554.

2. PetExec, "Pet Industry Trends."

when he cannot find an object of affection, whether it be a stray slipper, a random stuffed animal, or an empty water bottle to give me as a gift. He is a beloved part of our family. He never complains, except to get an extra dose of love in the form of a scratch on the belly or a dog biscuit. Many times I have said, "If the world were more like Titus, it would be a better place." Everyone knows that animals reduce stress, unify families, and bring health benefits to their owners.

However, the bark stops here. A dog is still a dog; it is not a human being. There is something wrong with a society that elevates animals to the level of human beings, that grants them the same rights, the same needs as people. While bonding with a domestic animal is generally a beneficial thing, there is a real ethical, psychological, and logical danger in substituting an animal relationship in the place of a human, person-to-person one. I would define the obsession the West has for animals, especially dogs, as *skilolatreia,* or dog idolatry. I would venture to say it is a sin.

The wake-up call for this dog idolatry came when my next-door neighbors gave me an invitation to the funeral for their 17-year-old German shepherd. It was expected that the two sisters, one childless and the other never married, would be distraught when their "son" died. The older one was especially intense in her grief, wailing and wearing black as they do to mourn the passing of relatives in their village in the south of Sicily. They kept vigil and did not leave the house until the day of the funeral. Although very frugal throughout their life, they splurged on the funeral expenses; they found a "permanent" pet cemetery in a posh northern suburb outside the city, with a dedicated plot, and marble-engraved headstone. I was expecting a quick simple ceremony, but I was shocked to find that the ritual was identical to one you would expect for an actual human being. First, the dead animal was put on view in a "wake room" so that everyone could pay their last respects. His miniature plastic coffin lay open so that all could view the serene body of Orfeus, his head lovingly resting on a satin white pillow. He had been delicately embalmed and was wearing makeup. A family member, before the cover of the coffin was closed, laid a wooden cross on its body in solemn gravity. Four pall bearers then carried the coffin on their shoulders to its final resting place. After the ceremony, the friends and family gathered in Orfeus' memory for a full-course lunch at a favorite Italian restaurant. Needless to say, the whole ceremony cost as much as a regular funeral, and then some, such as this particular pet cemetery which charged a monthly maintenance fee for the upkeep of the plots.

Although I can very well empathize with the loss of a family's best friend, to go to these lengths for an animal that technically does not have a soul is at best ridiculous and at worst sacrilegious.

The excessive love people show for their animals is indicative of the troubled times we live in. In many ways having a relationship with an animal, and one as faithful and self-sacrificing as a dog, is easier than having one with a human. It takes less work to have a good relationship with Pete than his master Peter. Animals are not mean, are not as moody, they will never abandon you unless you mistreat them. They will never run away with your best friend; they don't nag you to death (except if you have a cat maybe). They provide you with stress relief in contrast to most of our significant relationships which only pile on stress. And pets provide as much tenderness and affection as humans (if not more). But the buck stops at some juncture on the tracks of this line of reasoning. Animals, however warm and wonderful, are not human. They cannot serve as a substitute for genuine human interaction. They might ward off loneliness, but when they substitute for the potential in a person-to-person relationship, they become a crutch or a scapegoat for loving other humans. To replace human companionship for animal can be a sign of emotional unhealthiness. We have all heard of stories of the eccentric cat lady who keeps 150 cats in her two-bedroom apartment or the dog lover who bequeaths his entire multi-million-dollar estate to Fido.

In the 60's, dog worship entered new heights. There was an actual sect, the Dog Commune, an offshoot of the Universal Life Church, outside of Los Angeles that started by no doubt an LSD-hallucination/revelation that proclaimed that the reason for all the evil in the world could be directly attributed to the abuse and mistreatment of dogs. The reason behind the dogma? Because in English the word for GOD is DOG spelled backwards. Members of the Dog Commune herded dogs, raided animal shelters to liberate their canine deities, and were among the first animal rights groups in the United States to try to stop exploitation of dogs in scientific experiments.[3]

Although American society has come off the high of the 60's, it is still a pathetic state of affairs when people revert to channeling their needs for love, care, and acceptance onto animals. Because this signals

3. Stuart, "Entheogenic Sects and Psychedelic Religions."

that they have either given up or become so disillusioned with their fellow men that they would rather kiss their dog on the lips than venture into the dicey waters of genuine human love. Yes, there are the stories of those perverted few who look for sexual fulfillment from their pets too. (Wasn't Catherine the Great part of this statistic?) No cat can be the soul mate a woman yearns for; no cute Maltese puppy complete with manicured paws, smelling of baby powder can ever take the place of a bonafide baby.

This is why I see women pushing their pooch prams on the sidewalks of Park Avenue and wag my head in pity. For all the doggie bling bling and their luxurious penthouse suites, they are so very lonely. Frame this next to the drunk, scraggly homeless man who is lying on a piece of cardboard they are walking past in their doggie strollers and the image becomes ironic. In this country dogs have more of their daily necessities taken care of and lead a more glamorous lifestyle than human beings. How many lap dogs get more love and affection than the thousands of orphaned and abused youngsters in this city? How many canines have a direct, no-waiting line into the emergency room at the Bobst Animal Hospital on York Avenue than the hundreds of thousands of uninsured unemployed people who give up their spirit waiting for urgent medical care or are denied it because they lack insurance? For all the billions of dollars that Americans spend on doggie chew toys and all-natural organic dog food, if only a small sliver went to feeding the homeless and donating to children's charities or better yet forging a viable relationship with a needy youngster, there would not be such an obsession with animals. If as a society we garnered our energies and our resources for genuine acts of love toward other human beings, I believe we would not be so miserable and unfulfilled emotionally that we would run home to tuck our baby Chihuahua to bed. The one true way to genuine happiness is through the development of real human fellowship and philanthropy. Because our love for our fellow human beings has gone to the dogs, we are living in the extremes of pathetic perversity making idols out of our pets. When the love of one human for another is projected onto an animal to such an extent that it eclipses human connection, the hearts of men have grown cold. When God becomes a dog, the end times have found us.

To Choose or Be Chosen?

Several years ago, the Dalai Lama gave a public address in Central Park. Over 250,000 people were spread out on the Great Lawn, their radiant vermilion silks flowing in the golden sunshine. They came from as far away as Pawtucket, Patchogue, Piscataway to see the 14th reincarnation of the Buddha of Compassion. The Buddha of Compassion. I'm not knocking his message—we should get along, the world should live in peace and harmony. But I could not help but notice that Buddhism has become very popular at the break of the 21st century. It has become quite fashionable to be a Buddhist, especially in urban, upwardly-mobile, cutting-edge society of Manhattan. What with the clout and impetus that such high-profile followers as Richard Gere (who has become the self-proclaimed cultural attaché of the Daila Lama in the States), Madonna, and the like, Buddhism has become all the rage. In this our pluralistic, highly dynamic Western society seems to change its taste in religion as often as it changes its palate for take-out food during the week—Zen Buddhism on Monday, Jewish mystical Kabbalah on Tuesday, Neo-Hindu, tantric-vegan fare on Wednesday, Shinto-Vietnamese on Thursday, New Age save-the-whales on Friday, and an all-you-can-eat buffet of Reiki, tai chi, Feng Shui, tarot cards, spirit sticks, angel and spirit guided prayer circles on Saturday and Sunday. Being "spiritual," seeking for something other than this, is in style now (although there will always remain a staunch faction of die-hard atheists and couldn't-care-less pragmatist next to the sliver of a percent of Satanists or at least those who bang their heads to *Ozzy Osbourne*).

I'm not going to take up white space here for excoriating the fickleness in our society's spiritual inclinations. Neither am I going to expound on the reasons I feel Buddhism leaves much to be desired; I will not try to debunk nirvana (how can anybody especially these convenience-driven

Yuppies find any solace in zero, how the soul, even one which does punish itself, be satisfied with a reward of nothing?) Nor will I deconstruct the venerable Dalai Lama. What I'd like to tackle is the idea of choice in the human soul's desire for transcendence.

American society seems to think that their religious affiliation is a product of their own will. It's very democratic after all to have the right to choose a church or temple the same way you choose a candidate on the gubernatorial ballot. Check off which religion you would like to try for these next four years of your life, and if the candidate does not meet your expectations, if it lied or misrepresented itself or did not pan out on its promises, well, there's plenty more to choose from for the next four years until you become disillusioned and change your vote again. Unfortunately, in matters of faith, there is no democracy. With God there is no choice.

Faith is not something you choose to take, but something that is revealed to you, that you are led to by a power not your own. Ultimately, there is a choice in that you can accept it or reject it. (Was there ever a disciple who was called yet did not choose to follow?) God's presence is revealed through Grace and the Holy Spirit. It is not something somebody can catch, bind to an argument, and negotiate with. The tricky thing about Grace, as with love, is that it is freely given. Why one person is visited by the Holy Spirit while a million others are not is a mystery and God's inalienable prerogative. For those of us who have had the honor of having received Grace, we live in the splendor that this Grace showers our lives with. It is a paradox not easy to explain that by relinquishing your right to choose the way you would want to live your life, you have gained the freedom to live it in the way that most suits you. The same principle is at work in the exercise of our own personal will. In many cases, we have no force in changing our destiny.

Not to downplay the role of man's own free will. Ultimately, it is us who choose to follow the call or not. But very few I suspect with a really keen sense of hearing could hear the call and not respond.

There are many historical spiritual examples—Moses, the Virgin Mary, Joan of Arc. Moses made a reluctant spiritual leader. Imagine his life. To his knowledge, he was raised an Egyptian, a noble of privilege at that—with much politically and socially at stake for his position. He undergoes a personal transformation after what appears to be a heart-to-heart conversation with a burning bush. Much of what he held as "given" as known was eradicated. He was stripped of the outer trappings of identity. His knowledge of himself stripped to nothing, or worse, the complete opposite of what he imagined. He was born a Jew, and at that a slave. He embarks on a journey of self-discovery, and through that journey is drawn by a force both outside and within himself to an imposing mountainside. He does not know, logically, rationally, the reason he is compelled to climb the sacred mountain. All he knows is that he must. He is listening to a subterranean chord within himself that drives him to the pinnacle of the mountain.

At the summit, he has an encounter with the Holy. He meets God in a flaming bush. A voice commands him to take on a formidable task, a seemingly impossible task, much greater than himself. Moses's first reaction is "Why me? I'm not worthy of this task? I don't want this challenge. Find someone else."

Yet with some prodding, he relents and starts his descent from the mountain—once more a changed man—a holy man. One who is infused by the Grace of God, with a power greater than his own. Moses had little choice in the matter. Yes, he could have doubted the reality that a sage bush in the middle of the wilderness on Mount Tabor could talk, let alone could talk with the voice of God, a God who entrusted him with an insane task. Yes, he could have pondered the absurdity of his predicament—a slave Jew raised as a noble Egyptian, mandated to return and seek deliverance for God's chosen people, his own people, from the very hands that fed him. I'm sure, if he had wanted to, Moses could have engaged in a doozy of a lengthy existentialist monologue on the back of Mount Sinai. But he didn't. He had no choice. He was the chosen one—not the chooser of his destiny. Once that happened, he could no longer go back to being the same soul-seeker he had been before he had stumbled on the glow of the mountain.

It is the same with us. We cannot or should not choose in matters of faith. We cannot run through a laundry list of the varieties of religious experiences. The best we can do is be attentive, be sensitive to the cues around us so that the divine light can illumine the way. If we are sincere and patient enough, then perhaps Divine Grace will alight on us and roost in the eaves of our souls. But to take on the search for meaning as if we were bargain hunting for a chiffon blouse through the 75% off racks of Bloomingdale's results not in the discovery of a genuine article of clothing but a cheap trifle that will be flung off and go out of style next season.

The same lack of personal choice is at work at the crossroads between our own individual will and God's will for us. I have asked the question—where does a person's individual will fit within God's will? There seems to be, as CS Lewis points out, two opposing strategies for asking what we want. The one way is expressed in the Lord's Prayer as "Thy Will be done." We should not ask for our own needs and wishes to be carried out but trust in the Divine Will to execute what is ultimately best for us. The second way of prayer is expressed in the parable of the persistent (a.k.a. "annoying") widow—knock and it shall be given thee, ask and ye shall find."[1] Ask honestly and urgently enough and you will be granted what you need. So which is the way to pray? Which is the way to get what you want?

The answer I think comes from the supple lips of a most unlikely candidate for God's spokesperson, Mick Jagger who in the refrain sings, "You can't always get what you want. You can't always get what you want. But if you try sometimes, you'll see you get what you need." We think we know what we want, and know damned well that's what we want, so when we don't get it, like spoiled brats that we are, we sulk away in our bedrooms, slam the door and refuse to talk to our uncaring, so unfair parent.

Yet, after all is said and done, we have to admit that Mother/Father was right. We shouldn't have married Harry or Harriet—our marriage would have failed. We shouldn't have run away from home and become a groupie for Justin Timberlake. We would have wound up penniless and strung out on the street for a has-been anyway. God knows what is better for us. We just have to trust and hold out long enough to have our will meld with His.

And so the insistence on our choice lends way to our being "the chosen."

1. Lewis, *Christian Reflections*, 142-151.

Whore as Saint : a revisionist understanding of female Sainthood

close up of mixed media, Madonna Medea, 2019, by the author

Have you ever wondered why so many female saints led a life of prostitution? It has to do with the socio-political and class context they were born into. For centuries women had very limited economic opportunities. They were not educated like their male counterparts and so had few economic outlets. As a woman you were tied to the mercies of the males in your family. Your father, your brother, your husband. Women had little leeway for self-determination. This worked well and fine if you came from a decent family if your father cared enough about you to take care of your physical and emotional needs. This arrangement worked well and fine if your husband treated you half well. But if your fate tied you to a dysfunctional family, if you happened to marry an abusive partner, what choice did you have? Either you could join a convent or join a religious order as many educated women in the Middle Ages and Byzantium did. The church was one of the few avenues of opportunity for well-to-do educated women.

However, if you did not come from a wealthy family that offered you an education in the classics and Holy Scripture, then your only avenue for survival was prostitution. I believe it is naive to believe that the prostitutes were depraved and evil. Let's be frank, their services were in demand by men who paid them handsomely for it. Morality is tied to economics. Most of these lower-class women who traded their bodies for money did not have the moral privilege of doing something else. They could not find a job at an office because their societies with a strong patriarchal bent forbade access. The oldest profession has been a faithful backup business plan for many women across cultures. It is the one business route open to any woman who needs to be economically independent. The thick fog of misogyny pervasive throughout so many centuries interfered with the ability to see women as competent professional workers. Those women who were intelligent and attractive enough to amass fortunes through their commerce of their flesh stand out in history, especially church history.

Of course, I am thinking of Mary Magdalene. She was a shrewd businesswoman. Her conversion came at a time in her life when she was economically independent. At the point she encountered Jesus she had become financially secure enough to head into a different line of business. You could say she switched careers at that point and went into public relations or strategic communications. Ironically her conversion occurred just at the point she was most financially independent to make that choice. The seven demons Jesus cast out of her cleansed her of a lucrative trade and propelled her on a new career path.

The conversion stories of prostitutes touted by the church make more memorable exhibit chambers for the efficacy of the true faith. The more extreme the conversion, say a zealous Hebrew defender of tradition/persecutor turned Christian, the more effective for turning hearts. A similar rhetorical pull happens with the tropes of whore turned Saint.

This is not to detract from the genuineness of conversion. Even those who champion prostitution as empowerment for women cannot disagree that to commodify a sacred act between the sexes cheapens both of them. Whores who quit commercing in the trades of the flesh, however lucrative, and eschewed it for embracing the spiritual, bring a dignity to themselves. Quitting a certain epoch of your life into a new identity is what repentance is all about. But repentance makes sense when one has a choice. Christianity, while not perfect in championing women's rights, did offer the equity of salvation a woman was as worthy of entering the kingdom of heaven as a man. Her soul held the same weight as his. The dignity of the individual person, especially to an oppressed class such as women, would explain why so many women converted to Christianity.

Female saints who worked the flesh trade had little power to choose a line of work that would enhance their moral and spiritual character. In this light their conversions were born out of necessity and could not have been so hard to muster. It did not have to take a flash of blinding light on the way to Damascus for them to change their lives. It would have been a no-brainer.

Could it be that by preaching Jesus early female martyrs and equal-to-the-apostles were implicitly championing their rights as women? If Jesus was a rebel (incidentally, He was—the Romans crucified Him as a result), one of His radical acts is that He supported women of the lowest classes. He vouched for female empowerment by treating the most despicable and despised women of His society and had the audacity to not only converse with them, but to include them as members of His inner circle. Christ empowered women and that was radical for His time. If I were a downtrodden woman, I would snatch up that philosophy in a heartbeat. To support Jesus would be to support His political platform that included women's rights. The faith in Christianity gave many oppressed women the power and the passion to proselytize and spread the Gospel around the globe.

That socio-political-economic context drives female conversion is evident in the early church. As Isabella Double states, " . . .more women than men converted to Christianity in its early days, constructing a community with a very different sex ratio. Additionally, a higher percentage of girls would survive infancy in Christianity because it disallowed infanticide, and a higher percent of women may have survived pregnancy due to marrying at a "substantially older age," and a ban on abortions, which at the time were a "major cause of death among women."[1] Because there were more women in the early Christian churches, there was also more power in numbers. Women were the first adopters of the faith and

1. Double and Smith College, "Women and Their Roles."

were instrumental in its spread. Early Christianity congregated in home churches and these homes were the domains of women. "Women largely took on the role of "directing and running" meetings of Christians in their own homes, and those meetings served not only as worship for Christians, but also centers of conversion, especially when believers and non-believers lived in the same home," as they often did.[2] Women were therefore responsible for a large part of the construction of the Christian community before Christianity was allowed public meeting places"[3]. Besides, women converted their pagan husbands (remember Pontius Pilate's wife?) especially in the upper-class Roman society. Of course, they would raise their children as Christian to some extent (remember St. Augustine's mother?)

As Christianity was explicitly countercultural, women were drawn by the benefits that celibacy and singledom offered. "The Roman Empire made marriage mandatory for citizens between twenty to fifty in order to combat a declining birth rate, meaning that Christian emphasis on celibacy had legal implications . . . Also undermining Roman patriarchal values was the discouragement of Christian widows to remarry. Roman law required remarriage of widows under penalty of a fine, but if a widow remarried, she lost everything that she owned as it became the property of her new husband. Christian women, by refusing to remarry, maintained a certain level of autonomy that subverted the social norms of the time."[4] Conversion can be seen as much a function of the socio-politico-economic context of a particular place and time as much as a personal decision.

Women played a huge role for spreading Christianity in the early church as its tenets empowered their autonomy. I suspect this is the draw for many women in sub-Saharan Africa who have been flocking to the Orthodox faith so much so that the Patriarch of Alexandria has reverted to ordaining women deacons to handle the overflow of conversion. With time, women do lose their spiritual power within the institution of the Church, but that does not gloss over the need for their talents to be recognized. If Christianity is to remain true to its dogmas of equal partnering between the sexes, it must embrace women as spiritual beings with talents, intellectual gifts, and the drive willing to work tirelessly for the faith. They are not threats to the establishment and should not be treated as such.

2. Double and Smith College, "Women and Their Roles," 2
3. Ibid.
4. Ibid.

Is there such a thing as a Christian feminist?

A RECENT VIDEO BY Father Joshua Trenham entitled, "Virgin Mary: the death to ecumenism and radical feminism," he makes the argument that radical feminism makes the mistake of elevating maleness by mimicking it. That Orthodox Christianity sees the greatest truest Christian believer as someone who was a woman and a mother. He cites C.S. Lewis who argued that the most important of all jobs is motherhood and every other job that exists in the public square exists to support motherhood. To quote: "The Virgin Mary will always keep before the face of the Church the glory of motherhood which is a uniquely feminine reality. It is the glory of all women, and she never worked in the public square never receiving a single paycheck and she's the most prized woman in the world. The claims of radical feminism are bogus, and the Virgin is the model for everyone."[1] With all due respect to his office as priest, I would like to challenge some of his thinking.

LET'S GET OUR TERMS RIGHT:

First, we need to get our terms right. We need to the definition of "feminism" what it is and what it is not. Feminism is defined as, "the belief in social, economic, and political equality of the sexes"[2] Let's be real. There are many forms of feminism with many varying opinions as to what is warranted and what not.

I will define it as:

1. Father Joshua Trenham, https://www.youtube.com/watch?v=J7X1TwsaIN8
2. https://www.britannica.com/topic/feminism

- asking for equal rights of women and girls
- allowing woman a rightful place in society to be given the freedom to exercise her will, to live up to her potential and be encouraged to bring fruit to her spiritual, creative and intellectual gifts

Feminism is not

- asking for female domination, in fact some feminists take offense to using the term matriarchy as it amounts to substituting one dominance with the opposite gender
- feminism is not becoming a man; it is asking for the inclusion of a female perspective in problem solving, community building and law making.

I totally agree with the Christian understanding of men and women. The Virgin was the greatest example of charity, faith, and love outside of Jesus Christ. Men and women are different. But equal. Motherhood is put on the pedestal as the greatest vocation, but the realities show it very differently. As a single mother, besides my mother, I was given very little in terms of material support. I had to struggle to raise my child while juggling two or three jobs. When I most needed help from the church, it did not provide it. I had to take my daughter out of catechism and Greek school because I could not pay for the tuition, even though this parish was so well-endowed financially that they upgraded their restrooms with granite faucets and made a show of their new facade. Christianity might pay lip service to motherhood, but institutionally it does truly little to help mothers out. Where are the day care centers, the marital counseling sessions, the mother's groups? I find there is a wide discrepancy between what is valued on the abstract and what is supported on the real and down-to-earth.

SPLITTING OF WOMAN INTO DISTINCT TYPES: THE PROBLEM OF SEXUALITY

Christianity has an issue with female sexuality, if not all sexuality for that matter. I see woman's polarization as virgin or mother. But what about woman as a sexual being? What about us in-between? Sex even conjugal sex is not spoken about in the Church, at least not openly. I hate to break it to all the pious, but in the human world, most virgins cannot become mothers. Only our Holy Virgin Mary had that grace. Most virgins become mothers through sexual intercourse. The inability of society to accept a woman's sexuality, and by extension, a man's, polarizes these facets of woman: virgin, mother, whore/courtesan. By splitting a woman into parts that one can deal with one at a time, it simplifies the way you see her. This is not a true or wholesome portrait of real womanhood. It is the expression of male subjective perception of woman, not as she really is, but as he wants her to be. Women, like men, are complex creatures. By splitting them into constituent parts, you rob them of their personhood.

Where are the models for conjugal women? St Anne? Married saints take second stage to monastics in Orthodoxy. Joachim and Anna provide the one archetype, yet church teachings state that Joachim and Anna conceived the Virgin Mary via natural yet passionless love. What does that even mean? And worse, what is it inferring? That there is no place for a healthy sexual relationship in Christian circles? Is it a sin to have sex? In church I have always felt a tinge that it is so because it remains a taboo subject. Not speaking about something openly gives the impression that it is not welcome or wholesome. And forget about asking follow-up questions about what is deemed appropriate or inappropriate in terms of physical love. Sex that has always been associated with women (even though studies show men are more sexual in their nature and pushing the envelope in terms of sexual prowess). Because sex is considered sinful and tinged with the passions, by extension, woman is considered defiled and sinful. Could it be that the Church has conveniently gotten rid of the sexually mature woman as an archetype because men who run it as an institution cannot deal with her?

If that is the case, it has done women a disservice. By not exhibiting real examples that they can follow, in which they can see themselves represented, the Church erases the existence of a whole woman. The irony is that while society praises mothers and glorifies them, especially in the icon of the Virgin Mother of God, it ignores the elephant in the temple: human sexuality.

GENDER AND SEX ROLES: PIGEONHOLING THE HAWK

It would be nice if all men and women could neatly conform into the boxes for their respective gender roles. It would be nice for men to fit the bill as stoic, protectors and bread winners, and for women to be caring, stay-at-home nurturers making dinner. But people are not so simple. Gender roles, especially given the realities of a rapidly changing technocratic society, are in flux. Women must go out and make a living to support husbands whose jobs in construction have been halted. With the divorce rate at over 50%, the fact is men have become women and women men to do the job that was required of two parents. (Church going Orthodox Christians fare no better in this statistic.[3]) Frankly, is it so frightfully unorthodox to see fathers in the playground, changing nappies, going to the pediatrician with their kids?

We do not live in a world where gender roles are so neatly defined. Nor should we have to. Sometimes it makes no sense. Why should the woman in the house cook if she is horrible at it? Let Daddy cook and let her tile the bathroom if she is more artistically inclined.

A strict adherence to the traditional model of daddy provides, mommy raises the kids and takes care of house does not allow the liberty of expressing the gifts and talents of each unique individual. Women are not all built to keep house. Some of us actually have brains and talents. Why should we squander them? Making people conform to some rigid societal rules that state what women and men can or cannot do pigeonholes them in a way that might do damage to the full manifestation of their dreams and abilities. Who knows how many Shakespeares, how many Picassos, how many Leonardos in female form have been silenced or uncultivated because their destinies have been written off by their gender?

Don't think gender pigeonholing does not do damage to men either. One of the reasons why more men than women resort to suicide is that men have been conditioned to not exhibit their feelings and not "cry like a girl." If men cannot conform to the strict gender roles dictated by their society, they feel like failures or gulp! like "wusses."

FEMINISM IS A SYMPTOM AND REACTION TO PATRIARCHY, NOT AN EVIL IN ITSELF.

If only what Father Trenham said could be true, then there would be no need for feminism. Feminism is a reaction to the abuse, the neglect and

3. Justin Hoff, "Family Matters: Considering Marital Separation Divorce," 2022. https://www.ancientfaith.com/podcasts/familymatters/considering_marital_separation_divorce/

the undermining that women have endured at the hands of the men who uphold those structures that supposedly protect them.

The kind of world Father Tresham is positing for women does not exist. It is a broken world with incredible abuse on the most vulnerable: women and children. It is widely documented that:

- One in 5 women and 1 in 13 men report having been sexually abused as a child aged 0-17 years. 120 million girls and young women under 20 years of age have suffered some form of forced sexual contact according to WHO[4]
- Nearly 3 in 10 women (29%) and 1 in 10 men (10%) in the US have experienced rape, physical violence, and/or stalking by a partner and reported it having a related impact on their functioning.[5]
- At any given time in 2016, an estimated 40.3 million people are in modern slavery, including 24.9 million in forced labor and 15.4 million in forced marriage. 71 per cent of modern slavery victims are women and girls.[6]
- It means there are 5.4 victims of modern slavery for every 1,000 people in the world.[7]
- 1 in 4 victims of modern slavery are children.[8]
- Out of the 24.9 million people trapped in forced labor, 16 million people are exploited in the private sector such as domestic work, construction, or agriculture; 4.8 million persons in forced sexual exploitation, and 4 million persons in forced labor imposed by state authorities.[9]
- Women and girls are disproportionately affected by forced labor, accounting for 99% of victims in the commercial sex industry, and 58% in other sectors.[10]

4. World Health Organization, "Child Maltreatment."

5. National Domestic Violence Hotline, "Domestic Violence Statistics."

6. International Labour Organization. "Global Estimates of Modern Slavery: Forced Labour and Forced Marriage."

7. US Customs and Border Control, "Human Trafficking."

8. Ibid.

9. Ibid.

10. Ibid.

- A sobering report released by UN Women and the UN Office on Drugs and Crime (UNODC) on November 25, 2024 reveals that in 2023, 140 women and girls died every day at the hands of their partner or a close relative, which means one woman killed every 10 minutes.[11] https://news.un.org/en/story/2024/11/1157386

If men were true patriarchs, there would be no need for feminism. Feminism is not the ill, but the reaction to the ill. So many women live with the scars and the unseen wounds that their fathers, teachers, authority figures, yes, even priests have inflicted on them. They have had to stand up and get legal recourse for their rights. If they didn't have the right to vote, the laws would have remained the same. Rapists have parental rights in seven states. That means a rapist can coparent with his victim, has visitation rights and stays in contact with the child and mother.

The truth is women have suffered incredible injustice, economic, societal, psychological under the so-called rule of the patriarchs. (If I remember, there has even been a saint Thomais, ironically deemed the patron saint of women in abusive marriages, who was killed at the hands of her abusive husband.) When a person is not free to make decisions that affect her life, she has no other choice but to defend her rights. If women had not fought for their rights to be educated, to have an honorable means of employment, they would be exploited and marginalized to the one profession that has always allowed them entry: prostitution. Are we going backwards in time? By taking away a woman's ability to provide for herself and for her family, you are in essence rendering her powerless.

I do not think a Christian would argue that a sane and ethical society is made of values such as freedom, hard work, equality and prosperity for all its members. Feminists would say they want the same thing.

JESUS WAS A FEMINIST!

If you look back at the actions of Jesus and the history of the foundation of the Church, it is safe to say that Jesus could be considered a feminist. Jesus defended women and their rights as human beings who have intrinsic value in and outside their gender roles more than once. In fact, he defended the most victimized and lowly example of woman in his society: the prostitute. How many times did he get knocked by the Pharisees for hanging out with unclean women and prostitutes? For those times, when

11. UN News, "One Woman Killed."

women's activities were strictly bound to the home, Jesus's actions would have appeared radical. The woman who brought him a jug of alabaster and anointed his feet. The woman he saved from stoning was caught in adultery. The woman he asked for some water at Jacob's Well. That he cared enough to pay attention to a woman and a Samaritan at that, she belonged to a group of people considered inferior and with contempt on the part of the Jewish nation, shows the extent of His esteem for even the most ostracized. Jesus must have valued women in a way that was not the norm for his time. He chatted with the Samaritan woman at a well during high noon, a woman of dubious character who was shunned by her society (that's why she was at the well in the sweltering heat so she would not bump into anybody she knew). Let's not forget the BIG one: Mary Magdalene. The relationship between Mary and Jesus is after the one with his mother, the most intimate. Mary Magdalene, while she had rumors circulating that she was a high-class call girl, might just have been an intelligent businesswoman. Jesus brought out 7 devils out of her. She was one of his most prized apostles, touted as an "apostle to the apostles." She loved Him intensely. Why would it be a surprise then that He appeared to her first in His Resurrected form?

It was the women who saw the Risen Christ; the first witnesses of the Resurrection. That did not happen without good reason. After the establishment of the early church, women became equal-to-the-apostles for their spreading the faith: St Mary Magdalene, St Photene, St Thekla, St Helen, St Nino, St Olga. Women used their talents of speaking, creating, energizing to spread the Gospel of the Lord to all corners of the earth. They did not spare their lives for the love of God. They were not exclusively bound to the domestic sphere, but took part in public ministry in addition to their responsibilities in the home. It is obvious that their gifts were used for good purpose. They became saints through their efforts. They certainly defied the proscribed gender roles for their time. I think even from the historical record, it would prove likely that women were more dynamic back in the day as they are now. From this evidence, I think it can be drawn that Jesus and His ministry afforded women a high place. He deemed them worthy of care and showed them to be models of piety with precious souls worthy of salvation.

A CAUTIONARY CONCLUSION

Mixing politics and religion is dangerous. For someone who advocates separation of church and state, Father Trenham makes sweeping statements about social movements and political maneuverings. (There's another video where he outright thanks President Trump. Is this not an endorsement for a political leader who by all standards could be unethical and unchristian?) Using the pulpit to broadcast one's political opinions and tout them as "correct" under the mantle of sanctity is to confound separation of church and state. This is not what this country was founded on. A man of God should speak about matters of the spirit and theology not about sociology and political theorizing. In other words, Father Trenham, keep your political opinions to yourself and stick to speaking about matters of the spirit.

Unfortunately, the culture wars have entered beyond the nave. What with the right vs left, the Trump presidency, and the divisiveness that the COVID pandemic has wrought on parishes, it is impossible to escape politics in the pews. Ironically, because the one parish I attend has its monastery in upstate New York, I have attended trapeza downstate in the city where parishioners revile Trump and the following week attended upstate where parishioners extol him. And both claim that they hold the morally upstanding stance. My opinion is to "render unto Caesar what is Caesar's and unto God what is God's" (Matthew 22:21).

The Limits of Logic

"Don't always trust in your thoughts"
–a bumper sticker on a Chevy somewhere in West Virginia says.

Today as we commemorate the descent of the Holy Spirit, I muse about the mystery of expression, the capacity for clear thinking, and the limits of human knowledge without divine revelation. I like to think of myself as a writer, an artist, and a teacher. So much of my struggle has to do with the ability to capture the truth and deliver it in an eloquent, yet straightforward manner so that my readers and my students can grasp the nebulous, inchoate cloud of what I am trying to express. Many times, I come up awkward, sloppy, klutzy, or even empty handed. Sometimes thoughts wring me in a wrestling match where I am unable to disengage and arrange the words from the idea, the essence, the Truth of what I am trying to express. As much as I try sometimes the beauty, the exactness of the thought or feeling, I cannot accurately cloak with words. Words like a fabric cut too short cannot cover the immensity of the idea.

The other complication is that the vessel of thinking, our human mind, is also limited. Like a clay pot, it is so many cubits wide and long. While amazingly it can be stuffed with many things, strings of ideas, theories, memories, and even with imaginations that can spiral into entirely new galaxies, the mind has its boundaries. It can know only so much as its sentient powers allow. I argue with an atheist colleague about this all the time. You cannot know God or any spiritual reality if you rely only on the senses. Faith is a question of epistemology, how we claim to know the things we know. If as a scientist you claim to only know what you can derive from your senses, then it would be hard to make the deductive jump from the physical to the spiritual. The workings of the Spirit can be experienced through the senses but cannot be proven through them. My colleague insists you can only know from the material reality and as such because God cannot be proven from such, no thinking logical person can accept such a claim. God is a delusion, a figment of the mind. Just because you cannot see God who is unknowable with your senses does not mean he doesn't exist. But you can't make the claim that He does either, otherwise you can claim other unknowable beings are possible, beings such as purple fairies that go around painting polka dots.

The issue I have with my colleague is that he is not willing to admit that the human, material capacity for thought is limited. Believing that the human mind can know everything in and of itself is intellectual pride. It's like believing the clay pot can fit the entire known universe within itself. How proud to believe that your noggin can contain the Creator? That the oh so small container can comprehend the mind of its maker? The Desert Fathers and Mothers, wise early chroniclers of human psychology, made the case that our thoughts can be faulty. It is in the realm of thought that the spiritual war between good and evil takes place. The demons are noetic beings and can enter into our thoughts pricking them with dark reasonings. Satan they say is a smooth-talking lawyer able to make a convincing case for evil using the most logical most cogent argument. Human reasoning has provided the rationale for arguments for the Holocaust, war, genocide and other enlightened acts of reason. Human capacity for reason is tainted by the Fall, not just physically, but ontologically as well.

And here we are today at Pentecost. The Holy Spirit appears in the icon as swirls of blue waves of wind. Over the Apostles a flame of fire, although the word is "tongues of fire." What statement is this icon making on the subject of expression and thought? The truth with a capital T requires divine revelation. Without the Wisdom that comes from the Maker the human mind is but a noisy barrel, a broken pot. We cannot know the truth, cannot express the truth without divine intervention. With our thinking, we must aim at *kenosis,* at humility of thought, erasing our own assumptions of what reality is and making room for the Holy Spirit to give us the light and the tongue to express the mysteries that we cannot express with our own mind. The Holy Spirit is like a light that comes on making it easier to use our faculty of light. In other cases, it is like eyeglasses or even a microscope.

We cannot know the truth, let alone express it correctly, without the energy and force of the Spirit. There is a limit to human logic. Without the heart or *nous,* the innermost part of the soul to guide it, logic can become a powerful ploy of pride.

SECTION 2

The Struggle

Pilgrim making penance by groveling from the port to the top of the hill of the Holy Annunciation Cathedral of Tinos, Cyclades

Struggle to Have Faith

Anxiety
Oil pastel, 9X12, 2023

For some of us getting one year older becomes a struggle to keep the faith, to believe in the best of human potential and not disintegrate into a mass of hardened, disillusioned skepticism.

The big fight for those of us past the days of wine and roses is not to lose perspective of youthful exuberance, the joie d' vivre. It's another thing to physically get Botoxed and toned, but when the soul gets old and jaded, that in short is the bigger fight to stay young, to believe.

The truth is this can be a hard fight. Because the older you get the wiser you get. You can see through people's facades; you've lived through your share of disappointments, betrayals and broken hearts. Faced with the treachery, the hypocrisy, the folly in our fellow man we put up mental fortress and retreat into ourselves—for better or for worse.

This year I had a real big struggle not to lose faith in my fellow man in a very personal way. For many years I have been attending a Russian Orthodox Church. I found sustenance there and the priest was a dynamic speaker and an overall respected human being. Until there was a fall out. The priest had been spreading lies about his past, puffing himself up higher and mightier socially than his real origins.

That would have been all good and fine. Except that he never came clean with it. He never apologized or recognized his failings to his parish. This caused a rift, a divorce you might say, causing more than half the parish to follow another priest, the second-in-command to another church. Things weren't the same after that. So, I took the opportunity to reconsider my affiliation with the Greek Orthodox Church. After all, I am ethnically Greek, not Russian. The Greek chanting and language is beautiful.

I had distanced myself from the Greek Church because of all the power-mongering, puffiness, and hypocrisy. Most Greek churches I did not feel much spirit in; you were there to show off your status with your heavy minks and Louis Vuittons. The priests gave shallow sermons; very predictable and not soul-lifting, just Hallmark-quality messages with a few verses from the New Testament thrown in. The Philoptochos was more interested in collecting funds, not to feed the poor, who in New York City are plentiful, but to upgrade the bathrooms in the church with gleaming stainless steel fixtures and beautiful marble counters. I guess you are more sensitive to the sins of your own people as you are so up-close. They strike a chord a little too hard in yourself, maybe because you too might harbor them.

Few weeks later, after social shopping for a church, I found myself attending services at St Spyridon in Washington Heights. It was majestic; I felt the spirit. Most Sundays I would tear with the beauty of the place and the chanting. And the father, well, he was very respected and an imposing figure. He had what you can say "the spiritual balls" to call right, right and wrong, wrong. My daughter had a big Sunday school to attend.

It was wonderful. Until one Sunday when I returned from a vacation to Greece and found Father George missing. Another jolly, grandfatherly priest was officiating. He mentioned something about Father George being sick. And then the same thing happened the Sunday after. And the Sunday after that. And then while I was posting on Facebook, I saw the news. The "I Speak Greeklish" Facebook page was running with it. *The New York Post* had the scoop; all the juicy details of the priest, a respected clergyman, with a wife and daughter and a grandchild, in bed having orgiastic sex with a parishioner. She, it alleged, was his spiritual daughter, a convert of Hispanic descent, married to a Greek man with three children. The "kinky" priest needed cake and other things to get it on. The tabloid had even gotten access to a "sex tape" of the two and had blasted it all over the internet.

There can be no worse feeling than how I felt that Sunday morning. That Sunday morning I stopped attending St Spyridon's Greek Orthodox Church. I stopped attending every church that Sunday morning. It was a hard blow to even the staunchest of faithful. Sexual impropriety is one thing, but the hypocrisy. The not coming clean. It is human to err, but when a Christ-like figure (supposedly) does not confess, shows no remorse, does not ask forgiveness, like the majority of us shmucks who follow the cannons of this faith, but instead goes for years professing from the mountaintop like some larger-than-life figure, and has so much pride that he can keep a porn tape of his illicit affair in the hard drive of his office computer without fear that he could be caught, well, that's when you want to stop believing in everything. It's enough having to deal with the cut-throat injustice on the job, but when it occurs in the private realm, close to home, close to the heart, that's when it hurts the most. And these were one of your own; one of the best.

We need heroes to survive as a species. We need role models and fathers and mothers, responsible figures who do the right thing and show us the way. We need Jesus. But when a Christ-look alike is caught in flagrante with knickers down doing the dirty, what is there left to believe in? How does one find redemption in the human race? Even the best of us, even the ones we put on a pedestal, are all too human. (I think that's why JRR Tolkien had Frodo, the pure innocent fail just at the very last moment before flinging the ring into the river of Mordor; no hero is infallible.) When our very heroes betray us, it is then that we must look deep within ourselves. Because to be honest, if you peel back the layers of delusion, you will find that you too are made of the same shit as everybody else. That you can be as arrogant and proud and foolish as the worst of them.

Sure you can go on a search for the better family, the more refined marriage, the more authentic friendship, the more spiritual parish, but one way or another, you will come face to face with the reality of human shortcomings, the same hubris, the same pettiness, the same back talking, hypocrisy, slander, division and sin.

How then can you go on living with people, believing in them, let alone loving them when you know how utterly disappointing they are, how dirty, and crooked, and so utterly sinful? This is the crux of Christian love. It is the struggle to love people as despicable and frail as ourselves. That is the essence of being human. The struggle to find the icon of God within the mired mortal flesh. The hope that he or she will not let you down, even while knowing deep within, that they have already failed you. This is what Jesus had to go through by coming into the world. He loved humanity despite its folly, in spite of its stupidity and corruption. That is the real task of the human hero. St Passios says we should never judge others even as they are doing wrong. We can only judge ourselves.

"You've got to look at the whole tapestry," I keep urging myself, "and not the holes here or there. As a whole, it measures up to standards."

I recently heard an interview with Nick Yarris, a man who was put on death row for allegedly raping and killing a woman 20 years ago. He served 20 years behind jail and was unlawfully framed for a crime he did not commit. He was to be put on death row and face execution by lethal injection when the Innocence Project pushed for a warrant to have DNA testing done on him. He was pronounced completely innocent as charged. If there is a person who would most struggle to have faith in humanity and not turn into a bitter curmudgeon, it would be him. Listen to his interview and he is the opposite.[1]

Love. That is the answer. That has always been the answer. To get through the valley of the shadow of death, you have to have faith in love. That people will disappoint you is a given; you must love them anyway.

1. Mario Cacciottolo, "Nick Yarris: 'How I Survived 22 Years on Death Row,'" BBC News, November 16, 2016, https://www.bbc.com/news/world-us-canada-37974904.

The Lenten Fast and Cheese Doodles

We have started the Lenten fast (again!) In Orthodoxy if you calculate it, the year gets broken down the middle: 180 days of fast and 180 days of feast. "Oh you are a member of that fasting religion," a co-worker at the corporate lunch buffet mutters when he sees me pile the plastic plate with all thinly sliced meager lettuce leaves, tomatoes, and green pepper rings as I scrutinize the ingredient label on the "Classic Italian" salad dressing for any traces of Pecorino Romano cheese or any smidgen of butter. What can we do? My Catholic friends can get into heaven comfortably eating fried cod and tilapia on Fridays while we are mortified if we pinky pick into a dollop of sour cream or take a crumb of Feta. For 40 days we are to subdue the flesh by not indulging in any meat, dairy, wine, or olive oil, except for a few stray feast days when the calendar allows it. It's supposed to be a sacrifice, a purification, a way to get back to God by trying to subdue one of the greatest passions of all—eating. Eating, however innocent it sounds, is the reason why we got kicked out of Eden in the first place. "Of every tree of the garden thou mayest freely eat: But of the tree of the knowledge of good and evil, thou shalt not eat of it: for in the day that thou eatest thereof thou shalt surely die"(Genesis 2:16-17). Eating got us into big big trouble. It led to death. So, as church logic has it, by not eating certain things we will try to gain back our favor with God. By curbing our appetites, we will get back into Eden, albeit a few pounds lighter. It's not so much eating as it is obeying. Hey, the church's thinking goes, if Jesus could fast (i.e. starve) without food or water for a fortnight, the least we can do is survive without meat and dairy for 40 days and nights.

Now, out of all the passions that lead to the deadly sins, give or take a few, not eating, or controlling the stomach is one of the most challenging for me. You can lead me to walk through a football stadium full of naked buff Chippendale dancers, even throw in a couple of Kevin Costner, Brad Pitt look-alikes, and even the ultimate challenge—Robert Plant in his heyday with the Botticelli blonde curls pulsating his groin out to the riffs of the "Lemon Song"—and I swear, I would not touch a single body. I might shield my eyes now and then to avoid the sweaty, glistening six-pack of Vin Diesel or the Rock, a subtle thought would not waft through my brain; an evil chord would not pulsate through my body. No sir, no unclean thought, no below-the-belt titillation, no um-um-um desire would move me.

BUT, put me in a room full of thousands and thousands of unopened packets of cheese puffs and I'm done. Ooooohhhhh! That processed cheesy aroma would emerge like in some Woody Woodpecker cartoon where you see the smell of the roast transform into the long-nailed hand of some seductress and float into the nostrils of Woody, putting him in a trance, slowly elevating him through dells and hills to the source of his pleasure—cheese doodles! The puffy, slightly stale kind. Irresistible! Tantalizing! Impossible for me to keep away.

Ever since I was a toddler, I was transfixed by the crispy cheesy texture, the whole edible experience of biting into their air-filled creamy saltiness, leaving the processed cheese pasty residue on my thumb and forefingers that I would relish licking and scraping off with my front teeth. Maybe it was my Aunt Dafne who got me hooked. When she would visit us as kids, she would bring a plastic bag filled with shiny orange sachets of cheese doodles, the ones that carried a toy wrapped in cellophane in every pouch. I would pounce on her like white on rice. Oh, that cheesy pleasure of hearing the crunch of each puffy doodle, the slow savor of the cheddar creamy consistency in my gums, the methodical division of each doodle into three bite-sized chunks. I especially like the doodles that were a day or two old; they had just that right combination of texture and staleness that made them ripe for chewing. Never liked the crunchy doodles, just the puffy ones. So, help me God against the temptation of the Cheese Doodle.

Every day when I see first graders with Dora the Explorer backpacks munching on their packets of Wise or Utz, my mouth waters; my nose overwhelmed by that fresh cheesy fragrance. I look at the tiny cheese particles, the morsels that fall off the husks as they fly to the ground in grief. "Please, God, just a morsel; just a speck of the doodle detritus! It can't be that sinful, just a nibble, OK?"

I have dreams of devouring entire rooms of cheese doodles. I see a slow-motion clip of my falling into a pit (like the bright ball pit the toddlers jump into at the McDonald's indoor play pit) of oversized extra-cheesy, extra-orangey cheese doodles and drowning in their heavenly richness. I can give up sex, money, even sleep, but God, please don't, don't take away my cheese doodles!

Yet this is what we are called to do. To give up the stuff that most keeps us pinioned to the earth. The fast is excruciatingly difficult because of my penchant for cheese puffs. It is supposed to make you hold fast. Stick fast to the rules. I suppose it is supposed to make you strap the reins on your chariot of passions and not let them drive you into the abyss of your drives. It is paradoxically supposed to set you free by siphoning you into a very rigid scuba suit of rules. Only when you can follow the rules to a "T" will you finally be able to be free of them. It forces you to turn your insides out. And even though not impossible, it seems a do-able endeavor—"stay away from meat, things of the flesh, vain entertainments, sex for 40 days so that you can realign your focus on the things that really count, the things that are eternal, heavenly, spiritual." Fat chance! It is incredibly difficult. There is something in the world, in your inner self (some call it resistance, gravity, the "devil") that keeps you from changing, that keeps you from obeying a simple rule. "A little chunk from the chocolate bar, OK? Not a chunk, OK, then how about just a lick?"—your conscience's excuse generator kicks into overdrive. "If I only have the potatoes around the baking dish, but not the chicken itself, it's not like I'm eating the chicken. I'm still fasting, right?" "Oh Jeez, it's been such a hard day. I'm allowed a bit of milk in my morning coffee." Father says, "It's your 'but' that's gonna park you into hell."

The smallest of sacrifices is a Sisyphean task during Lent. The winter get-away all-you-can-eat cruise, your best friend's wedding, NYC Restaurant Week, all seem to get scheduled just around the fast period. It's during the fast, dab Nabit, that I quite unexpectedly bump into that long-lost friend who invites me for dinner and offers my favorite Indian dish, saag paneer, cooked to creamy perfection, only to have to decline because I cannot break the fast. Then quickly my "make-excuses-with-excuse generator" fills my mouth with, "Oh well now, can I really offend this very good, good friend? How can I not eat her homemade cheese with spinach in a cream sauce so lovingly sautéed with just the right number of spices?"

I don't know why it is so hard to change habits except that humans are habitual animals. The same way it is so hard to keep a fixed rule of prayer—I am supposed to pray morning and evening with a 15-minute Akathist here and there squeezed in. But I find as soon as I make a rule to keep an extra practice of prayer during the day, the sooner I break it. It's as if I go from walking on a flat plain surface to climbing up a steep sand cliff, losing footing with each step of the way, the minute I resort to following the fast and true way of the fast. To stay still, to stay fixed and resolved on what I set out to do needs the resignation of a saint. It requires heavenly help.

You have to deal with the enemy from within. Instead of relinquishing the power of food and flesh, I find obsessing more about it. "What am I going to have for lunch? Veggie burgers, creative salads? A juice shake? What am I going to have for dinner? Shrimp with pasta? Sorbet?" When will I stop by GNC or Trader Joe's to stock up on the smoked tofu, capers, and soy ice cream?" I find myself flipping through arcane web-pages listing vegan recipes, scouring the exotic spice racks at the gourmet shops for unheard of foodstuffs such as sharkfin dust, moonfruit olive relish. I am driven to devour things I would not have before had it not been for the fast: the ugly fruit like a face with a mean case of acne, smelt bread, quinoa spaghetti, crab crackers. I even attempt squid-flavored puff sticks—a far, wanna-be cry for a cheese puff. I eat artificial foods that harken to the taste of the real thing—fake bologna, fake milk, fake butter, fake chicken; things whose ingredient label sounds like the toxic inventory list of a nuclear reactor plant in Chernobyl.

It's the same resistance when it comes to giving alms, something else we are supposed to do during Lent. I have been deliberately delaying for two weeks already whether to deliver a sympathy card to the family of the local sanitation worker who was killed in a hit-and-run. "Oh I have to give that card to the secretary collecting donations," I keep prodding myself. The will is there but walking that flesh to the corner is weak. I want to give, really I do, but time, logistics, bills get in the way. It is so easy to spend $40 on boots but so hard to write a check for that much knowing full well it will go to feeding orphans or inoculating infants against malaria. A better bargain than gracing your toes with sheepskin or at least buffing them with pumice stone (better yet having someone else buff them). It seems such an easy choice, yet there is something that makes it so hard to make. The sneaky splash of frothy milk into the Cappuccino (it wouldn't be cappuccino without it). Is it the bastion of selfishness at the center of human essence? The "me-me-me" mantra unconsciously underlies everything, even the good things you do. "Let not the left hand know what the right hand is doing" (Matthew 6:3). I have to trick myself into doing something good for goodness' sake!

And those damning cheese curls! They beckon with the bend of their puffy little orange arms—"Come, eat us! Let us take you to that cinnabar land of lusciousness lubricated in just the right amount of processed cheddary-cheese bliss!" Just one puff, just one puff—PUFF! And you are there! Cheese puff heaven where you float on a giant cheese puff cloud with an orangey-rosy complexion and eat puffs from an ever-replenishing bag of cheese puffs to your heart's content.

In an instant, you fall into the 3/4th ring of hell. You float in a giant Utz foil bag with all the other cheese-puff damned souls, your belly bloated, your fingertips and lips cracked in that tell-tale color of shame forced to gorge on buckets and buckets of cheese curls for eternity. "Be wary, my son," the poet-parent will caution. "Be wary of the dangers of the flesh." All your forebears will say, "She traded her God for a cheap, air-filled puff of processed cheddar."

Ms. Grumble

MR. GRUMBLE

by Roger Hargreaves

Antoni Gaudi in his journals remarked that ““Life is love, and love is sacrifice. Sacrifice is the only really fruitful thing.”[1] Without sacrifice you cannot be too sure it is love. My problem is that I can understand this intellectually, but try putting this in practice and “Oh my God! Why am I the one that must bear all the burden!?! Why do I have to work so hard to keep a family? Why can’t someone take care of me for once.”

Sure, I want a baby–but the work! The sacrifice to my career, my lifestyle and social relationships. I don’t want it!

1. Austen Ivereigh, Godspy magazine, 2026. https://oldarchive.godspy.com/culture/Architect-Gaudi-the-Blessed-by-Austen-Ivereigh.cfm.htm

I am a reluctant lover. I want to eat the cake and not gain calories. Have the husband without the compromise of putting down my treasured Renaissance portraits and changing the softness rating of the mattress.

Most days I feel sorry for myself—"Oh how I suffer so much, that I carry so much on my shoulders that I'm getting nowhere with my life. That I have to endure so much injustice–my boss is so unfair she never gives me any credit. How can you make an honest living? How can you preserve some modicum of integrity in a world so engulfed in corruption, where one rises to the top by stomping on the backs of his fellows, where deception works better to lure friends and supporters than integrity and honesty? How can you still keep sane? How can you still keep the joy in a world marred by violence?

I started Monday morning by following the trail of splattered blood along the 125th Station down the stairs, across the platform to the turnstiles and into the corner behind the sign for the downtown 6, where a puddle of crimson lay curdling under the smeared ink of a crumpled *NY Post*. Some crazy man had randomly stabbed three people and had disappeared. You are on your way to your factory or office job at 6:30 in the morning and you get stabbed at random by a lunatic.

How can you go on living in a world where human life counts for so little–where fellow human animals devour each other without remorse? Where life is so cheap. Where few are friends. How can one survive morally in a world where only the most ruthless, unconscionable, aggressive survive? Is it feasible to be a Christian and still hope to make a stand for yourself in this ravaging world? How can you honestly turn the other cheek and not be considered a "sucker"? How will the lamb survive among a den of wolves?

This morning a difficult day dawned. I struggled to fight the tears. "Oh Lord, I am so exhausted of living here. Please let me die, let me die to gain entrance into Your country, that country whose borne twitters with the wings of the blessed. I have had enough of living in this hell."

It is at this time that I remember the words of my spiritual father, "You are an idealist. You will most likely get disappointed often." And when he said, "When you are feeling bad about your own situation, the best way to get out of your self-pity is to do something for someone else. Only by doing something for someone else can you get out of your funk, do you remember that you are not alone in this plight. You will find that others are going through the same struggle as you are. They are also exhausted, in pain, in dire financial circumstances."

Better yet, pray. In *Our Thoughts Determine Our Lives,* Elder Thaddeus of Vitovnica writes, "When our neighbor comes to us with his troubles, we take part in them, but if we do not know how to relax—to give all our infirmities and those of our neighbor to the Lord—then we bear this cumbersome burden in our own minds and hearts, and over time, we become unbearably stressed and nervous. We become irritable; we cannot stand our own selves, let alone other people around us—our family members and, of course, our co-workers. Our life becomes miserable and stressed, and our nerves become strained. This is because we have not taught ourselves to let go of our thoughts. When our thoughts are at peace, our body rests too."[2]

This is the problem. When I don't take time to pray, I get more irritated and more burdened by the cares that I have heaped onto my own shoulders. And then the burden becomes greater and I get more irritable, and nastier, and more hysterical till I am at the point of utter physical, emotional, and spiritual exhaustion and I just want to hang it all. It is at times like these when it is even more important to pray and pray more earnestly. Thank God for the Jesus Prayer; it's short and so sweet and it is so accessible. It is the thin, hair strand that keeps the scimitar from falling unto the nape of my neck. "Lord Jesus Christ have mercy on me. Lord, Jesus Christ, Son of God, have mercy on me. Lord Jesus Christ, have mercy on me."

My new year's resolution, therefore, is to not grumble and complain so much but to look for ways to get outside of my self-centered pity-party and do something good for someone else in Jesus' name. Amen.

2. Elder Thaddeus, *Our Thoughts Determine Our Lives*, 96.

The Demon Inside

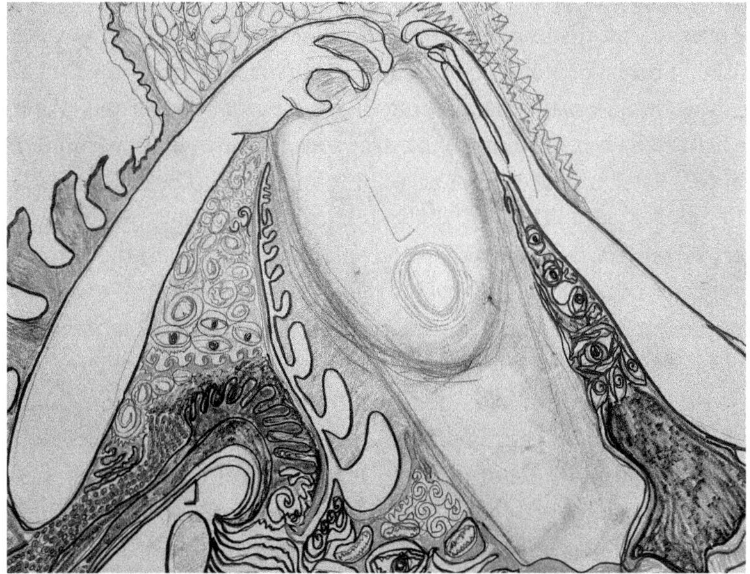

Eirene: Agone, 2020, mixed media on paper, 11X17 inches

THERE IS A DEMON that lives in me. That does not let me be. It rouses me to go fetch the mail, open it in an avalanche of paper—bank statements folded in quarters, credit card statements in triplicate, offers of free CDs and magazines—when I'm at the point of making a peanut butter and jelly sandwich because I have been so busy the whole day creating lesson plans, correcting essays, pointing out deficiencies between sentences and imposter sentences, while in the midst of inspecting the mail pile I discover an overdue car insurance notice—"pay the full amount of $1,214 by January 31st or else your insurance policy will be dropped, with possible prison sentence, etc., etc.," for which the demon prods me—"Go-go! Go find that misplaced checkbook that you last heard fall behind the computer's back and the desk's foam board."

And so I run, to shove the heavy computer desk crammed with my recent areas of interest—Quantum physics, Html Web Design, creative window treatments, and the history of cultural rituals in the Scottish Highlands, all partly read, but not one finished. But as I do this, I remember! "Oh my God! I have to add the bleach to the laundry!" I dash, dash to the washing machine to find I have just missed the wash cycle. Drats! "So where was I?" Oh yes, to find the checkbook, but on my way back to the bedroom to search for the misplaced checkbook to pay for the overdue car insurance payment I discovered while in the as-yet unfinished process of going through the weekly mail, I spot a stray sock that needs washing. So, the demon urges me to pick up the sock and take it to the bathroom and as I deposit the stray sock into the laundry hamper, by chance, I catch a reflection of myself in the mirror. Those blasted black chin hairs! Again! Those straggly stubborn hairs that grow on average every second day after I've completely plucked them out of the bottom of my chinny-chin-chin. "Must pluck them! Must pluck them!" the demon wheedles me. So, I open the medicine chest and start finely squeezing the thongs of the plucker just at the head of these black hairs, the plague of my Mediterranean womanhood, when Brrrrinnggg!—the phone rings. I stop everything and get the phone.—It's my sister. She talks on and on about her day and I about mine. Twenty minutes pass. "Em," I say, "I gotta let you go. I'm really busy. I have to write a check by today before they suspend my insurance. And I haven't eaten anything all day."

When I get off the phone, I turn around and go back to what I was trying to do. "What was I looking for? What was I doing?" Was it writing a check? No, I had to find the checkbook. Was it plucking my chin hairs? No. I was making myself a PBJ sandwich, while keeping an eye on the laundry. I look around the apartment. Dirty laundry in three disparate piles, half-in, half-out in various degrees of sorting. Computer shelves collapsed with an avalanche of books on the floor. An hour has gone by and the only thing I've managed to accomplish is find a stray dirty sock and deposit it in the laundry bin.

This is the demon that lives within me. I liken myself to "Taz," Bugs Bunny's nemesis, the Tasmanian devil who does not walk, but spirals and gyrates into a tornado wind ruffling, disturbing, and consuming everything in his path.

"Every time people ask me about you," my sister tells me on the phone, "I tell them a whirlwind. My sister is a whirlwind. Can never stay put in one spot, without doing something. Always going somewhere, always doing something. You have too much energy to just stay put and write."

Standing still is the hardest challenge of my life. I schedule too many appointments in one chunk of the afternoon, have too many to-do lists to do; have too many pots going on all at once on the range.

"You just don't know when to stop, do you?" an acquaintance remarks.

I only know when to stop when my thoughts race faster than I can think them, when before I've accomplished one daunting task, the demon sends me on a mission impossible to another, until I have spent every ounce of mental, emotional, and physical energy in my body and then—collapse. I exhaust myself to the point of comatose.

"You must think about this, Irene," my therapist prods. "Why do you choose to be so busy? Is there something you are trying to avoid by being less busy and having more time for yourself? What are you afraid of? What would happen if you just sat still?"

For many years, I never knew I was the one doing it to myself. I was making those choices. I started tasks without fully finishing any one like an ever-unfolding lotus flower whose first row of petals are not fully opened before the second row of petals opens. I made my life a chaotic disarray of loose ends where something is always happening, but nothing gets done.

"Your grandmother was a demon," a family member remembers. "She would be talking to us about something and then if she'd see a spot on the wall, she'd start cleaning it and if she'd see another she'd leave off rubbing off the one and head for the other." A demon, that's what she was. A fireball of energy. Couldn't stop talking or walking or cleaning.

For many years I never knew, there was a demon inside me, dictating, hanging me like a puppet on a string.

"Perhaps you need some medication," the therapist suggests.

"Medication?" I look back astonished. "What for?"

"I note some form of mania in your behavior."

"Manic? Me? How do you know it's mania and not just the way I am? I mean, I have a lot of energy and I do a lot of things. That doesn't mean I'm crazy, does it?"

"But not when it interferes with the quality of your life. Not if you get up in the middle of the night and can't control the urge to replaster your bathroom."

No, I don't go to those extremes. Yet, in my own way, I know there is a little demon that lives in me, that creates havoc when I enter a room, makes me begin talking to one person when I'm not yet finished with another, starts a chain of questioning even while I'm lecturing, going on in a roundabout circular fashion, so that in the end my students' faces are left blank—having lost the main point of my lecture (but I do bring it back by the end). "I know you," a Jamaican American spitfire tells me after class, "you are the all-around-the-world kind of teacher."

It has taken me a long time indeed to distinguish between the demon and me. But now that I have summoned it out of its black somnambulant hole, called it by its name, "mania, ADHD, mania, ADHD, mania," I have begun to tame it. Like those little red dancing shoes that drove their victim to dance to death, I've started to untie its laces.

"No," I say to those asking too much of me. "I can't make that appointment in time to keep the other one." I make sure to tell myself—"STOP! STOP! You're doing too much, too many things at once! Let's finish this before we go on to that!" I do not feel guilty about doing "nothing" anymore; now I call it "resting" or "reflecting." I've cut down my jobs from four to two. I am not ashamed to ask for help.

A remedy that has helped to temper those racing thoughts is the Jesus prayer. "Lord, Jesus Christ, Son of God, have mercy on me." I repeat the prayer on the *komboskini,* prayer rope, over and over. "Lord, Jesus Christ, Son of God, have mercy on me, the sinner." I repeat this unceasing, eternal prayer and still the tempest; beyond the susurrations of the demon, I embrace the present, the now, and in the ebb and flow of the prayer in my breast, inhale- "Lord, Jesus Christ, Son of God,"—exhale, "have mercy on me, the sinner" and touch the hem of the eternal, one stitch at a time. The prayer helps with metacognition; it is like having a coach over my thoughts as they do pushups and sit ups, keeping time, telling me to stretch more and watch my form. It is a sort of vigilant security guard over my senses. There is great power in invoking the name of God. His name calls him to roost in the nest of the *nous*, that thinking/feeling center of the soul according to Patristic teaching that is its center. It is the calling of God to enter the mind and help it unscramble itself, find the ends to its knots, and sort its whites from coloreds. It calms me down enough not to be yanked here and there by the tyranny of negative self-talk and thoughts that scramble like screeching monkeys across the canopy of my consciousness. "Lord, Jesus Christ, son of God, have mercy on me" exorcises that demon inside. As the ancients tell us, it is through our thoughts that the demons tempt us. The battle between good and evil takes place on the battlefield of the mind. You cannot trust your thoughts all the time. They can be wrong and downright dangerous. Some might not even be yours as they come from dark sources, launched by the demons to lead you into sin. By reciting the Jesus Prayer, I am able to "pray without ceasing" as St Paul exhorts, so as to quell the darts of the evil one. By reciting the Jesus Prayer, I am calling the physician of souls to come and put the wasp nest in order and cleanse me of the darkness that is not my own. By reciting the Jesus Prayer, I call God into the heart of me, and He is there.

Clear the Table

I am learning how to clear the table. To set the foundation. It is such an easy but easily overlooked fact but you can't build anything unless you have a table. The thing that is in the background but supports the whole show, the platform. I have had a life-long tendency of bombarding the platform. Filling it with things, cluttering the empty spaces. Now am learning—I have to let go of things, I have to clear the spaces, I have to empty the table.

Nothing can be built correctly on a cluttered table. This is what I have to do—declutter my mind, my life, and my living space. I have to figure out what is absolutely necessary, the most essential, and quintessential. Throw everything else out. I have to throw away whatever I have been clinging onto for years afraid that I will need it at some point. Our tendency to hold onto things, our hoarding instinct, stems from a position of lack. We stockpile things out of fear of loss, penury, that we will go without. It is the smart ant that hordes grain for the winter. On its own it is not a bad instinct. Those little clever critters scurrying with cheeks packed to their necks in seeds know it is a matter of life or death to hold onto resources. You never know when that will come in handy.

My tendency to hold on to things, to start yet another project, to do this and then that stems from my voracious need to do and know everything. I gotta have it all! So I go through life arms wide open embracing every good leaf, every patch of sky, every book and pursuit that excites and enriches me. Life is so full of wonder and amazement I want to pack my closets, shelves, and every cranny of my mind with it.

Except that I can't. The closets are bursting. My mind is so inflated it is stretched as thin as my super sheer pantyhose filled with runs. Frankly, I can't pay attention to everything I am interested it. I have reached the limit of my physical and mental powers. I cannot do it all. I have to focus on only what is important. The most essential.

What is that for me? I have some idea, but it will take time to sort through the mismatched socks, the puzzle pieces fallen behind the cracks, the chotckis of elves/marble cats/jaguar heads, dreamcatchers, lipstick cases, pillows, broken frames, piles of notebooks, drawers packed with random pills, notecards, keys. I am clearing the table first.

I want a clean long empty table. With absolutely nothing on it. A shiny white table.

Accountability

If I were ever condemned to hell, I know that the perfect profession for my eternal punishment would be "accountant." All the balancing of cents in, cents out; the sums and subtractions; the keeping the ledgers neat and clean and smudge-proof; all the focus on the dirty little details. It would be torture! It is like a straight jacket for those of us with the buck and buckle of the creative Pegasus bounding from cloud to cloud, absolutely refusing to be bridled or corralled. I have never been able to balance a checkbook. The most I do is pay the bills, write the checks, use the debit card, and cross my fingers and myself–hopefully, there is enough so that it all doesn't bounce. I do a little prayer in front of the ATM machine, "Please Lord let there be enough so I can afford a cappuccino." I have paid dearly for my inability or reluctance to be accountable, namely in hundreds of dollars of overdraft fees and a nasty credit history.

This refusal on my part to take careful note and track what is coming in and what is going out extends to more than just my finances. Take my caloric intake for instance. I can only take in 1,000 calories a day to keep from getting obese. I must lose a minimum of 500 calories on the treadmill or the aerobic studio three times a week to lose a pound. The nutritionist says there is no way I can lose weight if I don't keep a careful diary of what I take in (accounts receivable) and what I burn and take out (accounts payable). I must become fanatical about this balancing if I ever hope to lose the extra weight. First, I can never commit to writing anything down on paper. I usually blow the whole diet by scrimping on the calories on the whole wheat slice only to make them up triple-fold in the "low-fat yogurt" sundae worth 450 calories. It doesn't work. I have been the same weight for thirty years now.

Take my prayer life. I have vile and undisciplined habits. I might do my morning prayers consistently for a week, but then I skip out on the evening prayers. Or I'll do it in reverse. Hold fast to a regimen of evening prayers only to "forget" to pray in the morning. Never mind about the fasting bit. Sure, I can keep it for maybe two weeks and then my relish for cheese doodles takes over my will or the little voice comes on that says, "Oh well, but it's just a slaver of cream cheese. It's not really cheating. It's not like I'm having a ham sandwich."

I am as a Christian supposed to be charitable, not just charitable but as St. Paul says, "a leader at the forefront of good works." When was the last time I did something truly charitable? Something that cost me time, effort, a cringe in my pocketbook. What have I done to reduce the poverty of spirit that is so widespread in the affluent world? This too is a matter of accountability. I am supposed to give like a good steward back to the keeper of the vineyard. I am supposed to increase the dividends on the one talent I was given. If I do not, I will be bound and thrown out of the garden.

The problem is I cannot be accountable. I want to be a "more or less" kind of bookkeeper. If I have the impression that I'm doing things right or that I have given back enough, well then with a flick of the back of my hand, "Don't bother me. I have enough in the account to keep my body and soul together." However, the Lord expects me to be accountable. Very much so, both physically and morally. In this climate of low-cash flow and budgeting, I must be. Otherwise, I wind up like the prodigal son sleeping with the swine and sucking on corn husks. I am reaching the point in my bank account called the "red zone" where I will be in dire financial straits should something like an emergency happen. The red zone has caused my red blood cells to boil to the point you see in the Tom and Jerry cartoons-- the thermometer bulb bulges from the heat and blows up in Tom's face. "Take stock of what you have and what you really need," this voice tells me.

In the seven years of lean in Egypt, in the period of the Great Starvation equivalent to our Great Recession where resources are scarce and mouths are many, I must be accountable. It is as if the Lord is giving me a very pronounced lesson from life, "Take the reins in. Watch what you spend and what you eat, drink, and do." Pay attention to the details. To the little cents. It is the mites that are important after all. I am sure that this Great Recession has come to remind me about my prodigality and insensitivity to spiritual and physical poverty. To have to think about where my next bite of food will come from, if I am going to be able to pay for the electric bill by the end of the month so they don't turn it off, how to mend those shorts that ripped to save from buying another pair, these are things the poor deal with on a daily basis. It is in this time of need and missing out on the essentials of living-a car, a vacation, a PlayStation–that I am reminded of the great poverty that three quarters of the globe must contend with. It is a time to pull in our belts, restock our lives with what is needful and what is superfluous. Only when you need things, do you appreciate what you can do with a $20 bill, and you hit yourself over the head for what you could have done with all those $20 bills you spent on iced daiquiris and spa pedicures.

The Great Recession reminds us of our own poverty–our poverty of spirit; that in our gluttony to feed ourselves and our egos in conspicuous consumption, we have forgotten how the other half lives. If there are children who go hungry because of our selfishness and greed, we shall be accountable to them. Our lack of charity equates to their starvation. We in the lush suburbs of the First World who have so far luxuriated in the lap of luxury, we have been given a dose of our poverty of spirit. My grandmother used to say, "You need to eat of the loaf of poverty to understand the hunger of the beggar." This reminds me of the woman micro-entrepreneur in Haiti who won an award for her business --mud pies--bread baked with real mud inside.[1] Mud takes the stomach a long time to work so that curbs the hunger of the laborers. It is a quick fix to the constant stomach cramps the poor feel. They would be content to eat mud and not feel hunger.

I must be accountable. Out of my need I must give to those who have less. I must fill the poverty of my spirit with the fullness of God's loving kindness. I must rely on God even more now, for the essentials, for those things I took for granted when my belly was fat and my wallet fatter. And pray as I grow lean around the waist, I will grow fuller in the Spirit.

1. Rory Carroll, "Haiti: Mud Cakes Become Staple Diet as Cost of Food Soars Beyond a Family's Reach," *The Guardian*, October 19, 2022, https://www.theguardian.com/world/2008/jul/29/food.internationalaidanddevelopment.

Archery Lesson

"ἁμαρτία," from the Greek, "a"="not, without" "marti"="the mark, the goal"
(i.e. "missing the mark")

When I was four, and still a ruffian running wild in the cobble and dirt-filled square of my family's apartment building in suburban Athens, one of the neighborhood urchins created a ruckus. A throng of other buzz-cut rascals, their neck creases black in soot and dried sweat, had gathered around him and were jostling, poking, shoving at one another to get to the center of the circle and get a load of his new contraption. In one hand he held a thin piece of wood, maybe two inches wide, curved into a half circle with a string stretched taut from one side to the other. In his other hand he held a long, thin piece of aluminum chiseled to a point on one end with the tail feather of a pigeon on the other. "Give me! Let me try! It's Panagiotis–you can't grab it! Watch it! Look . . . How do you shoot it?" All these came out at once like a cloud of dust.

As I too was an urchin, wild enough to beat the best of them even if I were a girl, I managed to snatch it away from Giorgio and get a full three seconds of the contraption to myself to try to see what combination of space and motion I could use on the crescent and its bow to make the thing fly. The best I could do was weave the bow through the string and pull the string so the bow would fall to my sandaled feet, encrusted with dirt, ashy from the upturned dust.

Until my Pappou (God rest his soul) appeared on the scene and said, "Stasou!" (Wait a minute!), pulled the contraption from within my hands, and with the rims of his gold-plated filling of his front teeth gleaming in the sun, showed us how to shoot a bow the right way.

First, you hold the bow with your left hand (the opposite of your dominant hand) to the center of your body. Then you hold the arrow between the forefinger and middle finger of your dominant hand. You place the arrow point into the arrow rest in the middle of the bow's body; then you catch the arrow's butt or the "nock" into the string. You pull the string straight with your arm extending as far back as your elbow will let you go perpendicularly to the ground so that your right elbow makes the leg of an "L" with the arrow against the bow at anchor point. (In proper form they tell you your body showed be in shape of a "T" to the ground.) You measure the distance to your target by closing your left eye and approximating with your right and then just before you let go of the arrow, you creak the entire form 1/8th to a 1/4 inch upwards to allow for the arc of the fall in the arrow's trajectory to its object. Let go of the bow remembering to release the grip of your fingers both on the front and the back of the arrow shaft at the same time. (If not, you might get "arrow burn.")

Pheww! And the arrow flies into the cerulean sky–so boldly, so gracefully, so purely like a math equation magically made alive. It eventually dove into the ground and made a small cloud of dust. Wow! I had never seen such mastery of space and time. Like the arrow was a nimble dancer–cutting through the ether to arrive dead center into the heart of its target.

Witnessing the arrow's first flight has stayed with me all these 50 years of my life. The passion for archery has not faded. Think about it–the rules are so simple yet getting them right is so hard. Align your body with the target, sharpen your eyes, flex your muscles esp. those lower trapezes, measure distance, account for the arrow's fall and the things that get in its way, and then you get out of its way. Viola! It is gone. You must try to replicate each precise motion and action–all for the one object of desire–to get into the heart of the target, the center of the bull's eye or the hart's heart.

The archer's quest is a fit metaphor for the Christian spiritual struggle. So much concentration, so much precision, so much patience and perseverance, the entire mind, body, and soul goes into getting the goal. An archer will attempt to perform the same sequence of steps, isolate the perfect form, the precise angle to get closer and closer to the mark. The same motion, the same movement repeated again and again but with differing results. That's the ultimate frustration of the archer. You might get the bulls' eye once every 150 tries. Your aim is to replicate that exact combination of movements that resulted in the hitting of the bull's eye. In essence, the challenge in archery is to repeat the same performance, the perfect performance, again and again, no matter what changes in variable, no matter how many failures, to produce the same result–the arrow piercing through the heart of the object of its desire. It is the futility of perfection; no matter how many times you try it it is impossible to replicate the exact constellation of actions that led to a bull's eye. You might get lucky and be perfect occasionally, or close to perfect, but you cannot be precisely perfect all the time.

This is the lot of all who seek perfection, who seek to replicate in act, form, and intent, the *summum bonum*. I can try very, very hard to be like God. I can aim all my faculties, gather all my energies, physical, emotional, and facultative, take aim, have eyes on the prize, and still fall far from the mark. Again. and again. The reality is as an archer and as a human being, I will fall short of the mark countless, endless more times than I will hit it.

When I look back to all the times I have tried to meet the mark, my own failure has been made all the clearer by the outcome. Here are some of my failed attempts to meet the mark.

"Mark!": I will remain quiet in the face of others' contempt or criticism.

"Form!": "Shut up! Shut up!" I tell myself mentally when my mother complains about the way I put the groceries back on the shelves. "Don't let me speak," I coach myself. "Don't open your mouth. She's an old woman. She's been through a lot. She is not going to change." But the urge to keep quiet is not as strong as the will to assert dominance to prove someone wrong.

"Don't tell me how to put the things back in my kitchen!" I hear myself bark back at her. "You never in your whole life know how to organize a house. Look at all the damned plastic bags you keep stuffing behind the radiator. You clutter every amount of free space in the kitchen shelves!" If my mouth could stop there, it would be bad enough. But no, it goes on and on and on. "No wonder Daddy left you! You never knew how to run a house. Your house was filthy and out of control."

I was trying to be helpful to her by putting groceries (groceries she had bought for me) away esp. in those hard-to-reach spaces where her arthritic hands cannot reach. I tried to keep silent to be patient and loving.

"Result!": I fell far from the mark.

Mark: At the beginning of the week, on a Sunday afternoon, having been strengthened by Holy Communion and the sense of combined spiritual endeavor from sharing time and conversation from my church parish, I vow, "Lord, I will pray consistently to You–every morning and every night. I will keep the fast. I promise."

Form: Monday afternoon. Pangs of hunger exacerbate the annoyance of not finding available fasting food in the school cafeteria. Fish fillets have processed/imitation American cheese swathed in their middles; salad bar has Parmesan-laden breadcrumbs. I cry, "Oh God! Oh God! I can't! I'm starving! I need sustenance. I have been called all kinds of "b****" from my students and my principal made an infamous ambush-observation on my worst class. I Need Foood!! I'm having a hard day. You will understand, right?"

I take a generous helping of the salad and another generous helping of the fillet-o-fish.

Result: I have fallen far from the mark.

Mark: I will be more generous in almsgiving.

Form: I have kept two envelopes with alms–complete with stamps and signed checks–in the back of my writing desk for close to six months now. I make all kinds of excuses why I don't have time to drop them into the mailbox at the end of my street corner (the one I pass by twice a day).

Result: I have fallen far from the mark.

Mark: I will be the better person. I will not get angry at my daughter. I will speak to her respectfully.

Form: "Hi, Christina, how was school today?" I greet her when I come in from work.

"Fine," she mutters within a bag of Doritos. Without eye contact.

"Do you have a lot of homework tonight?"

"Can you please get out of my room?" she answers.

"I am only here for a few minutes. I just want to know what's going on in school and how your day was. I care about you."

"Nothing, nothing is happening in school. It's the same old routine," she returns pushing my shoulders into the threshold of her bedroom door. "Everything's fine."

"You cannot push me out," my tone starts to escalate. "I am concerned about you. I am your mother."

"My life is none of your business," she retorts.

"Oh really?" I say. "As long as you are in my house under my roof, you are my business. As long as you are in my pocketbook, I am going to be in your business. You are only 14 years old. You come into my room all the time taking my stuff, my pearl ring, my eyeliner, my blush; it's only common courtesy that you allow me in yours."

"I do not take your stuff!" she protests.

"Yes, you do," I return. "Where is my eyeliner?"

"I didn't take it."

"Oh yes you did. That's why you have your eyes outlined with my Lancome that cost me $35! It's OK that you want to use my things, but you are so messy and irresponsible you never return them in their rightful place. God forbid I take anything out of your room! You will have my head!"

"Yeah, yeah, I'm always irresponsible and messy. You don't appreciate all the things I do around here. Get out of my room~!!" she screams.

"Don't you dare scream at me like that!" I scream. "I refuse for you to answer me in that tone of voice!!!"

"GET OUT OF MY ROOOM! THIS IS WHY I NEVER WANT YOU IN HERE. All you do is complain how messy and irresponsible I am. Move and leave me alone!!!"

"Oh don't worry about that. I won't bother you again. You can stay and rot in your room, you ungrateful wench! With all the things I've done for you! You should be ashamed of yourself! You are going to stay in there and not come out until you know how to treat elders with respect! Even God put that in the Ten Commandments: Respect thy mother and thy father. You don't have to love them but you sure in hell better respect them!!!" I am totally out of control, hysterically slamming her door behind me.

Result: I have fallen far from the mark.

Mark: I will not scream or cuss or complain about little things. I will be grateful for things, even difficult things, as God allows them to happen for a reason.

Form: Why doesn't this f***ing stove work?" when I go to make the morning coffee and the pilot light refuses to come on even after five repeated counterclockwise attempts at the "Light" arrow and the annoying strings of "tik-tik-tik-tiks" that go along with sparking the flame. "God damn this freakin' dog!" the first words from my mouth when I step on one of Zhou Zhou's "accidents" in my bare-naked feet on the kitchen linoleum as I prepare to come to life with a cup of coffee. "Gamoto tin ora kai tin mera pou genithika" (Greek, "F*** the hour and the day I was born.")

Result: I have fallen far from the mark.

Mark: I will be charitable. I will do more acts of mercy, esp. for the poor.

Form: There is a homeless man close to the subway station that I take to work. I will make it a point to give him some money or at least make a sandwich or a bag of food for him on a daily basis. He is of Greek descent. He is part of our community. As one of our own, we have a moral responsibility to take care of him. God knows he is a good-natured bum. He is like the Cynic philosopher around here. People talk to him about their problems. He never comes out directly to ask for cash, but his glance and his demeanor let you know he needs it. He wears long hair to complement a long scraggly beard. He wears leather sandals with both hands stuffed in his 3/4 denim overalls replete with the grime of the city street. Sort of like a Greek hippie. He is mild-mannered and talks to the locals about life. He says if we are the ones who are free, how come we take the subway every morning and night wearing faces of disgust and tiredness? He is above and beyond the "rat race" that enslaves our souls. He is the one who is free. He doesn't want to find a house or job and lose his freedom and the joy in his soul.

Result: While descending the steps from the elevated subway, I spot him at his usual place under the spray-painted covered bridge that makes an overpass for the Acela train to Boston and beyond. I start feeling a sense of discomfort–the time has come to make right on my promise. But I feel very shy all of a sudden. I get the willies. How do I give him a handout without insulting him? Will he start to see me in a different way esp since I am a woman? Will I start getting unwarranted attention from him if I do? On second thought, it is dangerous or at least unseemly for women to be giving bums under bridges money. If only there was a homeless association I can give money to that could take care of these people around here? Yeah, that's it. That's what I'll do instead of giving him money. I will start this sort of civic feed-the-homeless-around-the-block association, specifically to feed bums we are afraid of.

My thoughts fly like arrows as I walk by him demurely, my shoulders hunched, my eyes skirting the cracks in the city's pavement. My sense of dread subsides with each step as I get farther and farther from my mark.

Once when he was looking across the street to the other side of the painted bridge, I snuck a $10 bill in the folds of his backpack resting on a grey blanket. Even then the words of my spiritual father echoed within my head, "We think we know how to love. We give a homeless man a sandwich and we think we have fulfilled our moral duty. We have no idea how to love." And again in another confession-session, "Even the righteous man sins a thousand times each day."

Result: I have missed the mark.

It is futile. This endeavor to aim and get to the center of the mark, again and again and again. I am reminded every time I release that arrow that I am doomed to fail. I see it sweep through that infinite distance between the intention and its outcome, and cringe at its falling. I see so many of my failed attempts at my aim, the tell-tale holes in the target paper. It is a wonder I don't despair. The paper is riddled with holes some in the 200, some 400 some 600 some even 800 zone while some altogether miss the board entirely. There is no getting around the fact that in 99% of the tries, even in my best form, the arrow will fail to reach its mark. The pursuit of perfection is an exercise in failure and futility. It is particularly painful for the perfectionists who so desperately in good faith want to reach their mark.

But–ah!–for that one good shot. That arrowhead that makes it to the perfect center of the board. That transversal that penetrates the heart of the unattainable. It is that perfect shot that makes the perfectionist try and try (and fail and fail) again and again. It is the possibility of perfection that keeps the archer at his bow for hours (even as poor Orion is fated for eternity to circumambulate the globe in hunt for the eye of the Bull). When the act of failure becomes the very inspiration for success, maybe then we will have learned the lesson of the Supreme Archer. As humans we are doomed to err, but in our endeavor to emulate the divine, we surpass our short-comings and get that wondrous chance, that miracle of all impossibility that we pierce into the center of the perfect circle and become like God himself, perfect and divine.

We get over our failings and our fear of our failures and strive for excellence in spite of ourselves. This is the lesson from archery. We are wretched and even in our greatest form, we will fall far from the mark. In our imperfection we will never reach perfection. But we have to attempt the impossible in any case. It is the struggle to achieve perfection that gives this sport its meaning, its beauty, its resilience. It is the act of trying even in the inevitability of failure that brings us one step closer to perfection.

My Spiritual Diet

Pears, Oil Pastel on paper, 2024.

I HAVE BEEN ON a diet for the last 45 years. In fact, when I think about it, my efforts at losing weight parallel my attempts to achieve a spiritual life. The two efforts are both exercises in ascetic self-control. They are both anchored in the need for the body and soul to change. They both take a lot of work and are slow and grueling. They test your endurance and your tenacity at sticking to a goal even in the face of disappointment and no outward gratification of results.

You see, the idea that you go on a diet starts with a dissatisfaction with how you look or feel. You compare your body, Michelin-man rubber tired around the waist, chicken flaps that wobble under your arms when you walk, your turkey neck with more chins than a Chinese phone book—and you say "Enough! Something has to change! I can't stand walking by a mirror to catch sight of my unattractiveness. I am going to change how I eat, what I put on my inside so I can change how I look on the outside. I'm going on a diet! I am going to keep to a strict rule of working out 3 to 4 times a week, varying cardio with toning. I have to change the way I look and feel about myself."

This is the same realization I get when thinking about my spirit. I analyze my heart—the quick temper that recoils with rattlesnake vengeance to the guy who took my parking space, my constant grumblings and unappreciation, "Poor me! I hate my job! I don't drive a fancy car. Why wasn't I born rich! The wallowing in my own unique brand of self-misery, the self-centeredness, vainer than a supermodel's glance in the mirror—and I say, "I need to change. I need to be more patient, more loving, more generous, more joyous and thankful even for the crosses. I will change my ways of thinking to be more positive. I will adhere to a strict fast for body and soul. I will pray the Jesus Prayer as much as I can. I will stick to a strict rule of matins, vespers, and compline prayers."

Do you know how hard it is to lose weight? You have to radically change your life. It takes tremendous willpower, commitment, constancy, vigilance, and work! From the moment you wake up, you have to keep track of what you eat and count the calories. Even when exhausted after a day of work, you have to push yourself into the torture contraption—the treadmill—and push your legs till they become Jello taken out too early from the fridge, until you can count the streams of sweat that slither down the groove in your back just above your haunches, until you can't bear the excruciating heat in your triceps and biceps and you feel like screaming and then you actually do, "Oh my God! This is torture!" gritting through your teeth and you collapse crying on the gym floor, all muscles wiggling like squished worms and expire. You feel such utter desperation. And you look at the calorie counter and all it says is "250." And you want to give up because you can see that all your hard work hasn't made a dent in your fat thighs. And you curse yourself again and again—"You fat f***! You will never change!"

The struggle to change my soul is as hard, if not harder, as the struggle to lose body fat. There is a deeply entrenched brick wall in all of us with the word "*resistance*" sprayed in graffiti bubble letters on it. Try as I might, and I really would like to, really I would, it is excruciatingly difficult to change. Especially since humans are such creatures of habit.

Prayer, like 30 minutes at 4.5 speed at 11 incline on the treadmill, is hard work. You must constantly remind and check yourself, "Was that a thought of envy about your girlfriend Helen's beautiful body that skirted through the dark perimeter of your mind?" Your next-door neighbor refuses your offer for a coffee and then you spin into hypersensitive mode: "Oh my Gosh! Did I do anything to offend her? She doesn't return my phone calls either! Hey! wait, she's done this before. I gave her a present and she never even called to say thank you. Am I going to be the one who constantly offers? That's gratitude for ya! I'm not going to waste my time or effort making nice-nice to her again. Especially since my kindness registers as weakness for some reason. Then the hell with her!"

It is almost impossible to stop an evil thought in mid-tracks. It just slithers out of my head like Medusa's banana curl before I can, with a swift hand, chop it off at the nape of its neck. When I try to change my habits, I meet with resistance "Get up!" I goad myself at first hearing the buzzer on the alarm, that kind that signaled a fire drill in grade school. "You have to pray! You have to go to an early liturgy." Oh yeah, the spirit, it is willing alright, but heck, the flesh is weak. Very weak. "Please, just another 5 minutes and I'll get up." I hit the snooze. Again. And again. And again until 5 minutes have become 50 and by then, well, what's the point of getting up? It's too late to make it to church on time so might as well go back to sleep.

The struggle to keep focused on the goal, (I must lose 30 pounds by summertime, I must get into the kingdom of God) is relentless. You must change the way you shop for food, you must learn about the finer points of food chemistry, you must keep a journal and daily log, you can't forget to drink lots and lots of water, three one-liter bottles per day. You have to contract the help of friends and family not to tempt you with open bags of cheese doodles and not to bring the host presents of white pastry boxes tied with twine filled with sticky sweet baklava and assorted custard combos. Losing weight involves a radical rethinking of yourself, how you eat, how you burn energy. Plus, you have to keep true to this change of plan for a long-darned time. Without seeing any results for what seems like ages. And then you give up.

This sounds just like making strides in the spiritual life. You want God but without the sacrifices to meet Him. You try to do right with the right hand and then erase that good with the left. To save your soul, you have to let God do some major (de)construction in your essence. You have to pray constantly, watch what enters through your five senses, watch what comes out of them too. You have to keep a daily log of rights and wrongs. You must attend liturgies and go to confession on a regular basis. You must go out of your way to do good even when that good will come at a great cost to you (i.e. you might overdraft your bank account because you made out a check to a charity). And you cannot do this alone. Because it is so hard to change, you need the help of an experienced spiritual guide just as you need a nutritionist or trainer or a friend you are accountable to or a gym buddy. Someone who will act as your life coach. You also need the help of a spiritual community just like a weight-loss support group. A community with the same goals who faces the same challenges you do, to provide you with encouragement or a candid, "Hey, have you been doing a bit too much midnight snacking?" A community who is there to give you the "lift" under your wings when the journey gets tiring and overwhelming. Salvation and fitting into a size 5 are so difficult you can't do them alone. You need help.

And then there's the treachery of temptation which is the same for both endeavors. You cannot give in, not even to the slightest provocation—"Why don't you shove it where the sun don't shine?" the nasty teacher who shares my room tells me when I ask her to change the seating arrangement. I want to send her to hell in a handbasket with her room chart flapping behind her. Instead, I bit my tongue and managed a cold but cordial—"Alright, let me see if I can change rooms." And when I see the fat bottle of Nutella waiting for a victim to plunge an engorged finger into its depths, I excuse my nibble and say, "It's not made of real milk but some chemically test-tube concocted processed milk whey something. It's not the same thing." The pangs in my stomach keep me up at night. I swear there is a furry overgrown blue muppet the likes of the Cookie Monster that grovels about in the pit of my stomach and yells up from the depths—"Cookies! Cookies! Feed me! Feed me! I want ice-creams! Give me! Give me!" Against my better judgment, I throw down a half dozen chocolate donuts to appease the monster. "Gee!" I think, "I just blew my diet. I went back not one or two but maybe three days of grueling workouts at the gym. That means I have to make up for it by going 5-6-7-8 times next week. It's no use! There are not enough days in the week to work out that much. I give up!" I hang my hands up in despair and curse the cookie monster in my stomach. "I'll always be a fat slob no matter how much I try."

I'm cool and nonchalant with my favorite person to tempt one with—my adorable, ego-maniacal big baby of a 45-year-old brother.

Until he walks into the house without knocking after 9:30 at night and demands that I move my car from my driveway so that he can park. And that's when I blow—"Get the hell out of my house you miserable piece of turd before I call the cops!" Let's face it—I can recite the Jesus Prayer forever and a day, I won't ever become a saint. I'm the same undisciplined, grouchy, self-centered nag I have always been. I cannot change.

I glance up at the size 8 chiffon dress I used to wear—the one with the scooped neck and the dainty lace around the cuffs adorned with the softest pale blue flowers. I see an old photo I have in my 20s basking on the beach of Santorini. I was hot back then. I look up at my icon of the St. Mary of Egypt. She is skin-thin, her eyes deep-set in black kohl outlines but teary and wide. Her hair is disheveled and wild as the scraggly goat-hide covering her privates. She used to be a prostitute. She tempted a boat load of young men on the voyage to Jerusalem. She engaged in group orgies. She too came from a dysfunctional family. The love she never got from her father left an emptiness so deep in her she tried to fill it with the embrace of thousands of strangers.

Then there comes the time when I face the wall. What is it that keeps me from living my authentic self? Am I more afraid of success than failure? Why do I run away from what I most want to become? Every time I open the refrigerator door, I'm looking for happiness. Every time I skip services, I have cheated my soul of its fulfillment and that deep inner peace that cannot be found in any other place. Why do I search for peace in the hustle and bustle of the mall when I know where I must go to find it? Why is it that I most shun what I most need? It is because I am afraid of change? Am I afraid of the latent power within me? Am I afraid to shine? To be the gorgeous, 125-pound bombshell. To be that beautiful soul radiating with compassion, patience, love.

In your heart of hearts, you know the absolute necessity of losing weight to keep healthy and seeing to your salvation are non-negotiables. These are the most vital acts you must accomplish. Changing your body can save your life and bring enormous benefits, emotional, physical, and psychological. Good health is one of the worthiest aims somebody can strive for. Saving your soul leads to eternal life. This is the soul's ultimate quest to unite with its Maker.

God calls us to change. Radically change. The kind of change needed to lose 45 pounds and temper your soul is the kind of change that happens from the inside out, not the outside in. It is the only real change worth striving for. For through the groans and creaks of this change, there is a transformation of body and soul into a creature of glory and brilliance. It is the only type of change we should be striving for as Christians. To become beautiful like our Maker, for our bodies to shine with the uncreated light of the universe, this is our destiny. Our bodies twinkle with stardust and our souls with a hard gem-like flame. How can we stand to be anything but the true stunningly beautiful creatures we were meant to?

This is the gist of the anecdote related by the Desert Fathers. Abba Lot went to see Abba Joseph and said: "Abba, as much as I am able I practice a small rule, a little fasting, some prayer and meditation, and remain quiet, and as much as possible I keep my thoughts clean. What else should I do?" Then the old man stood up and stretched out his hands toward heaven, and his fingers became like ten torches of flame and he said to him: "If you wish, you can become all flame."[1]

We must never be shortsighted about the goal of our Christian life with all its efforts. It is nothing less than *theosis,* union with the Living God, becoming "all flame." Whether to lose 45 pounds and fast for righteousness' sake, for body or for soul, we do everything for the love of God, to achieve perfection through and by Him alone. For the spirit to conquer the flesh in both dieting and fasting, so that we may burn without burning. Let us burn calories and passions and become as Abba Joseph said " all flame."

1. Ward, Benedicta. *The Sayings of the Desert Fathers: The Alphabetical Collection,* 1975.

This Strange Rock: A Cosmic Contemplation

I WATCHED "GASP," ONE of the episodes of *One Strange Rock*, a 10-part series from National Geographic. It happened! That numinous moment when the veil of conformity and taking-things-for-granted lifted. The realization that WOW! The complexity and interconnectedness of everything—the simple act of breath is an accumulation of several cosmic and chemical events. Oxygen the ability to hold oxygen in the atmosphere that thin layer made possible by ozone; the dust from the salt beds once sea beds filled for half miles with the carcasses of trillions and trillions of diatoms in Africa gets lifted up by mighty winds that transport it to the Amazon where it settles on the forest floor feeding it with the most luscious layer of fertilizer. How water is pulled through the underground networks and sucked through a trillion trees that make oxygen the product of photosynthesis. How fragile yet how complex life is for the simple fact that oxygen exists in the atmosphere. Too little and there would only have been one-celled creatures to make earth home; too much and oxidation would make earth a roaring bonfire. Salt deserts that feed rain forests, glimpses of flying rivers from watch towers higher than a skyscraper. Twenty seven million tons of dust from the salt desert in Africa winds up on the Amazon basin. One tree produces enough oxygen to support two people. The Amazon, so full of oxygen, uses it all up to support the diversity of life there. Diatom blooms, microscopic up close, are seen as blotches of moving blue from space.[1]

Juliana of Norwich had a vision wherein God revealed the cosmos as a hazelnut in the palm of her hand: "He shewed me a little thing, the quantity of an hazel-nut, in the palm of my hand; and it was as round as a

1. Graham Booth, dir. *Gasp: One Strange Rock*, 2018, National Geographic. Prime Video.

ball. I looked thereupon with eye of my understanding, and thought: What may this be? And it was answered generally thus: It is all that is made. I marvelled how it might last, for methought it might suddenly have fallen to naught for little. And I was answered in my understanding: It lasteth, and ever shall for that God loveth it. And so All-thing hath the Being by the love of God.

In this Little Thing I saw three properties. The first is that God made it, the second is that God loveth it, the third, that God keepeth it."[2]

Perhaps I am taking a great leap of faith here but my poet's soul cannot help but clutch my breast at the awesome mystery of this—that nowhere else in the cosmos would it have been possible to have just the right conditions, enough oxygen, for one, to allow for life and consciousness to evolve as we know it. And the miracle is this—that we can contemplate this little nut that holds the cosmos in the palm of our hand and know that Providence governs a thing so small just as the hugeness of the universe, our nut of a galaxy, in the palm of God's hand.

We are everything, from the infinitesimal to the infinite, a manifestation of the Divine Presence in the cosmos.

How can anyone watch these documentaries and not get a sense of awe—that this Created reality we live right now is nothing short of miraculous, whether you attribute it to God or chance? The more I know about the working of the universe, the more I feel the presence of the Divine, that Spirit that ties it all together. We as mankind in our dirty dealings with one another have shaped this world into the hell it is, but by God's Providence it is not so. Look at it as Chris Hatfield the astronaut did from inside the space shuttle and it is a wonder, it is earth from heaven. The Creator must have had a soft spot for us indeed to have fashioned the conditions just right. "Without the energy from oxygen life couldn't grow any bigger than a pinhead," the astrobiologist Dr Felipe Gomez Gomez cites in the documentary.[3]

Gasp! The contemplation of this miracle leaves you holding your breath.

2. Juliana of Norwich, R*evelations of Divine Love, Chapter 5.*

3. Graham Booth, dir. *Gasp: One Strange Rock,* 2018, National Geographic. Prime Video.

East vs West Mindset: a snatch of journal

Every morning when I get up my mind races to the things I have to accomplish for that day. I make an ambitious to-do list replete with the steps to the grand life projects I have planned for myself. In fact in American society, we have made a science out of planning, organizing, and phasing out. Books, seminars, tv programs, Ted Talks, life coaches, efficiency gurus, they have made a good living teaching us how to break down our lives into manageable steps, how to tap into our inner strengths and translate them into achievable goals. An entire multi billion industry is founded the art and science of fulfilling your dreams.

I am no stranger to this American obsession of getting things done effectively efficiently, of not wasting a dull moment. America instills the wide-open sea of limitless possibility of vast vistas of dream accumulation. "You can do it," is the slogan. "Just do it." "You have the power." "You are the master of your destiny." You are made to believe that somehow if you do not accomplish your goals, if you wind up living a life less than what you have imagined, then it most probably is your fault. You are not trying hard enough. You have not taken the right number of classes, you went to the wrong school, you don't know the right people. You haven't planned your life right. Many times when you are not able to live to the grand plan you have sketched for yourself you wind up feeling miserable dissatisfaction. "What's wrong with me?" I am a failure.

I fall into this western way of thinking very often. My ruminations over what I haven't scratched off of my to do list, of what I have not become, put me into a funk.

But then I remember I have an eastern side. It is the wisdom of the deep Greek east that sits me down in a pew during a three-hour liturgy that has me realize man plans and God laughs. It is a sin of subtle pride to think you can plan your day and can create your life out of your own ambition. It is a fallacy to think you are the center of your own life and that you can steer it this way and that. Mortal fool, God the universe laughs at you, you think it was your doing, but it was the universe that led you here all along.

The people of the East have a different understanding of plans. "If God wills" is the addendum for any plans uttered by the Christian East. A devout Muslim utters a prayer at the door of her house upon leaving asking that she might be granted God's favor to return. She is humble enough to understand that every step, every breath is not a given. A Zen saying states, "the obstacle is the path." How profound. How in total opposition to Western thinking. The very stumbling block in your way creates the way you must walk.

And when I meditate deeply on the course my own life has taken, the Greek East undoubtedly captures the more complex truth. It was the struggles, the suffering that propelled me to the path I walk now. I never wanted to be a teacher of emotionally disturbed at risk youth. I wanted to be an international correspondent. I never wanted to go to a city college, but after I lost the scholarship to an Ivy League because my mentally ill father had a breakdown and moved us back to Greece, that was the path open to me. That city college turned out to be the largest producer of teachers in the state.

Sometimes as the western and eastern sides of me wrestle in the tortured arena of my mind, my life becomes a composite of my choices. I whip myself for not having a successful business like my friend down the block. Why haven't I advanced in my writing career? What about that not for profit that flopped? I didn't do the homework. I didn't get enough contacts. It's me. I have to work harder. I obsess over myself because I believe I have control over my way.

But I don't. As I grow older and wiser, I realize how much is out of my control.

I am limited by the way my mind is wired. That's not in my control. I am limited by the circumstances of my birth, the place and time and my social class. Those are not in my control. I am limited by the nuances of my temperament and personality. Those are out of my control. I cannot control macrocosmic events that I am vulnerable to--economic recessions, war zones, natural disasters. I cannot control the manifestation of trauma or the aftereffects of accidents on my psyche. For the life of me I cannot figure out why some with less intelligence and talents and less moral turpitude wind up making it in the eyes of the world while others with more smarts wind up struggling.

Indeed, as I huddle under the warm flame of a candle, the only thing I can control is my attitude towards the uncontrollable. Considering how many things I have no control over, I thank God/the universe that I am standing here today. God has taken care of me regardless of the disappointments and myriad failures of my not satisfying the plans for my life according to my terms. If I surrender to the greater Wisdom of the universe and allow the Grace to move through me, I can accomplish more than ever I could have schemed.

Oh Martha! The one thing is needful, chimes the Gospel like a broken record. (It seems every time I'm in church this is the Gospel reading. Is the universe trying to tell me something?)

Peeling Away the Delusion

Relief Print on Paper, 2026.

Love is a grand delusion. It is necessary to not see someone as they are but as one wants them to look. We create our lovers in order to fall in love with them. Without the magic potion of erotic love, the other would be a bumbling ass as the Bard pointed out. The chemical concoction by which each one of us is bamboozled into physical intercourse with an otherwise repugnant body works like a charm to propagate the species. And it is for the pure necessity of procreation that so much ink and air is spilled on this topic of love. One has to be deluded to be in love with someone else. Love acts as a wool-over-your-eyes. It shields you from the brutal truth that the love of your life is a stinking selfish bastard at worst and an average schmo at best.

By extension we create our own reality, like a sort of carry-as-you-go makeshift booth from the insides of which we paint our own private scenery. We carry around us constructs to help us live our own version of reality. Without our delusions, we would be terribly unhappy. Everyone to a certain extent has to tell him or herself lies in order to be happy. Think about it. The lies we tell ourselves to live with others, and even with ourselves are as ingrown as our skin. Each of us thinks of him or herself as upright, intelligent, hardworking, an overall good guy/gal. But only with the Grace of God can the thick skin be pulled back to reveal the monstrosity within. That what we do for others—to be nice, generous, self-sacrificing—is but a way to reinforce our own sense of goodness. Who is good anyway? How can we by our own discernment know that we are good? Only God is holy; only God is good; the rest are but penumbras.

The saints know not to put too much stake in our own thoughts. They can be erroneous, delusions. Who but God can peel away the multiple layers of skins to find the core of truth at our center? No one is good, no one is holy, no one can be virtuous without the pickaxe of the holy to reveal apocalyptically what we have inside.

We can try to do our own long form of psychoanalysis, but it is with the wisdom of God through the Spirit that the truth about ourselves can come to light. For example, my seeming sense of humility has been but a mask of pride. My lovelorn delusions of my own importance and what I can accomplish through my gifts, how I have driven myself to pieces trying to accomplish so much, excel at so many things, and my angst at not having been able to be a grand writer or artist or some other exalted sense of my own importance—this too has been a grand delusion. I have created cut out dolls of my false selves for decades. Failed journalist, failed writer, failed mother, failed wife–I have felt so sad by my own failures. But that sadness was puffed up by a gargantuan pride that filled the sails of my moving through the world. I was sad because I could not become what my pride dictated I should be. Failure is the ultimate call for humility. I am a nobody but indignant that I am such, the notion does not humble me but saddens me to the point of acedia. Until I truly become humble so that failures become right fitting footsteps in my own advancement, I will never truly be free to be me—the soul God needs me to be.

Only when the light of the Spirit sheds our false sense of selves like so many severed cobwebs can we stand at the Lord's hand like clay for molding. I am asking God that this should happen—that He will allow me to shed the shadow selves to accept my failures as part of my authentic self and not struggle so much to be what I am not. God give me discernment to know myself truly. And to accept myself as such.

I am asking God to help me love other people, those who have done me much damage. Those who have abandoned me. Those who hate me. Those who do not care that I live or die. It is by divine plan that the one to betray the Master was one of his friends, one of his closest associates. Only those intimately connected to us have the power to destroy us. Living in the world leaves one all too acquainted with the ways of it—as Hamlet has lamented.[1] What is the use of living it if it is full of the proud man's contumely, injustice, apathy? How do you love the people who make your world hell? I have not gotten to this level yet. It is impossible by human standards. The story of Jesus's betrayal by one of His brethren serves as a cautionary tale—that those closest to you will betray you, brace yourself. They will throw you under the bus even when they know you are innocent. When innocence is sacrificed at the hand of evil it creates a negative balance in the balance sheet of the universe. It purges the evil out of it. But how does one love the one who is bearing the blade to his throat? How does God expect us to love our brethren when they become the embodiment of evil? That is unconscionable and impossible for me. I have learned to guard myself from the evil that lies within human hearts by keeping my distance from them.

So, you can't trust your own thoughts sometimes. One, they might be false; cognitive distortion is the fancy psych word. They are false notions that we unequivocally hold as true. Things like we are ugly or that the world is a horrible place. Some thoughts get played back over and over like the buzz of a relentless mosquito; most are negative, sabotaging. They pop up when you are doing the dishes or on the bus. It is as if they get inserted into our consciousness by some outside force. Some are so dark and insidious, we cannot think them out loud so they get buried

1. Sean McEvoy. *William Shakespeare's Hamlet: A Routledge Study Guide and Sourcebook*. Taylor & Francis, 2023.

deep; they slither and slide one into each other like a brewing broth of eels just under our radar, yet they influence how we feel and what we do. (e.g. Why do I feel like smacking certain people who I have never met before? Something in them triggers something dark in me).

Yet the very worst of our thoughts are those we do not realize we have. "The dark and evil powers operating diabolically in my members" that the night prayers ward against. I do believe the devil lurks in our subconscious. It is the dark thoughts that entangle us in our own thoughts, even luring logic into the web of equivocation distorting the darkness and crocheting it into light. The passions, the lusts of the flesh, and the manifold peacock flashes of pride, these lie under our consciousness. It is the enemy you do not see and cannot even sense that is the most dangerous. The subconscious, that cauldron of repressed desires, violence, and most barbaric rages, the underbelly of the rotting log, fires up the fleshy side of the human animal. It is, I believe, the vestige of our evolutionary history. The evil spirits use the darkness of that subconscious to conjure up false impressions, falsities in the guise of truths, and to push us into believing that our basest wishes are warranted.

Sitting with My Demons

from a sketch of "Grieving Mother" by Kathe Kollwitz, charcoal on paper by the author

"Demons are spirits (*pneumata*) or noetic beings *(noeroi)*, which are evil and whose main aim is to darken man's intellect (*nous*). Being spirits, they are more difficult to deal with than human persons. They hate the good and it is they and man's consent to them, not man himself, who are the cause of evil. They sow the seed of sin within man and "force us· to Sin" but they cannot predict the consequences of their sowing, they cannot know the future of our innermost thoughts -except, as the Macarian Homilies imply, by virtue of the fact that they have been with us for so long. But God knows (*epistatai*) that they cause

> sinful thoughts and that, at times, they act without man's consent. Their main characteristic, as will be seen below, is judging, discriminating against others-etymologically, *diavellein* means to slander, to throw over, to separate, to divide; in fact, people become "diabolic" by acting in this fashion. It seems that man, too, can become demonized and thus act against himself as well as others.[1] --John Chryssavgis

FOR THE LAST THREE weeks, I have been attacked by demons. The demons of my daughters and my own. My daughter, now 26, according to psychological literature, would be diagnosed with some form of personality disorder. She has reviled, slandered, and verbally abused me in tone and word for over 15 years since early adolescence. She acts out of her pain with such vehemence I shudder in her wake. It has reached the point that I can no longer endure her darts. Especially since now I have her 14 year old half-sister who is following in her wake. My younger daughter refuses to live with me, having gone to her father's house in the summer. She shows me the door when I visit. She is silent for Mother's Day and my birthday.

To have both daughters revile me and refuse to have any connection with me is a torture I could not have imagined. This is the period of unbonding. I have become distraught. My sense of guilt and inner turmoil have plunged me back to full-time smoking, nights of sleepless anxiety, and periods of gasping grief. What have I done wrong? Is it my darkness that I have bequeathed to them? Is it normal to hate your mother so much? Yes, I have done something to them that they are reacting this way. It is my constant criticizing, my need to control them, my intensity that registers as anxiety? Is it because it is just who I am. She says I emotionally abuse her. That she does not feel comfortable around me.

How? What? Because I beg them with letters of forgiveness. I am sorry for anything I did or did not do to hurt you. It was never my intention. I love you so much, please do not shun me. To love someone and have them wash their hands of you is so painful; I sleep and wake up choking from sobs. The pain is unendurable. I do not know what I have done. She cannot really explain it either. "Because you don't cook for me," she says. "That's because I am not a good cook. Even when I cook you will not eat and buy food from outside." "You do not buy me clothes,"

1. Chryssavgis, *The Monk and the Demon: A Study of the Ladder of Saint John Climacus*, 754.

she says. "That's because whatever I buy you will not wear. I put money in your bank account instead." I think she is creating a "false mother," a projection of her own delusion to have a reason to hate and spite me. It is easy to hate anyone, even your own mother, if you create an image that is black enough, compliments of your selective evidence.

Or maybe it is true? Maybe, I am abusive and do not even realize it. What does "abuse" mean anyway? It is open to interpretation and subjective definitions.

What happens when I am under demonic attack is that the onslaught of the demons from the outside awakens the demons from the inside. Is my ex-husband saying evil things to get her against me? Could it be that their accusations of "abusive" are true? Have I passed on my trauma to them subconsciously?

Their hurt irritates my hurt. The pain of rejection as a mother starts me on a war path:

The miserable ungrateful b******.

I am going to disappear and show them what it is to not have a mother.

I wish I were dead

God will punish their disrespect.

What have I done to deserve this treatment?

I regret ever having children.

What if they never come back again?

I have lost my children.

I have found relief in a spiritual father and a loving Irish Catholic therapist with over 40 years of experience. Both have told me the same things:

Don't react.

Reflect on how you may have contributed to the situation.

Learn to sit with your demons.

Stand apart, fall back but do not disappear.

They are going through a lot of pain.

Be loving and understand that those demons although they will hurt you have a reason for doing so.

Learn to endure their assaults without retaliating in kind.

Don't try to escape.

Sit through the temptation.

Practice patience.

Say the Jesus Prayer.

Pray unceasingly.

So much of mental illness comes about through the demons. If the definition of theologian John Chyssavgis serves us, it is in the noetical plane that they wage war. The warfare of the mind. The dark thoughts that turn man against another and even his own self. No saint can ever become holy without them. I am learning to accept the temptation of the demons. I am holding on to the prayer of the Publican because I know I myself am not free from their infestation, "Lord, Jesus Christ, Son of God, have mercy on me."

One of my favorite quotes is "When you face your dragons (ie demons) they turn into angels." That is what demons are really--dark angels, angels who have warped the energy of light and love into darkness and hatred. My demons wreathe my thoughts into ones of retaliation. When I am spurned and rejected, I spit venom back. Or else I pull a geographic and retreat from the battlefield altogether. Or I just ooze into a cesspool of self-pity, inconsolable sorrow, and enervated doubt.

This time I will not react as I normally would.

I will not pursue a violation of custody petition in family court

I will not bring an order of protection against my oldest.

I will not flee to another country.

I am going to sit with my demons, both those who attack from the outside and those from the inside. I am going to sit, breathe, say the Jesus Prayer, and ask for humility, for enlightenment, for the wisdom of God. I am going to sit still and just be present. I will take the lacerations, the loneliness, the agony—until they see that it is useless to make me like them. I will not turn into darkness; I will not rage like fiery coals. I will trust in the love of God that has compassion even on the demons because even they, however evil, are to be pitied.

And I will pray like the Canaanite woman, for a crumb of mercy from the Master's table. That the Lord will hear my prayer to heal my suffering daughters from the demons that possess them.

As the wise Father Symeon the New Theologian stated:

"Learn to love temptations. as if they are to be the cause of all good for you. The demons have no power by themselves; they do what they do because God allows them to do it. In this sense, they are to be seen as instruments used by God for man's salvation. Ultimately, they are a cause of crowns, and the more there are of them, the more abundant are the crowns. Without sorrow there can be no salvation."[2]

2. Hilarion Alfeyev, *St Symeon the New Theologian and Orthodox Tradition*, 2000.

Gratefulness

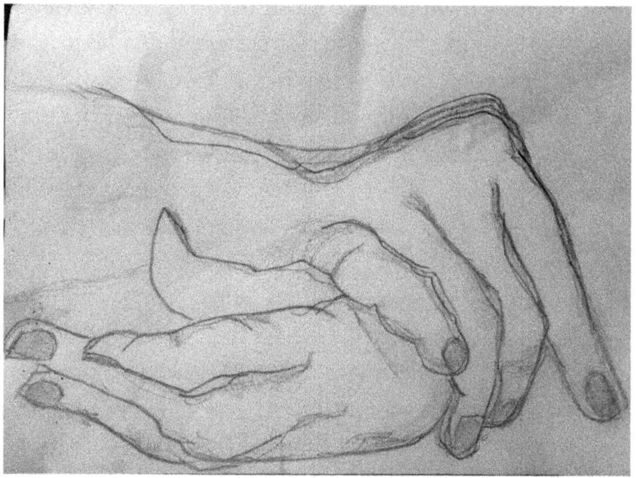

sketch of hands by the author

"In daily life we must see that it is not happiness that makes us grateful, but gratefulness that makes us happy." – Father David Steindl-Rast[1]

As I hover on the brink of 40, that apex of life's panorama which affords the most pleasant of views (you have the benefits of both hindsight and foresight), I have come to realize that, indeed, true joy must come from within. You cannot hold on to the fickle churnings of fate and fortuitous occurrences thrown slapdash into your life's path. If you want to become happy, you can't wait for that good news phone call or that random act of kindness to be showered down your way. No manner of external rewards—titles, medals, bonuses, awards, baubles—can bring on the

1. Steindl-Rast, David. *Gratefulness, the Heart of Prayer: An Approach to Life in Fullness.* Paulist Press, 1984.

eternal glow of happiness. That happiness must radiate from within. It must not fluctuate like the glow of a campfire on a windy day, but burn steadily like a hot iron. It must be self-exploding, sort of like the phoenix that auto-combusts. Or like a steady streaming star. Does the edelweiss or the desert rose seem less lovely and less fragrant for the lack of someone to witness or smell it?

The "peace that surpasseth understanding" the Holy Bible speaks about comes from the Kingdom of heaven within. Once you give up waiting for things to change but look to change the internal landscape inside, then you are on your way to acquiring true peace. The way of the world is vanity. Things change on the surface, but underneath things are the same. How long have human beings been evolving only to stay the same warped species? One calamity will rise and take the place of the former. All waxes and wanes, waxes and wanes; in both the large, universal scale and the individual scale, things change but remain the same. You are happy one minute and then sad the next.

I keep longing for things to happen, for things to change so that I can get happy. "If I get a better job, then I will be happier." "If I get a raise or make more money, then I will be happier," "If I drop by 20 pounds, then I will be happier." "If I move to a bigger house, then surely, surely I'll be happier." "If I find the love of my life, then truly I will be happy beyond my wildest dreams." These are all external conditionals that make happiness dependent on a conditional. But then I find that the more I hope and wait and wish and pray that if I get this or if I do that—if I get a new degree, if I move to a better neighborhood, the list goes on and on—then then at that magical time I will be happy. Ironically the more checkboxes I cross off on my "Life's Things To Do to Get Happier" list, the farther the prospect of being truly happy gets. Happiness, and the myth of attaining it, becomes as elusive as El Dorado.

As I was maneuvering my way around a snow-jammed parking lot, I saw "MD PhD" on the license plate at the back of a white Mercedez. "Sure," I thought," that guy/gal must be very very happy, very very proud that he/she has to show off the external trappings of his good happiness for all to see." How many people I know, accomplished, professional, intelligent people, who hide the grim face of their unhappiness behind degree titles, bank account bottom lines, Platinum credit cards, expense accounts, business plaques outlined in gold on a mahogany desk. How many people I know have mansions in the Hamptons with echoing halls and deftly dressed maids and yet behind their façade they are empty and extremely sad. They are completely and miserably, feelingly unhappy. Their emptiness could fill voluminous caverns of their penthouse apartments in LA, NY, Paris, till they were overflowing with despair. Their faces scream in silent agony. Joy, true joy, escapes them because all the while the search for their happiness has been outward, when really it should have been inward. Or rather, inward to the source of what makes them human. And what is it that brings the glow in the heart that turns on the furnace of felicity so that through you the world around you becomes beautiful, radiant, and alive? That joy comes from God and God alone.

I stop my pity party in its tracks. This is *acharistia* or ungratefulness. This is grumbling about the Cross. I'm like those old Jewish women in some joke who do a lot of bitching and complaining, that nitpick everything on the menu. It is a real struggle for me to be satisfied, content, and grateful, not bitching all the time. It has always been my struggle—even when I had it good, in hindsight of course, I always found something to complain about. Let's be honest: if you look hard and long enough you can always find something to bitch about. Always.

It's a matter of perspective and changing heart. Before when I was younger, I thought happiness was some mythic Eldorado that you had to search for and stay in hot pursuit of. I trekked down many highways, scaled mountains, and perused complicated maps in search of the stuff. I thought you had to look for happiness across continents like some buried box of treasure. It was something out there, somewhere over the rainbow, under a 4-leaf clover; happiness was what happened to other people, never to you. Unless you went after it in hot pursuit, it would escape through the tips of your fingers like so many tiny minnows. I went looking for happiness by moving from one city to another, passing from one border into another. But just when I thought I'd found it, it moved like the sun's shadow; it encroached ever so quickly into another's time zone, into another neighbor's lawn, leapt up in another's bosom, sprouted from another's patch.

But now that I have matured, I've realized joy is not some elusive province in a far-away country, it lies within you. It is buried deep in the confines of your soul's closet. It is not something you search for 1000s of miles away but like some burnished tin box you buried somewhere under your kitchen stove whose cover you brush off with your fingertips and see the brocade work. And you open the box to find little toy soldiers from your childhood, a half-eaten candy bar, a photo of your first love, and a penny from 1942.

Happiness is something you must work inwardly for. Instead of grumbling because this two-year-old dumped a tube of yellow paint on the plants, smeared her hair and the dog with it, to be grateful that I have had a child so late in life, to thank God for the gift of a healthy, exuberant child, to thank God that I am still able to walk and work and be exhausted for everything in my life. I get so caught up in wanting to live someone else's life that I forget that I am living my own and that this is the only life I will know and live. My neighbor with the three kids and the huge house and the BMW convertible in the garage with a loving productive husband—that's not my life.

Someone sent me an email once that went something like this—

A group of graduates, well established in their careers, were talking at a reunion and decided to go visit their old university professor, now retired. During their visit, the conversation turned to complaints about stress in their work and lives. Offering his guests hot chocolate, the professor went into the kitchen and returned with a large pot of hot chocolate and an assortment of cups – porcelain, glass, crystal, some plain looking, some expensive, some exquisite – telling them to help themselves to the hot chocolate.

When they all had a cup of hot chocolate in hand, the professor said, "Notice that all the nice looking, expensive cups were taken, leaving behind the plain and cheap ones. While it is normal for you to want only the best for yourselves, that is the source of your problems and stress. The cup that you're drinking from adds nothing to the quality of the hot chocolate. In most cases it is just more expensive and, in some cases, even hides what we drink. What all of you really wanted was hot chocolate, not the cup; but you consciously went for the best cups… And then you began eyeing each other's cups."

Now consider this: Life is the hot chocolate; your job, money and position in society are the cups. They are just tools to hold and contain life. The cup you have does not define, nor change the quality of life you have. Sometimes, by concentrating only on the cup, we fail to enjoy the hot chocolate God has provided us. God makes the hot chocolate; man chooses the cups. The happiest people don't have the best of everything. They just make the best of everything that they have. Live simply. Love generously. Care deeply. Speak kindly. And enjoy your hot chocolate.

Prayer for Daily Bread

LORD, HELP ME FIND joy in the everyday things, in the quotidian nuisances of picking up dog poo and toddler sneakers from behind the stove. Let me find the crumbs of unexpected joy—the ones you find while walking across the street and hear a cardinal twitter above you, the unexpected joy of sneaking a swig of mint between your breasts so you smell fresh all day long. The sneaky little happiness that wiggles on tiny mouse feet when you are sleeping on the couch watching an old version of *Sanford and Son* and you remember the match trap you made to get rid of the baby mouse when you were ten.

Jesus Prayer

THERE CAN BE NO joy, no lasting joy at least, experienced without God. Only the joy that the Holy Spirit brings is a joy that cannot be snuffed out like a brief candle, cannot be torqued by the vicissitudes of time, chance, or mood. It is the ever-burning gem-like flame that burns from within. I must realize that only by getting closer to that eternal flame can my heart light never go out. By drawing ever closer to that source and experiencing its presence in a deep-felt way can I learn how to be happy. Happiness is not some fleeting luck of the draw dependent on externals; happiness is a skill and as such it can be learned, practiced, and mastered. It is practiced in the recitation of the Jesus Prayer, again and again, like the breath, "Lord Jesus Christ, Son of God, have mercy on me." This prayer, this focus of the mind and heart's energies on the source of true happiness connects us with that Source and keeps us happy. It's like being plugged in to a powerful generator; your batteries will never die.

This prayer is not so seemingly simple as a cognitive trick; it's not so facile as what cognitive-behavioral psychologists say to do "stop thoughts" and replace them with something positive. Although there is something of this that is true (changing our thoughts can change the way we see the world which in turn changes our mood and even our life). And religion is not just a generalized coping strategy to get through a shitty life. True happiness has a source. And the trick is to know how to tap into that source and keep it in focus. It is almost like coaxing the Holy Spirit as a dove to roost into the nest that is your soul. It is that joy, the Joy that comes from the Holy Ghost, that is immutable, eternal, unquenchable. To know God is to be truly happy. How can one not be happy? Indescribably happy. The greatest heights of ecstasy have been reached through pursuit of divine love, not humanly. To know the Source of love, of life is the greatest joy there is.

It is knowing this joy that radiates outward and makes the whole world, as dark, greedy, hostile, and sinister as it is, "suffused with the grandeur of God."[1] The quest of the eternal is in the everyday. The extraordinary is in the ordinary, once I realize that this is the manifestation of the divine hand. That ordinary tree over there opened to the sky branches open in a prayerful hug to the sky, it can teach us a thing or two about the "extraordinariness" in everyday life. The sun rises and sets every day, an ordinary start to another day. Yet it never ceases to astound me—the pinks, magenta streaks, the hues and subtle tonalities of the morning rose-gold glow. It is amazing! The wonder in the world comes from opening the heart from within. Like love, happiness is not acquired but created. Like the pomegranate it must be smashed to reveal the stash of its rich ruby reliquary. And like the Little Prince said, "Everything is like the other if you don't love it."[2] It is this day, however cold and gray; it is this job, however tedious and dysfunctional; it is this spouse, however annoying and needy, that is beautiful and worthwhile.

I pray that I will be allowed to connect to that Source of Joy, of Light, of Love so that I too can give off joy, light, and love to all those I meet around me.

For me who complains that I never have time to think, to write, to pray, then I must grab time from the forelocks and put her in a sleeper hold, and yell, "Stay! Stay! Stay where you are! Don't move!" I have done that this past hour writing this insignificant little rambling in the coffee shop around my way, the one I never have time to visit because I am alas, always chasing, always busy.

The Lord in His mercy has taught me a hard lesson. You see, I'm the type of person who complains—a lot! My entire life I have tried to find that mystical and mythical pot at the end of the rainbow—I have been searching for the perfect job, the perfect house, the perfect school for my kids, I have been a restless soul always on the lookout for the next big thing. No matter how many blessings the Lord has bestowed me with, I have had cause to grumble. Why can't I be happily married? Why can't I live in a big house in the suburbs? Why oh why oh why? Why can't I have a well-paying respectable job? Why me?

In my thirst to better myself I have trekked around three continents, changed addresses 35 times, dreamed of packing my belongings

1. Gerard Manley Hopkins, "God's Grandeur," https://www.poetryfoundation.org/poems/44395/gods-grandeur.

2. Antoine De Saint-Exupéry, *The Little Prince,* Chapter 21.

and moving to jungles in Costa Rica or island villages in India. I am absolutely nuts! I have never been happy with what and where I was. My daughter who has suffered through all my mad dashes to "get ahead" which have resulted in her changing elementary school four times before she got to middle school (changes that included a mid-transcontinental move to the Midwest and a transatlantic move to the Middle East) has summed up the matter for me very succinctly-"Mom, it doesn't matter where you are or what you do, you will never be happy anywhere." She is absolutely right. I am so restlessly unhappy I cannot find fulfillment anywhere.

Now that I am older, the glasses are off and the stark reality of hard-won experience has set in. There is no heaven on earth. A woman can travel the whole world over looking for something but in the end has to return home to find what was missing.

That "home" is the true heaven, the one we can only find through a close intimate connection to God. Christ has taught my soul a deep lesson—that one thing I was looking for was Him. No one can find peace without the only peace possible and necessary. It is the peace that lies within. Every attempt by human beings, however ideal and well-meaning, to create a communal utopia, a heaven on earth, has ended in delusion, disappointment, and worse, tyranny. The closest I have seen to utopia is a monastery. And that is because the focus of such a community is God. "Thou hast formed us for Thyself, and our hearts are restless till they find rest in Thee," St. Augustine remarked.[3] Our soul will not find fulfillment till it has established a home for the Holy Spirit within it.

Now that my life has become really brutal—now that I have come to grips with really a bitch of a boss, with real economic uncertainty, and real deprivation—I look back at my grumblings and want to kick myself in the butt. How stupid! How foolish I was to confuse blessings for troubles. How ungrateful! What an overbearing grumbling tiresome woman I must have sounded to the Lord. No wonder He's put me through "hell" to make me see how in all things I must glorify God. Now when people ask me, "How are you? How's your job? How's your kids?" I stop myself from complaining and say, "Doxa to Theo," "Glory to God, I am good." For now I have learned that it is not what troubles and persecutions you are put through that determine whether you have it "good" or whether you can have peace or not, but rather the spirit of holiness, of patience,

3. St. Augustine of Hippo, *Confessions,* 1,1.5

and gratitude that makes you happy. "The kingdom of heaven," the Lord has said, " resides in you." And in order to acquire heaven, peace, or "home," I have had to learn to stand still. I cannot move anymore. I have neither the money nor the time and three children act as pretty good anchors.

I have been taught the hard way to seek the Lord quietly, methodically, patiently—like a bird watcher or one who wakes early to see the sunset creep and then explode in majesty before them. Through my daily prayers, through the cycles of the seasons and feast days of the church, through my obedience to the counsels of my spiritual father (he warned me about moving to faraway places), I am learning to make heaven out of this plot of hell I am standing on at the moment. And there is no heaven without listening to the voice of God, that whispers in the secret chambers of silence, that curl into sinuous swirls of eternity like some Caribbean conch. Only by learning to bless even the darkness of my pathetic, sin-filled life, only by learning to bless what I once cursed, can I find the heaven that exists in the everyday hell I live through. "Be ardent in your labor and you will find God in your cooking pots," St. Theresa of Avila said.

And I know the closer I come to the Lord, the more the spirit of peace I will acquire and the joy, that ineffable joy that I lost through the dark journey through Mordor and the valley of the shadow of death, that joy will return again. And I will with a joyous heart filled with peace cry out to the Lord for the whole gift that has been my life—"Doxa si Kyrie"—"Glory and thanks be to You oh Lord. I am truly thankful."

Morning is a Miracle

Morning over Mt Graham, Safford, Arizona

MORNING IS SUCH A miracle. I take it for granted on most days. There is no guarantee that I will rise. Or that you will for that matter. It is God's mercy that allows my bones to creak and groan and rise, like a crumpled, crooked marionette, pulled to life and standing by those invisible strings. My mind—forgettaboutit. It takes 21/2 cups of strong coffee and 45 minutes to fully come to life.

Morning, like breath, is so important, yet so underappreciated. You take it for granted until you stop breathing or you can't rise from the bed. So much of what we believe comes from our own energy is really borrowed energy. It is a wonder that the sun rises, give or take a few minutes, depending on the season. I heard a story about a dancer once. She would rise every day and rush to do her practice exercises, plies or whatever else dancers do, without doing her prayers. Until one morning she found as hard as she could, her legs were stiff. She tried to stand off the bed and collapsed. She started showing symptoms of a slowly degenerative muscle disease. She lost her ability to dance. But with time, therapy, drugs and prayer, she gained it again. "I never rise without doing my morning prayers," she confessed. "I cannot start the day without thanking God for it. I will never take it for granted that I can rise and use my legs again."

To start the day with prayerful thanksgiving is so necessary in this world plagued with the "to-do" list, the cares of "how will that deal and that appointment scheduled for today go." The beasts of cares with claws pounce on that sweet sleep that emerges from the peace of unconsciousness and shred it to pieces before it has a chance to fully wake. The birds know more than us. I heard the song of spring on the throat of a bird walking to the subway. Even in this concrete jungle, the magic and mystery of nature do not fail to break through. Yet this bird in the urgency of its deep-throated chant was praising its Maker.

The morning is a petite resurrection. We lie in a sleep, the petite mort, for eight or so hours and then by some inner stirring, the morning breathes into us, calls us into action, and we rise. We rise like Lazarus from the dark cave of slumber and are refreshed enough to face the muck of the world afresh.

By Jesus! We need to feel that small resurrection every morning, that comes as such relief. The blessing that comes with the morning—that we can begin again like new. That we can hope for something better in the newness of another day. That we can put behind the disappointments, the agonies, the sorrows, the exhaustion of the day before—and live in the hope, the chance that today might be better than yesterday. The relief of forgetfulness that comes with the night—even for just the two-to-three-minute stretch when our soul is born onto the stretch of the terry-cloth white possibility of an empty day.

Every morning serves as a reminder that even if you wake up to the same place, to the same circumstances, to the same problems, (to the same shit), the same skin, the same self, there is a chance that this day, perhaps, this day things will be a little different, a bit better.

MORNING SONG

How my heart waits patiently for the morning;
How my soul expects the unfading dawn!

My heart leaps up like the lark
Because it remembers its Lord
As the first rays of morn delight the eyes
My heart leaps up with joy

In the morning light
In the daybreak chorus of song
My heart rings out
Emanates in gladness and madrigal

For it has not been consumed by the darkness
Its eyes have been uncovered to witness the glory in yet another day

Oh bringer of light
Who walks in shifting cinnabar, salmon-coral, royal purple, rose golden robes of damask
Whisking clouds and hyssop bushes with each footfall on the horizon

Bridegroom whose countenance is secretly unfolding behind veils of chiffon, tulle, and lace
You who walk upon the dew and baby breath of earth just waking, apucker and wrapped in shawls of dreams and intimations of immortality

My heart is glad because it sees Your light
You have trampled down the darkness
You have banished the shadows of the night
The nightmare visions replaced by nightingale warbles
The sweat and blood on the pillow
The doom bell of the midnight hour

How my heart waits patiently for the morning;
How my soul thirsts for the unfurling dawn—
To meet the sight of my Bridegroom and light-giver
Who comes walking across the fields of gold
And envelopes me in His warm hands
Bathing me in the hope of light
Exuberating my spirit from its slumber, from the shadowy realm of its unconsciousness
Resurrection reams from the unfurled scroll of the day's accounts
Oh how my soul leaps up like the lark at the dint of day
Oh how my soul rises up in time with the Son!

We missed you

Lord-let us seek You. Let us ask not for the bread that fills the earthly body, but for the *epiousion*, the quintessential, the over-essential, the bread that fills the eternal spirit. For in this age of consumption and that conspicuously so, in so many Jimmy Choos and Mizrahi suits, Lamborghinis and Norwegian cruises, iPads, iPods, Alexas and X-Boxes, we need to find your ghost floating over the water. We are famished for Your Spirit. We are like skeletons whose skin sticks to our bones. We walk the streets with a beggarly hand outstretched pleading for alms, for mercy. Feed us, oh Lord, Feed us. We are hungry. We have forgotten that we are not just flesh. Our spirits are emaciated. We seek You asking for the Murano or the promotion at the job, but we miss You, the deep connection of You. We see You as a cosmic go-fer. Get me this! Do me that! We fail to see You. How did You get here? We didn't see You ride on the water? We can't find Your boat or that of Your apostles moored on this side of the Sea? We missed You entirely.

We do not know how blessed we are. We cannot comprehend the mystery of You. That You are the Unseen made Seen, the Unknowable made Tangible, the Eternal made temporary just for a short while enough for us to get a glimpse into the magic castle from the French door before they draw the curtains. We have missed You or looked right through You. Like straining to snatch at the broken shells and discarded pebbles at the receding shore while missing the glory and majesty of the great wide Sea. We missed You, Lord. We miss You.

God vs Satan in Me

I HAVE SATAN AND God living in me, one pulling me away, the other pulling me in. I am pulled taut by two contrary forces. Like they taught us in physics class. There is the force that pulls objects into its center, the centripetal force and the force that pulls objects out and away from the center, the centripetal force. Basically, they dwindle down to the big two—the tendency towards order and the tendency towards disorder. I struggle constantly against the forces of chaos and disorder within and without.

The devil is the great stirrer of the black cauldron. The perpetrator of chaos. He is the one that makes the earthquake, smashing walls, burning buildings. He is the one that spoils the butter, permanently loses the other red sock, makes it impossible to fix the bloody incessant leak in the back of the toilet. The force of chaos—the 2nd law of thermodynamics. In an open system, the textbook states, things tend to go from order to disorder. Thoughts start spiraling out of control, hysteria makes the seams of my soul tatter. Chaos—the body breaks down, black spots appear under the fingernails, supple skin once glued together with the force of life sags under the weight of gravity, books stacked in a neat line on the shelf fall off, get misplaced, sweaters get holes right smack in the center, papers yellow at the edges, shit stains on once pristine underwear, towels fluffy and fresh, now smeared with sweat and urine, laundry lined with dirt, piled higher in huge messy mounds on the floor strewn with shedding dog hair and drool. The devil is behind maggots eating the insides of dead cats.

The devil is the voice whispering, "I'm a failure. I can't keep it together. I have so much to do. I look like shit. I can't keep the thoughts in my head." Before one ends another starts—"Boil the pasta" I start the pot and another, then, "open the filing cabinet and search for the car insurance paper." I do not close the accordion file within the cabinet before another thought, "Organize the sock drawer" makes me move on. The devil, the great stirrer of the pot, who tangles the chords of the puppets, so they dance maniacally. The force that rips open the canyon and makes the rainwater roar in a zigzag maddening pattern through it. He is the one who hurls the great big asteroid, kicks it out of its elliptical course, hurling it straight into the earth's orbit in a blazing foul ball that bumps earth's head bring it a huge "karoubalo" (head bump the kind Tom gets when beaten on the head by a bat thanks to Jerry). The chipper of the fine china, the hider of the remote, the one that makes your left foot stumble on the front step that sends you flying to the curb in a mass of broken bones and stitches down the eyes.

Chaos is the demon who makes your last quarter fall through the open grate to the black swamp of the sewer at the curb. He is the force behind Uncle Jimmy's rude comment about Jesus and Mary at the dinner table that leads to wine glasses smashed, dinner chairs waved threateningly above Uncle Jimmy's bald head, little Billy's thumb throbbing, and Grandma's best china breaking with her heart.

He is the unsettling as you ruffle your papers trying not to look, trying not to hear, at the nasty look and dirty motion of mouth of the guy on the subway seat across from you. He is the force that hides the passport behind the folds of the Con Ed bills and unopened bills that winds up ruining your plans for a Bahama cruise. He is the force that makes you want to unscrew your head and lower it into an acid bath.

And then there is God. The force of order, of unity, of synthesis, symmetry, and balance. He is the force of prayer, the still point in the turning world, the eye of the storm. It is the whisper that yanks my heart strings and says, "Go ahead. Give that homeless man your last ten dollars." The force that quiets the crazy spiraling thoughts and says, "Peace, now, let everything go. The landlady can wait. The child is more important than her chores." The force that forces me to stop and take notice—there is a sparrow bopping on one leg on the chain link fence, the light how beautiful it falls on the rumpled white comforter. There in the words of the Psalms, "You who bring light out of the darkness and light out of death." The peace of the Prince pervades through the words into my soul and brings balance. The devil is in the details, but God wraps up the whole. How beautiful this tapestry is even if frayed and tasseled at the inseams. "Peace—eirini imeen" the spontaneous joy that rises out of the chaotic smoldering Gehenna and sings a morning madrigal.

God is the one who balances the lampshade, who shakes the egg whites just so that the soufflé comes out succulent to the tongue. God is the harbinger of smiles, the one who makes you chuckle to yourself when you see a kid with no front teeth. The chimes in the falling leak against the rusty pipe. The halo around the lapis lazuli mosaic in the metro. The force that makes you answer with love—"I know you have been working very hard, dear, with the house and your sister, but can you see in your heart just a couple of hours more so that Mom can finish the DMV business and then drive you to the mall?" God, that sorely needed cheer me up call comes from the friend you lost touch with.

The synergistic smiles you share with the stranger on the "A" train. God is the force that glides the liquid eyeliner across your upper lid so it matches perfectly with the lilac glow eye shadow that goes with your purple leather pumps. The force that binds the disparate parts of things into one cohesive whole. Who pulls all the creeping things, the winged fowl, the 2-legged, and three-legged, 4-legged walkers into one tight web. The one that makes sense out of things. That wind that moves the wings of the butterfly and the waves on the sea. The force that binds all things with drawstrings into one button on His breast pocket. The one who draws all into one mighty center point from which all things are born and reborn. He binds your bones together and keeps the baby from falling out of the breast. He holds you tight, hugs you, contains you unto Himself so that you don't fall apart into the millions and millions of little pieces you would become. He is the glue, the center that holds, the high pillar, the strong sanctuary. He is the gentle sleep. God is the force that keeps my wits together. "Jesus, Son of God, have mercy on me." I repeat his Holy Name again and again in an effort to keep myself together with His glue.

When I begin to fall apart, when Satan the destroyer, the hider, the spoiler, the corrupter, the entangler, breaks me up and shatters me into a million shards, scatters my thoughts like soda cans and makes me begin something and never end it, God, God, bind my soul.

On Corruption

In the name of the Father, and of the Son and of the Holy Spirit

I have been thinking a lot about death lately. Maybe as I approach 40 the possibility becomes more likely or else it is just that the thought of death and people who tend to be spiritually inclined go together. Death of course is the big question—the biggest one there is. For someone who tends to think globally and needs to know the end sometimes before tackling the beginning or the middle (I always used to peek at the end of the exam during my school days—start somewhere in the beginning but always have the handle of what the end, what the whole would be like, before I kept plodding on). In college, during the Survey of English Lit 1 class, we read a poem by an anonymous poet from the Middle Ages whose haunting refrain, "Timor mortis conturbat me" ("the fear of death astounds me")[1] still echoes within the grey oubliettes of my breast.

I saw the image of corrupting bodies that a forensic paleontologist unearthed during the Serbian-Crotian genocide. It was chilling—the brute visceral truth of the body decomposing, just torsos contorted into macabre embraces. This is what happens to the body when you die? It's the corruption, the utterly abysmal truth of corruption. That the form you have kept, the symmetrical proportioned order of the body will break down into composite pieces like a crazy jigsaw. The destruction of the body registers like the shattering of a glass pitcher into a million shards—and where is the soul? Where does it go? If the decomposed rotting pieces of flesh is all that is left of a person, where does the soul go? If it ever existed to go anywhere, that is.

1. William Dunbar, Academy of American Poets. "Lament for the Makaris." Poets.org, n.d. https://poets.org/poem/lament-makaris.

The consumption of earthly flesh by the earth, (the case of the two-year-old murdered by her mother in Florida was settled by the evidence of the number of worm larvae and fly eggs hatching from the decomposed pieces of her body left in a trunk of a car for 2-3 days). And the smell! I have never smelled a dead human body, but from what they tell me, once you do, you never forget, or rather, even if you have never smelled one, the moment you do you know it is a dead body. The stink is so penetratingly powerful.

In the dull moments of quotidian life, the stark stentorian warning bell strikes, "You too shall die. One day will be your last." When folding the white tube socks or unsticking the threads of crisp spaghetti from the bottom of the pasta pot, the thought of death confounds me. This is the human lot—fear and trembling—because the knowledge of the inevitability of death consumes every passing moment of our earthly existence.

There are days when I take this as a relief—alas! There will come a time when this "too too sullied flesh would melt/Thaw, and resolve itself into a dew"[2] ("To be or not to be" soliliquoy from Hamlet) and the horrors of daily living will cease, a relief to the end of suffering. There are days when I actually look forward to my passing because if I have kept my soul in good order, I will have the mercy to meet my Maker. This is "a consummation devoutly to be wished." There are days and nights when my "spirit is crying for leaving" as an old rock ballad mourns. And then there are those days, when the worms, the fat wriggling worms, eat in and out of the tissues of my brain—and the stink and sight of my own corpse in my mind's eye keeps me from the restful balms of sleep. And I toss and turn and writhe in mental agony on my couch seeped in sweat. I can't take the sheer thought of corruption. It disgusts me how the body must stink and dissolve into its most basic building blocks at the supple mouth of the decomposers. And not just me but everyone, every living thing will succumb to this fate. What can we hope for—even if the soul survives after death and is immortal, the body decays in such a way that makes all good people vomit.

It is the few, whose virtuous life full of disciplined asceticism and sacrifice for the fruits of the Holy Spirit, who escape from corruption. Like the veritable Seraphim Rose, whose corpse was said to be supple and from whose bones a sweet-smelling rose-like myrrh emerged. Or like his spiritual father, Saint John of San Francisco, whose flesh has not

2. William Shaskespeare, Hamlet, 1.2.133-34, Folger Shakespeare Library." www.folger.edu. https://www.folger.edu/explore/shakespeares-works/hamlet/read/1/2/.

withered but remains intact. I have had the mercy to see this—both smell the myrrh instead of the stink of rotting flesh and see the supple flesh on bones. But few, few will receive this grace. There is little hope for me in my sinfulness to not suffer from corruption. But how I wish I could—how I wish to glorify the name of God even in death through the fragrance in my bones. How I wish my body could be transfigured so that it does not break down but remain intact to stand as a living icon for the love, the power, and the life that the holy name of Jesus Christ imbues to those who love Him. This is why the Holy Fathers tell us to be mindful of death, because it is through this consistent mindfulness that informs our everyday life and makes each decision of our quotidian days become powerful way-markers in our journey to heaven. There is no more important time like now because it is at this very moment that we decide for ourselves our future fate. The consciousness of death sheds a stark yellow spotlight on every single, albeit trivial, action of our daily life imbuing it with the weight of eternity. Now is the time, whatever deed we are doing, whatever place we are standing, whatever thought we are contemplating—that decides our fate for forever.

And yes, we have hope for the resurrection of our souls and bodies. We will not remain as stony carcasses in the desert or weighty skulls on some professor's desk or in some depressed poet's hand. Our skulls and skeletons will not merely exist as tokens to start philosophers on a long monologue on the vagaries of life, the futility of human action, and the sad punctuation point of action. They will come back—both body and soul. As Father Seraphim Rose expounds in *The Soul After Death*:

> "One day this whole corruptible world will come to an end, and the everlasting Kingdom of Heaven will dawn, where the souls of the redeemed, joined to their resurrected bodies, will dwell forever with Christ, immortal and incorruptible. Then the partial joy and glory which souls know even now in heaven will be replaced by the fullness of joy of the new creation for which man was made; but those who did not accept the salvation which Christ came to earth to offer mankind will be tormented forever-together with their resurrected bodies—in hell."[3]

St. John Damascene, in the final chapter of his *Exact Exposition of the Orthodox Faith,* well describes this final state of the soul after death:

3. Rose, *The Soul After Death*, 19

> "We also believe in the resurrection of the dead, for there really will be one, there will be a resurrection of the dead. Now, when we say resurrection, we mean a resurrection of bodies. For resurrection is a raising up again of one who has fallen. But, since souls are immortal, how shall they rise again? Well, if death is defined as a separation of soul from body, the resurrection is the perfect rejoining of soul and body, and the raising up again of the dissolved and fallen living being. Therefore, the very body which is corrupted and dissolved will itself rise up incorruptible. For He Who formed it in the beginning from the dust of the earth is not incapable of raising it up again after it has again been dissolved and returned to the earth whence it was taken by the decision of its Creator …
>
> "Now, if the soul had engaged alone in the contest for virtue, then it would also be crowned alone; and if It alone had indulged in pleasures, then it alone could be justly punished. However, since the soul followed neither virtue nor vice without the body, it will be just for them to receive their recompense together …
>
> "And so, with our souls again united to our bodies, which will have become incorrupt and put off corruption, we shall rise again and stand before the terrible judgment seat of Christ. And the devil and his demons, and his man, which is to say, the Antichrist, and the impious and sinners will be given over to everlasting fire, which will not be a material fire such as we are accustomed to, but a fire such as God might know. And those who have done good will shine like the sun together with the angels unto eternal life with our Lord Jesus Christ, ever seeing Him and being seen, enjoying the unending bliss which is from Him, and praising Him together with the Father and the Holy Spirit unto the endless ages of ages. Amen."[4]

May the Lord Jesus Christ make us worthy of His love and eternal life spent in His Presence to resurrect both our body and soul and make them both incorruptible.

4. "Excerpts from *The Soul After Death*," http://orthodoxinfo.com/death/excerpts_death.aspx

Thoughts Upon a Gravesite

There is nothing like death to try your faith. Seeing your father's lifeless face asleep and swollen in that pale glow that death washes over the body and then his coffin lowered into the pit is enough to give pause to your faith in any belief system. When you see the open pit, the rocks and rubble embedded in red earth waiting for the submersion of the lifeless corpse, it is then that doubt creeps into the steady anchor of your faith like rust around the edges and gnaws you till you find you cannot sleep in the darkness but pass out just at the first glimmer of dawn, and not just one but several nights on end. It is the darkness that enshrouds your peace of mind, the logic and order and the clarity of the bright day, so that the night becomes the blanket and the lid that bears down upon your coffin.

Could it be that faith is just another blanket—the blanket that covers the consciousness from feeling the terrors of the pit, the agony of the consuming night? Could it be that death is the end, the period, the turning of the key within the door and the fading echoes of footsteps down the stair? Could it be that faith is just a teddy bear that we clutch to release our terrors of that dark and awesome night? That open pit makes everyone stop and take note. The Doors' beginning lyrics to "This is the end" starts as background in my head. And in the chorus of another song, "all that lives is born to die." This is the law of life, the commandment of all sentient creatures.

It makes me wonder—really makes me wonder. Perhaps that is the natural state of man—to live in a constant state of fear and trembling. In a state of gnawing unknowing. Except that no stable civilization could be created if the entire world were composed of neurotics terrified of the next bustle in the hedgerow. I am sure many philosophers, psychologists, and thinkers have surmised such theories to account for the origination of organized religion. "All deities reside in the human breast," cried Blake. Sigmund Freud said, "Religion is comparable to a childhood neurosis" and "Religion is an illusion and it derives its strength from the fact that it falls in with our instinctual desires."[1] It is rooted in neurosis and makes the individual thrive in wish-fulfillment as opposed to the cold reality that must be faced in order for each person to advance in his or her maturity level. So the theories go.

But when you experience death with the heart, not just as a lifeless logical enterprise from your armchair, but with your whole spirit as a poet or musician would, then how raw, palpable, and visceral life becomes. Life and death become different sides of the same coin. Ironically, it was after the days following my father's death that I felt most alive. What was left of his family—sisters, brother, children, wife, nieces, nephews—we all sat in the ground level apartment of my Thea Poppy's and talked and talked and laughed and cried. We remembered how the family had lived in the stone hut in the remote village at the back of the Cycladic Island, Ios, where he was born. How they would sneak out for a swim in the afternoon by busting out of the bedroom window and making sure not to bang the azure wooden shutters. How his two sisters, both under ten, had walked two hours from the Chora, main town of the island, and had brought him Christmas dinner in the leaky stable where he alone, a boy of 11, had been left for weeks to keep watch over the family's cows and oxen. They had shared a Christmas meal and shooed away his loneliness and alienation, his feelings of abandonment as he was a sensitive boy dutiful to his parents who took a bit too much advantage of his obedience and subservience. He was so happy to see his sisters –he cried openly.

According to the story as it unwound from memory from Theia Poppy, it was raining so hard that day that they went to sleep huddled on the same mattress over the stone extension. It was raining so hard the roof made of thatch collapsed and they slept watching the rivulet of water splatter from the low-lying roof onto the edge of the mattress. We remembered how the family of six children, four boys and two girls, would sit in the "aloni" or the circular stone grinder where the "giadouri" or donkey would pull on a pulley attached to a huge six-foot round stone round and round the grinder until the wheat stalks separated the grains from the chaff. They'd eat handfuls of olives pulled from their

1. Sigmund Freud, *New Introductory Lectures on Psycho-Analysis*, 2013.

olive groves, chunks of cheese they would make from the goat's milk that they'd leave to strain in old burlap sacks they'd tie to the ceiling of the kitchen, red tender grapes whose pits disappointed the bite of sweet flesh. They'd pull apart the country bread they'd make from the stone mound oven fired by branches and tree branches and brambles and pass around the "karveli" or round loaf from one member to the other. Raw tomatoes, cucumbers, everything made from the land and their own sweat. They did this under the light of the moon and the stars; no electricity existed on the island till the 1970s. Giagia Eirini had to haul two buckets she'd pitch across her strong shoulders along a bowed branch with hooks on the left and the right; they'd dangle as she walked to the only well close to 100 yards from their house every morning before the sun shone too brightly to fill them up. Those two buckets of potable water was all she had to cook, wash dishes and clothes, scrub the faces of six filthy children and make the Greek coffee for her husband Niko who she did not have the slightest feelings for.

We talked about the stories of the past and told story upon story for hours—I sat in a chair from 4pm on the day of the funeral till 4 a.m. in the morning of the day after. It was as if with words we were forging marble memorials of memories for him. We stitched the legacy of his life, hoping to immortalize him. How his two faithful hunting dogs, Zouzouli and Kounistra, the ones who'd ferret out wild hare from their underground burrows through the marble rocks, had died within two weeks of his leaving the island to pursue his fortune in Athens. How he had learned the machinist trade thanks to the good word of his aunt Argyro who worked as a housekeeper in the Athenian townhouse of Mr. Gatzi, the industrialist factory owner. How he had met his bride on the beach of Aghia Marina in Aegina and promised to marry her in a double wedding with his sister who had met her husband on a beach in Corinth. (The priest, old with problems of short-term memory, kept joining the wrong bride with the wrong groom). How he had taken up the offer by the South African government for skilled metal and iron workers and moved his bride to Joe-berg. With his savings he would send thousands of rands back to his father who put a down payment on an "oikopedo" or land for building in a quiet northern suburb of Athens, Ano Patissia. Month by month, the ground floor apartment he build for his sister, then the second floor for himself, and the third level for his other sister. How his first daughter, me, became the apple of his eye. How after the birth of his second daughter and his long-awaited son, he took up his brother's invitation to come to America so he could get "rich and richer." (That was never to happen). His sister Katy said before she left our family reunion, "Your father was a hero. Look at all he built for you. May you live to remember him. Both for his good and for his bad. "

And we remembered the bad. How he spent the majority of his life struggling with bipolar disorder, the rapid changer kind. He would go from gentle to extremely explosive and aggressive. He'd start vociferous, even brutally violent confrontations with people over the wrong way they looked at him. Extremely paranoid, he'd ward away any evil eyes in the supermarket by giving people strange hand gestures like placing palms one on top of another and moving two thumbs. "Look at the fish, you bastards, look at the fish," he'd say. His illness had cost him many jobs and many opportunities for advancement. He was sacked from his factory job in New York because as the boss said, "Jimmy is very smart, and an extremely hard worker but unfortunately he can't get along with anybody." His illness made him into a raving lunatic who would holler and make every surface shake; his voice bounced from every building facade once it escaped from the open window of our apartment in Astoria into the surrounding courtyard of two-family apartment complexes to the consternation of the neighbors. "Don't talk to that madman," they'd tell their children and we would be shunned as we carried the stigma of the "trellos" or madman. He could swear better than the devil and use words to strike into your weakest point and render you paralyzed. He abused us emotionally and psychologically, my father did. He cost me a scholarship to an Ivy League school because he would not let me study away from home. He gave my sister recurring debilitating migraines from seven years to the present. My mother he trashed and blamed for everything, for how we turned out, for what he did and didn't do in his life, for putting the salt shaker on the wrong side of the table so it was not conveniently in his reach.

But this is what a person amounts to—good and bad. And this is all we have left. We shall try to keep this immortality of memory upright as long as we remain vertical. And then what then? When we too shall cease to exist, how will his memory be sustained? Who will remember us to remember him? Alas this is why the poet bemoaned, "Vanity, vanity all is vanity." Everything shall pass to dust. This is why my friend Lilia has a small sand garden, a made-in-China chachka of bourgeois Buddhist spirituality. You make tiny sand drawings with one pen and then you erase them with a hoe. Nothing remains. The inevitability of death, the slow erosion of memory, the withering of empires—what does it all mean? All is vanity. Everything is dust.

Except that after the funeral, there comes a strange silence, a silent peace. That glimmer of the other worldly infuses the earthly every now and then. That faint passing of the shadow that leaves a penumbra of light—the relief that overcame us the second day after the funeral like a glazed underlay, the thin coat of lacquer icon painters use to prep wood with. Through the ecstasy of sorrow, the serenity of relief and surrender to the inevitable. The soul even with the heavy weight of knowledge of death scales to that part of the mountain that gives the panorama of the higher principle. That same force that drives the wedding sheet binds the shroud as the poet has said. The pain of death, of Crucifixion releases the soul to see what it could not see before. That it is a part of all it has seen, of all it has touched, that it is a part of every living and non-living thing—the sea, the earth, the sky. The body becomes created to be recreated –and is forced to decompose into its basic constituents—the angry thistle, the smooth white stone on the shore, the swallow and the bee, the sun as it strokes the olive trees tresses, the wide cerulean sea. And my spirit swells up intoxicated with this knowledge of the truth—that a life is not so easily obliterated, that the soul is immortal and can transcend into a level of consciousness we on this plane cannot really comprehend as of yet. It is that force that governs all things—even death—that makes it tolerable, natural if not permissible. Death too is part of this creation. Until the time comes for the New Creation when all will be refashioned in a new light in a new energy. Until that time, we must accept the sting of death while knowing that it too will die.

So now, while the memory of my father still lingers and his soul hovers above the stories and the living room chandelier we weave of him, I must bid him farewell as I knew him. "Geia sou Baba and pleasant dreams" until we wake from that deep sleep and become the light.

I will close my reflection with an excerpt from the dear Elder Paisios of Mount Athos from Volume 1 of his collected counsels entitled *With Pain and Love for Contemporary Man* :

> "Today, increased knowledge and trust in logic has, unfortunately, shaken our faith to its foundations and filled our souls with question marks and doubts. This is why we don't have miracles anymore, because a miracle cannot be explained logically, it can only be experienced. But faith in God will bring down divine power and overturn all human expectations. It

will perform miracles, resurrect the dead and astonish science. From the outside, all things pertaining to the spiritual life seem upside down. Indeed, the mysteries of God will be impossible to know and will appear strange and contrary to nature as long as we don't overturn our secular mindset and see everything with spiritual eyes. Those who believe that they can come to know God's mysteries through mere scientific theory, without a spiritual life, resemble a fool who thinks he can look through a telescope and see Paradise."[2]

2. Elder Paisios of Mount Athos, *With Pain and Love for Contemporary Man*, 245.

SECTION 3

Musings on Specific Feasts

Saturday of the Myrrh-bearing Women: Anastasi to the ladies...

As an Orthodox woman, I have always received communion on Holy Saturday, the Saturday of the Myrrh-bearing women. For me, the truth and the light of the Resurrection comes earlier. I greet my friends and family with "Christos Anesti" even before the midnight Paschal service which is the "official" pronouncement of the Anastasi. Why can I get away with it? Because I am a girl. Anastasi comes to the ladies first!

The Myrrh-bearing women like most women of most cultures are responsible for tending to the details of daily living: the grunt work that keeps life turning, shopping for food, cleaning up dirt, wiping up feces and snots, tending to the sick and elderly, and of course, readying bodies for burial. In following the cultural dictates of the Jewish law, they had to rise early, before dawn (how many women do this on a daily basis?) to bring ointments, aloes, and myrrh to anoint the body of the deceased. Women's work in this regard has always been relegated to the private realm; they are responsible for the background work and as a result they are not granted the credit or praise they deserve. That's just "women's work" the society signals it. In general, most societies degrade and devalue their work. Unlike men who hold high offices and are very visible in the public arena, women work in the shadows.

Yet, on this sabbath morning, when they come in deep mourning to look on the lifeless body of the one they love, Christ in His righteousness gives them the good news first. Here is the Scripture, with a few shortcuts:

"Now after the Sabbath, as the first day of the week began to dawn, Mary Magdalene and the other Mary came to see the tomb. And behold, there was a great earthquake for an Angel of the Lord descended from Heaven and came and rolled back the stone from the door, and sat on it.

His countenance was like lightning" and clothing "as white as snow" told them: "Do not be afraid; for I know you seek Jesus, who was crucified. He is not here, for He is risen even as He said . . . go quickly, and tell his disciples that He is risen from the dead, and indeed He is going before you into Galilee; there you will see Him. Behold, I have told you. (Matthew 28:1–7).

This account brings up several points. One, the first people to get an "official" pronouncement of the good news of Jesus' resurrection were the women. This is not coincidental. In keeping with the social justice bent of Christ's ministry, it would seem fitting that women, those substandard, sub-human second-class citizens, would be granted the joy of the resurrection first. It seems fitting also that those engaged in the most quotidian, "simple" tasks, the bearers of myrrh, would become the bearers of the miracle. Christ's message is then transmitted via grassroots or the bottom-up approach through the second sex, the women.

Yet, even so, the official, public pronouncement does not occur until the Apostles get whiff of it. Unfortunately, when the women did tell the disciples that He is risen from the dead, they did not believe them. Why? Because they were women, of course! Women ontologically are not taken as witnesses, their testimony counts for nothing because their society has always viewed them as less than men. Women because of their sex are not taken seriously—even when they tell the truth. Ironically, the first person to meet the Resurrected Lord is Mary Magdalene, a woman. Her testimony is also discounted. Is the Gospel making a statement about who receives truth? Perhaps women are more inclined to understand deeper spiritual truths than what they are given credit for? Whatever the case, the status quo of the society of that time is maintained as it is after midnight when the official news of Christ's rising from the dead is understood by His disciples that we greet Holy Pascha.

Thirdly, the message of the joyous resurrection came first to those who need it most. So many women suffer from emotional distress, the balm from the despair of death, the mothers, sisters, female companions, got it. For women, the Crucifixion is an emotional one, ("I see a sword piercing your heart," Simeon's prophecy to the Virgin). Their souls needed the light of the resurrection as their grief plunged into abysmal depths. It was not that they were not afraid, they were very afraid as the Scripture told, but their love was greater than their fear. Clinical research shows that women in general suffer twice as much on average than men from unipolar depression, generalized anxiety, OCD and associated mental illness.

Two, for all the bad words and insults that men use to put other men down by comparing them to women—"pu**y" "don't cry like a girl" etc.—it is the women who show the most courage to visit the tomb and support the person they love. Besides St. John, all the other apostles ran and disappeared, booked, abandoned their leader in the time of most need. Isn't that acting "like a girl"? A scaredy cat, a pussy? Ironically, it is the "weak" sex that shows up and stands with the hero as He is getting butchered. They did not betray their Master by running away. They were there, living the pain and despair with Him at the foot of the Cross. They were not afraid to look at the horror happening in front of them; I am sure many would have taken the Cross and the nails and the beatings had they been allowed. This shows that women, while physically no match for the muscle of men, carry a deep emotional strength that men lack. Who can walk into the mouth of the grave in darkness to bathe the body of a corpse—and not just any corpse, but one's own son? That is a tall order. Yet these women did it.

For all these reasons, I believe women should start celebrating Pascha earlier than men. They received the good news of Christ's Resurrection first. Sometimes those who are underground and silently oppressed are the first to know the news.

So, Christos Anesti! For the women and girls, ladies first.

Psycho Sabbato and Orthodox traditions (Koliva) for commemorating the dead

Table with Kolyva trays, St Irene Chrysovalantou Church, Astoria, NY

Tomorrow is Psycho Sabbato, Saturday of All Souls, when the living remember the dead. This service, which follows in a succession of three Saturday mornings, serves as a safeguard for all souls who perhaps because of the hasty circumstances of their death did not have a proper burial. But in addition it serves to commemorate the recently departed or those whose memory we hold dear no matter how many years they have passed. The custom is to make a koliva plate for each of those who have fallen asleep. The Church lays out long banquet tables in the aisles of the nave where hundreds of koliva commemorative plates, like snowy mounds of powdered sugar with four or more blanched almonds arranged in the form of a cross from the center of which burns a beeswax candle. The koliva plate captures this marriage of the mystery of death and life. On the outside they remind you of tiny graves. Koliva is made from the seeds of the earth—barley, cracked wheat, raisins, dried nuts, pomegranate seeds—symbolic of the stuff the body is made of, of earth to earth. But the koliva double up as living plates for the living. They mark the place setting for ones living at the table of life.

In taste the koliva symbolizes the exact flavor of life—bittersweet-like the ruby seeds of the pomegranate, some of which rest in the mix of the earth underneath the sugar-covered mounds. A thin layer of soft, juicy flesh envelopes a bitter, inedible, hard seed on the inside. In that seed, paradoxically both dead and alive, lies the mystery of all that the service is trying to communicate. The pomegranate seed, the ancient symbol of the underworld waiting to come to the light of the living day. Like Christ, who had to descend into Hades, shed the outward layer of flesh to reach the bitter depths of death and reemerge alive. Christ, like Persephone, the seed both alive and dead. The seed holds the core of this mystery, that what it is to live is to die and what it is to die is to live. This is the meaning of the service.

During the service, the priest remembers the names of the dead. In fact, the majority of the service is made up of the priest reading names. He reads from a huge stack of "For the Departed" sheets of paper. "Eis mnimi tou Theou, Marias, Georgias, Persefonis, kai ton siggenon. Andreos, Charalambou, Nikolaou, Cleopatra . . ." A litany of names that goes on and on—probably unto eternity.

It is a mystery; this banquet that brings together both the presence of the living and the dead. For the dead, although lacking bodies and breath, are alive in spirit, kept alive through the prayers of the living. And the living, through the gift of the dead are reminded about the value of life. This is what the dead offer the living—the realization of the preciousness and fragility of life. For what is death and life but sitting on opposite sides of the same table?

It is so uncanny, but life and death follow in each other's footsteps. I am here to commemorate my father who passed away eight summers ago. Yet within three months of his death, his favorite child, my sister, announces she is pregnant. "It's a boy," I tell her intuitively. Which of course it is. He will be named for our father—Dimitrios. He will probably be born around the two weeks' time our father passed away. And way before that, I remember squeezing my head between the rails of the kitchen balcony in our flat in Athens, looking up to the streaming face of my mother on the phone. (You never do forget the times your mother cries when you are a child.) Her sister was on the phone telling her that their mother, Emilia, had passed away. It had been less than a week since the day Mama came home from the hospital herself, bearing her second daughter, Emilia, pudgy, red as a tomato in a woolen grey blanket, in honor of her mother who was on the verge of being born into a new world.

The litany of names goes on forever—"Stamatios, Argirios, Athinas, Konstantinos, Annis, Ioannis, Eirini . . . " If you listen long enough, you will hear your name no matter how rare and unusual you think it is –"Konstandoulas, Ectoras, Athinis, Avgerinis, Anthipis, Efsevios, Parthenas, Baisanias, Garifalias, Elizabeth . . ." The plates of koliva stand as a silent reminder of the presence of the spirits of the dead who have come to feed at the table. Though they outnumber the living—there could not be a banquet table long enough to seat all the departed—they fit in the space provided.

Their presence fills the empty spaces so that no one dares go close. A banquet table is comforting because it involves food and Greeks love food. Food is sustaining for both the living and the dead. The dead are fed by our prayers and vice versa. The dead and the living form a pair of two separate hands locked in prayer. No one alive is present without the fullness of the memory of one who has passed away, as one past away is sustained through the memory of the living. Such is the mystery of death that millions and billions of souls can fit together around a mystical banquet table. But the weight, the sheer force of the countless dead overpowers the living. The cloud of departed outnumber those alive.

This service in our Church is very wise. The memory of the sleeping helps to wake up those supposedly awake. The petty concerns of our everyday lives, the headache of finding parking, the grumbling of the gossipy neighbor, the daily grind of dealing with difficult people, pale in the presence of the mystery of death. What errand so pressing, what squabble so pervasive, what worry so nagging that it does not dissolve in the darkness of the grave? The mystery of life entwined to the mystery of death in this service.

The service ends with "Eternal the memory—aionia I mnimi, aionia I mnimi, aionia i mnimi." And even if the memory of those lying asleep is so far away in the past that no one living has a memory, the reminder is the same.

For the living, live as if you are going to die, and for the dead, sleep with the knowledge that you live eternally.

Transfiguration and the Artist

> At that time, Jesus took with him Peter and James and John his brother, and led them up a high mountain apart. And he was transfigured before them, and his face shone like the sun, and his garments became white as light. And behold, there appeared to them Moses and Elijah, talking with him. And Peter said to Jesus, "Lord, it is well that we are here; if you wish, I will make three booths here, one for you and one for Moses and one for Elijah." He was still speaking, when lo, a bright cloud overshadowed them, and a voice from the cloud said, "This is my beloved Son, with whom I am well pleased; listen to him." When the disciples heard this, they fell on their faces, and were filled with awe. But Jesus came and touched them, saying, "Rise, and have no fear." And when they lifted up their eyes, they saw no one but Jesus only. And as they were coming down the mountain, Jesus commanded them, "Tell no one the vision, until the Son of man is raised from the dead." (Matthew 17:1–9)

TODAY WE CELEBRATE THE Transfiguration of Christ. What does this mean? To transfigure means to change form across media. In Greek it is "Metamorphosis" or a change of form. According to this account given us by the Church, Christ climbed Mount Tabor, a high place that takes effort to arrive to relative secrecy, and there in front of three embodied human witnesses and two disembodied old ones, changed form. While He changed form, he did not change essence. What He did is manifest his divinity. The glory he kept hidden under cellular bonds and cotton folds. He showed those in his inner circle that he was human, AND he was God. It was I believe an apocalypse, an undressing, a taking back of the curtain to reveal what is secretly underneath. It revealed the mystery of Christ's glory for those who had yet to understand that within He harnessed the power of a thousand suns. He is the One.

For some of us, those who are used to keeping our power under wraps, so as to not to offend others or walk with inflated sense of self, it is good to ponder on the Transfiguration. For some it is necessary to contemplate the icon of the Crucifixion, of extreme humility; for others it is necessary to think about the Transfiguration. The Church provides them both. For one who has no sense of self, someone wounded as a child, for someone who lacks self-regard or self-esteem the contemplation of the Metamorphosis is absolutely vital.

What the transfiguration presents is that a human being, par excellence embodied in the figure of Christ, the ultimate hero of heroes, has two sides, the human and the godly. The human side is the one that struggles, that curses, that hungers, that feels itself short, limited, insufficient. It is the side that doubts itself and others that complains, "Why can't I be more? Why can't I do this faster, nicer? It is the side that sees the limits in its own capacity and others. Had you come faster, master, our brother would have been alive. It is the human side with its foibles and idiosyncrasies that we laugh at during each episode of *Seinfeld* or *Big Bang Theory*. The human side keeps tabs, huffs and puffs as it climbs up the mountain.

But there is another side, a side rarely seen because it is hidden and unknown in each person. That side is the divine. That is the side that glows with such bright light, the uncreated light, the light behind the light of the Sun that explodes spontaneously with the burst of a billion points of light. It is the light that sets the galaxies and universes into being, that crouches waiting to explode within each atom and *atomos*. It is that side we see symbolically painted in the icons. That divine side that shakes out like shook foil that is made up of the energy of the cosmos. That divine side that shares in the divinity, that holds so much power, force, and beauty it blinds the human side. It is this glorious powerful all light blinding side that we forget we hold in us. It is so shocking because it is so unexpected. We keep it hidden, unknown, because the surge of that power is so forceful and overwhelming, it could destroy the very container that stores it.

On this day, Christ took three of his disciples, Peter, James and John, to a high remote place. He revealed Himself in His true form: that He is not only human, but God also. The disciples so overcome by this revelation are groveling at his feet, holding on to their innards, keeping themselves from puking by covering their mouths. How did they escape getting blown up into smithereens by the energy of this light, the uncreated light of God—the light brighter than the sun, the light that set the light of the sun shining? There is contention in this. Some theologians like Balaam claimed the light that came from Christ on Mt Tabor was not the uncreated but created light. While very bright, we humans still have the limited capacity to look at the sun even for several seconds. The disciples could muster a few seconds of this light. Others like St. Gregory Palamas maintained the light was the uncreated light of God, but the disciples were given grace to perceive it. This supported Gregory's larger argument that although we cannot know God in His essence, we can know Him in his energies, as He reveals Himself.

While they were at the top of the mountain, they were joined by two Old Testament prophets, Moses and Elijah, who built stalls for the occasion. (This parallels the Jewish tradition of erecting booths.) The Old Prophets stood as witnesses to make more authentic the reality of this phenomenon—that the Christ is God of the Old and the New, of past, present and future, of the living and of the dead. And if that was not enough, the voice from the heavens made the announcement yet again, "This is my beloved Son, with whom I am well pleased; listen to him." (Matthew 17:5).

Some of us need to see that Metamorphosis happen within us. We have been conditioned to hear the criticisms, the shortcomings of our personhood—not _____ enough, too much ____, too little ____, do this more, do that less. Some of us tragically have been denied not just the power of their godly side, but have been conditioned to doubt even their human. So starved have they been of affirmation, of love, they walk in the world slithering on their underbelly, hoping not to get stepped on, begging for a crumb of mercy. Some of us have grown up completely riddled with self-doubt and immobilizing un-confidence that even choosing what to wear becomes a monumental decision. Some of us have been stripped of so much human dignity, we no longer appear human to others, not least to ourselves. These are the wastelands of the abused, the taken advantage of, the poor, the helpless, the powerless, the vulnerable. They appear in newspaper stories, pop up on street corners, sit at secretarial desks, live in group homes. The ones who are the last to stand in line, to speak up in a crowded room, the ones who whimper their losses away at night, the ones who believe they take up too much space on the subway platform, so they squeeze themselves into a slippery slope; the ones who shoot up, take pills, and shoot themselves or else drop from the top of tall buildings. Even the ones with fashion empires that wind up dangling from crystal chandeliers in their penthouse suite.

But herein is the Mystery of mysteries as revealed to us in the Transfiguration: that the human can be divine. Somewhere crouching in each of us is the light that can shatter the suns of a million galaxies. If we tap into that power, into our potential for the divine, we too can become children of light.

This reminds me of that famous quote by Marianne Williamson, "Our deepest fear is not that we are inadequate. Our deepest fear is that we are powerful beyond measure. It is our light, not our darkness that most frightens us."[1]

So true.

We have so much light endowed by our Maker; we are blinding! Do not despair of your human weakness, child. But beam out with the force of a thousand unfolding suns.

Become luminous, all-powerful, beautiful.

Walk towards the light, strive against your own darkness.

You are a child of light. It is hidden in you. Remember that. Be the light.

1. Marianne Williamson, *A Return to Love*, 190.

Epistle Reading

The Reading is from St. Paul's First Letter to the Corinthians: 10:12-22:

Brethren, let anyone who thinks that he stands take heed lest he fall. No temptation has overtaken you that is not common to man. God is faithful, and he will not let you be tempted beyond your strength, but with the temptation will also provide the way of escape, that you may be able to endure it. Therefore, my beloved, shun the worship of idols. I speak as to sensible men: judge for yourselves what I say. The cup of blessing which we bless, is it not a communion in the blood of Christ? The bread which we break, is it not a communion in the body of Christ? Because there is one bread, we who are many are one body, for we all partake of the one bread. Consider Israel according to the flesh: are not those who eat the sacrifices partners in the altar? What do I imply then? That food offered to idols is anything, or that an idol is anything? No, I imply that what pagans sacrifice they offer to demons and not to God. I do not want you to be partners with demons. You cannot drink the cup of the Lord and the cup of the demons. You cannot partake of the table of the Lord and the table of the demons. Shall we provoke the Lord to jealousy? Are we stronger than he?

St Paul's Letter to the Corinthians speaks to the struggle common in this globalized, ecumenical postmodern world. How do you guard your values, your standards, indeed your very faith without getting tainted by others whose values are far from what you believe? "You cannot drink the cup of the Lord and the cup of demons," St Paul says. That might seem straightforward in writing, but in practice it is challenging. In a country such as the US, and ever-increasingly in other cities where tribes of other faiths have entered and pitched their tents, it is common and necessary to rub shoulders, to have dinner, and commune with others who do not believe in Christ. As civil people, out of politeness, we must interact with these members. But, to a point. I believe this epistle is a warning not to get too close; to keep one's boundaries. If we pray with them even in gestures of goodwill, will we not be complicit in following their values, in symbolically accepting what they accept as sacred?

Because I am a huge lover of all things exotic, I have been drawn in my youth to other faiths and customs. While a student, I chose to live in the international dorm building where I was exposed to many people from the East. My roommates were from India, Persia, and South Carolina. I wore saris in grad school and joined the Indian Student League where I attended sitar concerts cross-legged on the ground. It was good fun; I learned so much. I hung out with medical students who showed me how to make the best tandoori chicken, how much masala is enough for saag paneer, how not to get juubi stuck to my fingers. The Hindu community was full of international students studying engineering, computer science, or medicine. They were polite and gentlemanly. Sharing space and food with another culture opened my mind and my world. I became more accepting and tolerant of other people. I even had a Hindu boyfriend. He took me to the open-air stadium one night and under the light of the arena he started reciting poetry from Tagore. I was smitten! There was so much truth and so much wisdom in the words of this ancient culture. Here was a way of thinking so foreign to my own it was addictive. I could not get enough of the music, the words, the food; India spiced up my life and thinking. It was thrilling—until I had my first encounter with the gods of the Hindu temple.

Gargantuan, in white elliptical domes hovering over Bowne Street in Flushing, it seemed otherworldly that such a structure would exist in this far out corner of Queens. There were husks of broken coconut at the entrance where penitents made offerings and bright garlands of marigolds, chrysanthemums, and daisies wrapped in bunches in straw baskets. A lanky priest, bare to the waist except for a long necklace of wooden beads, wearing a cotton cloth wrapped between his legs and tucked into itself at the side, stood in front of a woman wearing a bright pink sari whose ends she had lifted to reveal her earthy legs up to her knees. Her palms together in a gesture of prayer, her eyes closed, she was muttering prayers as the priest extended a clay oil lamp with a dancing flame over her head in circles. He incensed her with an incense stick, and she cupped her hand over the flame taking its heat and with a flourish of her hand brought it to her face then over her head and swiveled around her shoulders. He smashed the coconut on the second stair leading into a hidden room where he would retreat into. The temple had two marble stairways leading into a main hall that held a raised second level with two structures that seemed like sanctuaries only the priest was allowed to enter. A giant statue of Ganesh, the elephant god, fat with round tusks, sat in the far interior. Palms, flower petals were strewn everywhere, and red votive flames flickered along the grooves along the periphery.

This is the most exotic structure I had ever entered. My mind was doing cartwheels trying to process the extent of the unfamiliarity. My curiosity buckled my perturbation enough to get me to walk to the extensions and inner rooms on the periphery. There were niches cut into the stone in what seemed a neat line all along the side of this room. In the display spaces, as big as those you would find in the store window of a jewelry store or at the reptile section of the Museum of Natural History, there was what looked like a doll dressed in a bright pink dress. I walked slowly, hesitantly closer to discern what was displayed: a little black monkey with pink painted cheeks and kohl eyeliner. There was a whole line of these monkey idols that looked like baby girls in puffy pink dresses. I was floored. These people actually revered these little monkeys in poofy pink dresses with gold sequins and coins dangling from them? I could not understand for the life of me how a people, so educated, so advanced, could still believe in a pantheon of half-human, half-animal figures. What did these monkey gods represent anyway? I mean, ancient Greece believed in a pantheon of gods, but they were anthropomorphic; yes, there were a few hybrid creatures, but they were not gods. They were not honored and prayed to. They were monsters.

I could not understand how it could be possible in the 21st century for millions of people to take stock in a religion of polytheism? Where was the spirituality in elephant gods, monkey gods, raging purple faced goddesses with skulls and bones sticking their tongues at you? You could not say that Hinduism was an atavistic throwback either because India's belief system has not advanced to revert to an earlier form. True, I have not studied Hinduism to know the answers, but it seemed so strange. What kind of culture can believe in tiny monkeys dressed in pink tutus?

I had come face to face with the grounding bedrock of faith that the culture I had adopted and grown to love: it was a tiny monkey dressed in a pink puffy dress. Clearly the buck stopped there. That is when I realized I cannot break bread with people who believe in idols. I cannot share a bed with a man whose beliefs are so different. To do so would be to deny Christ. This is I believe the message of today's epistle: love and respect others, even those very different from yourself, but don't trade in Christ for other spiritual truths. Our faith in Christ is a non-negotiable. The boundary is clear. In today's world the boundaries can get fuzzy; many Christians visit mediums, practice yoga, go to meditation retreats. Sometimes it is hard to seem impolite or guarded in a pluralistic world that values acceptance of differences. You might be labeled as close-minded or even stuck up when you refuse to go along with the spirituality of the day. But it must be our deep love of Christ, not only as a concept but as a living person, that must keep us rooted to what is right. We cannot give away what we know is the Truth for a swirling passing multi-colored veil of truths. To do so is to deny Christ. It is His Blood in the Cup we receive. Only Christ, Love incarnate, gave His blood willingly on the Cross to redeem mankind. Which monkey god ever did that?

We cannot mingle His blood with the blood of idols.

No, we cannot drink the cup of the Lord and the cup of demons.

Christmas: setting up lights in the darkness

Altar Boys synchronizing the Great Entrance, St Glykeria Church, Attica, Athens, Greece

Today it is Christmas. On the corner of Astor Place and Lafayette on Christmas Eve I overheard a young man says that in a couple of more years Christmas will not exist. It will be over. Yes, it might seem that way looking at my block, half or more of it covered in darkness, the other half with blinking red and blue lights, "Let it snow" signs, and animated reindeer whose heads move side to side.

Growing up in Astoria as a child I remembered the awe of riding in the back of Baba's Oldsmobile as it turned the corner of block after block of two-story attached houses bejeweled in necklaces of light —a fanfare of glittering magic and larger-than-life Nativity sets. As a child, weaving my eyes around house after house as the car inched down the blocks, I felt the wonder of Christmas through the spectacle of speckled lights and the chutzpah of each neighbor outdone by the ego of the other. Today, these same pockets of streets are dim or dark— the evidence of a changing demographic. Some are out-of-towners, renters who have no time or energy to deck their front yards; some are millennial hipsters who have better things to do than deck their windows with cheesy Christmas cheer. Some are Muslim or Buddhist without a tradition for these sorts of things. Still others are agnostic or against the whole faith thing whatever.

I can see the turn in the times through the changes of the block. Yes, I am sad that things have changed, a sure sign that I have gotten older. But to live without the tradition is to be handed a gift box without a gift. Why would anyone want to live this way?

"God is dead" the new world texts, so don't expect him to be born on Christmas day. "Don't delude yourself," the intellectual says. "It's a story like many other stories compiled by old men," the feminist says. "Don't hold on to the past; grow up and out of this fairy tale. "Like the myth of Santa, it's time you put childish beliefs away," says the post-modernist.

Today it is Christmas and this is what I know–love came into the world and took the form of a babe. It is that love, that hope in swaddling clothes that has made all the difference. It is faith that the God-Man, the very embodiment of love, was born to live an earthly life with all its suffering and sorrow to make my life meaningful.

There is no greater gift than this. In our God-forsaken age (not because God has forsaken us but that we have turned away from Him) the greatest gift is Christ himself. The greatest gift is faith. It is a gift to believe in God in the 21st century. To hold a flickering light of faith in a sea of dark doubt. It is indeed a gift to love the figure of the God Man, the hero of all time and space in an age that blots Him and seeks to erase him from all of history.

I can not argue to an atheist why I believe. Try explaining to someone who does not love your fiancé why he should love her too. "It's subjective," they would say. "I don't see in her what you see." You can't convince anyone about the truth of your love the same way you can't convince them or force them to love you. Love like faith is a matter of the deepest center of the heart. It defies logic.

But my point is beyond this. My point is that on the day we give gifts to the Messiah the one who has given of Himself in the most intimate way, this God-Man has gifted us first. He has given Himself to the dark cruel world knowing full well that it will despise him, it will obliterate him. He has come to allow us to live and live more abundantly through His love and loving kindness.

Let me repeat again–the greatest gift in a godless age is faith itself. It is a grace, a gift. The Greek word for grace is "charisma" the same root for our English word charm. It translates to "gift." Grace is something you are gifted with. Beyond something you can will on yourself. Those who are gifted with the grace of faith these like the Magi hold the charm of the season.

On this day the Nativity of Christ, the Lord, let us glorify him. Let us give thanks that he has given us the gift of Himself. In the reciprocal act of believing Him, this faith has made all the difference. It's the difference between setting out a flickering display of lights for the passersby to see and be glad and letting it all be a bland infernal blackness.

Christ is born. Glorify Him.

"Will there be faith left on earth when the Son of Man returns?"

To be a Christian today is like being a part of a diminishing minority. The post-modern world has evolved to one not only that apostatizes itself from the holy, but one that ridicules and scorns those who believe, and not only those who believe in Christ but any power outside of themselves. To harbor faith is seen as infantile, deluded, misguided, passe. A faithful person in the post-modern world is considered an anomaly, a misfit. Very soon I suppose having faith will be included as a disorder in the DSM9. God is not only dead, but considered an obstacle to peaceful, logical living. Just look at all those believers – starting wars, blowing themselves up, believing in the afterlife and all such nonsense. During the funeral of my father, I quoted a verse from Scripture in the car where my cousin was driving me to the memorial lunch. "Are you sure there is life after death?" my cousin asked in a sarcastic way. "Yes, I am absolutely positively sure," I responded. "Are you absolutely sure?" she squinted her eyes as if to nudge me into really considering my naivete. "How can you be so smart and still believe in God?" read the undercurrent.

In a world that is fixed on believing its own course of mind, it is impossible to convince of the truth of God's existence. Logical thinking is a consequence of the Fall, the holy fathers and mothers teach us. We cannot put a full stake on our own mental powers of cognition because our very thoughts can be wrong. It is pride that pulls us into thinking that we can be correct in our own mind without tampering from other sources. The Desert Fathers, who were acutely perceptive psychologists, warned us not to put too much stake in our own thoughts; they can deceive us. Faith is paradoxical because its source stands outside of the individual mind; faith starts with God and then the individual responds to that energy. I might be wrong in this of course. But this I know, it is a grace from

God above to still harbor faith in these times of faithlessness. To believe in God is a radical act of going against the norm. It is a mystery, a gift that some people can have faith in God while others cannot accept it as real. Both sides see each other as deluded and flawed. In my life, I can confess that faith has made all the difference. That gift, because it is a gift and not some self-determined decision, has kept the votive flame of my heart kindled with light, warmth and joy. It has imbued my life with Meaning, the centeredness needed to survive in the shifting sands of a frenetic world filled with brokenness, instability, sadness, and malice. That faith that defies logic brings me into communion with a divine stratum of existence that cannot be felt through the five senses but experienced with the living heart, the center of the human being created in God's image. To live without faith is to live without meaning. Call me a fool, a delusional double-maker, but it has been the fixed point, the compass center, the Big Bang of my short existence.

Faith, true faith, the kind that leads you to sacrifice your first born on top of a mountain, looks crazy on the outside but makes sense from the inside. Faith in the post modern world is the ultimate gift from God. In the eschatologic times, very few of faith will be left upon the earth. This is why the Desert Fathers and Mothers prophesied that late Christians of the Church will not be able to achieve any feats of ascetic practice: they won't be able to fast or hold long vigils; they won't be able to escape into the desert and devote themselves to God; they won't be able to bear tortures like getting their skins flailed or burning in oil vats or getting their nails taken out. All they will be able to accomplish is just keep the faith in God. For this they will be honored more than the early martyrs who suffered so much for Christ. Imagine that! The Christians of the late church will not have to suffer on the scale that the early Christians had; all they must do is keep the faith. To live in a world that is so contrary to God's commands, when everyone is free to work out their own will on others without so much as scrutiny, when one is ridiculed for having faith—these will be the martyrs who will suffer the most and be exalted above the others. You get all the glory just because you believe. That is enough. The Irish monks would stand arms outstretched in the elements or would push themselves into thornbushes; St David of Thessalonika lived for 30 years at the top of a walnut tree (how did he manage to relieve nature without making a fuss of himself?). The ascetics of Nilus survived on a crust of bread for weeks. Meanwhile I can't keep a prayer rule, feel like fainting if I go without eating for more than eight hours, and sit at the slightest ankle pain during all-night vigil. Don't tell me what to do—I will fight till I get my way. Yet, will I receive more glory? Yes, that is the power of keeping the faith.

“For a thousand years are but a day in your sight”

Time is subjective. For many years in my adult life I felt as if it was a precious spool of thread. I only had so much of it. I lived my day as if it had an expiration date, as if it would run out. When you live in the material plane, you feel as if time is running out all the time. This causes you to run faster and faster to catch up with the dregs of time. Carpe diem keeps you frenetically sopping up experiences, ticking off lists of things to do. When you live as if you have no time or very little, your days speed up faster and faster and ironically, you lose it. But, if you enter into the world of the holy, that immaterial dimension where time is like air, you calm down. Faith in God torques your notion of time. With God time does not exist or rather it exists always, sort of like those Renaissance icon paintings where the episodes in a saints’ life appear all at once—she is born into a humble hut, she leaves on an ocean voyage, she encounters God and repents, she enters into the desert and lives naked among the beasts, she receives holy communion, she dies and is buried in a pit of sand. You see all these sequential events as happening at once. Time when you progress to the spiritual level does not dictate your actions; your actions are subsumed into the larger tapestry of time. Time is a human construct; God dwells in eternity. Taking on a spiritual perspective allows you to be plucked out of the river of time. Because of this changed perspective, I am not in a hurry to do this or that; I am not obsessed with living life to the last minute. I luxuriate in a sort of temporal ether like the sky. My words and actions will echo into eternity, so it is best that I slow down and contemplate—is what I am about to do the best use of my time? Now time rolls from under me like a red carpet. I feel so less stressed and more at peace because I know that in God’s time, I will fulfill what I am meant to do.

What is more, this shift in sense of time allows me to focus on the internals instead of the externals. So many times, running after goals, accomplishing objectives pinions me to what is outside of myself when I really should be taking care to tend the inside of myself. Letting go of time forces me to look at what is truly needful—the things that transcend time. What transcends time? The essential self, the self made in the image of God, the soul. The saints in the desert lived the same day for decades—on the surface. Many people of today would deem that the holy Desert mothers and fathers who lived lives of austere asceticism in long hours of prayer had been wasting their time. They accomplished nothing on the physical plane with the exception of establishing a monastery or a hospital here or there. They have not earned degrees or founded companies or raised families. But what they have done, to cultivate their inner life, is more difficult than any high-powered degree-bearing CEO can: they have tended to their souls. They did the inner work necessary to bring out their soul's fragrance as is pleasing unto God. They pulled themselves out of the rat race, the cities obsessed with making appointments on time, to enter the world of ever-expanding eternity. Time does not exist in the desert: it is the same day for centuries. Human industry has a way of making time speed up to a frightening frenetic pitch. Take stock of your day: how many things have you done? How many errands, meetings, phone calls, emails, orders, purchases and what not have you put executed in three hours? This busy-ness has a tantalizing tendency to speed up the turbines of your mind so that they spin hot smoke. In the post-modern world so much business and busyness forms people who cannot sit still enough to understand their most essential selves. They are lost in the dust devils of their own activity.

Yet a thousand years are but a day in God's sight. I am trying to slow down instead of speed up. I am trying to accept and feel the beads of time one by one without feeling guilty for standing still. In my life I have found that my greatest external accomplishments could only have followed my internal accomplishments. Too many of us run around substituting external activity for what is truly needful—internal awareness. Only when I have the courage to sit still long enough with myself like the Bedouins do in their tents with strangers sipping small cups of roasted coffee spiked with cardamon on slow-burning coals can I truly know myself. Only when I know myself and my calling deeply can I then exit the tent and conquer the world. Prayer is like sipping coffee with a Bedouin. Except that Bedouin is God. That strange exotic stranger somewhere deep in your soul. For some of us encountering that beautiful stranger is the most frightening thing. It is easier to apply to an MBA program or fill in applications for a condo. I know. I have been guilty the majority of my adult life.

Only by living one day as if it were eternal could I live it truly.

The Cross

Holy Cross on the grounds of St Anthony's Monastery, Florence, Arizona

As a Christian I struggle with the idea of suffering, even worse than the idea is the experience—the soul-wrenching skin piercing visceral experience of pain. This is the paradox that the Orthodox Church presents for our meditation today. The Cross—the excruciating physical, emotional and spiritual agony that our Lord suffered on behalf of us, the most undeserving and miserable ones–it is through this Cross, this agony that we are led to salvation.

Most days I do not want to accept this. I do not want to suffer. I do not want to witness suffering and injustice. The blown up bloody bodies of innocents strewn against the morning paper—the greed I see around me that gives rise to heinous institutionalized inequality. Blatant racism, sexism, corruption of every society. When I reel in loneliness because I know that in my most painful moments, I too will be alone; and not just left alone, but even mocked and ridiculed. Who wants to suffer? It is counterintuitive; it is unhealthy, even self-destructive, the self-help books tell me.

But the Church teaches me that there is no way to heaven—the only way is the Via Dolorosa, the Sorrowful Way, the Way of the Cross. This is the rub—that the way out of the pain is through the pain. The only way to heaven is through hell.

At the foot of Golgotha in the Church of the Holy Sepulchre, I have knelt in front of the Cross of the Lord; have witnessed the stones torn in two. I have tasted that bitter cup of agony, if only in the lightest dose. Having attended the pageant of pain at that holy site, I have scabbed the bitterness of death, have followed His shrouded body to the burial cave, have witnessed the blood on the pavement, heard the lashings and the beating of the nails through the bone. It is the shrieks of infernal pain unleashed in the darkest hell, the agony of despair, that reverberated through the Praetorium while the soldiers played dice over the white gown. The lurid circles and Xs inscribed on the floor of the dungeon where He was awaiting His doom.

The bloody pool, mockers with grimaces wagging fingers. I too have felt the deep cut of the sword through the heart. The emptying, the utter relinquishing of will to something or someone that must have felt utterly sinister and pointless.

It is death incarnate that we must stare deeply into to understand that this is what life is about. Suffering is life. No one can escape it. Only when we comprehend this can we realize that just a few feet away, a few days away, lies the site of the Holy Resurrection. From the mouth of the abyss the light floods out. It is the very same revolving door from within which pass both birth and death, light and dark, agony and ecstasy. That is the paradox that we are forced to swallow—that death is life crouching to be born; life carries the seed of the bitter knowledge of death.

It is the Lord, our hero, who has paved the Way. The Via Dolorosa leads to the stairway to heaven. The instrument of death has become life-giving. Such is the Mystery that our minds might like sieves attempt to hold.

Let us raise up our Crosses and take on the same agony of Crucifixion that leads to the ecstasy of Resurrection.

The Desert

"My soul yearns for you like water in a parched and desert land" –Psalm 150

Camels on the road to St Katherine's Monastery, the Sinai, Egypt

THE DESERT. DEATH VALLEY. No man's land. The nihilistic plain. You walk into the desert and you die. Or you survive. It is a place of transformation. You come face to face with God in the desert. And the Devil.

The period of Great Lent is like walking into the desert. The desert trope has had a long history in the Orthodox tradition—both physically with the establishment of the first monastic communities (Nitria, Sinai, Jericho,) and symbolically.

The experience of the desert, not just as a metaphor, but a real physical entity leaves anyone transformed. It is a place that invokes fear and awe. In my life I have been honored with translating the Judean Desert and the desert of Sinai. Rolling rocky hills reveal a desolate landscape, but at the same time unveil the utter stark elemental power of the most essential stuff of earth—sun, rock, sky. In the desert you notice things you had not seen before—the subtle changes of the red orange glow at sunset; the scuttle of scorpion; the shadow behind the stone.

The Desert is a paradox of undulating proportions. It is only in the silence that you can hear the voice of God. It is only in the nothingness that you can be creative. It is in the barrenness, in the stark deprivation that you will find what is necessary to sustain your soul. In your nakedness, you will clothe yourself. It is only when you stand still that you realize where you are traveling to.

I think of St Mary of Egypt who walked into the desert a sinner. I see her naked, emaciated, brown form wandering through the dust clouds and heat waves of infinite dunes. In the desert she became a saint. She completely metamorphosed into a thing of psychic beauty.

Our post-modern world full of digital bombardment and information overload has made it impossible for us to know our souls. Always active, always reacting to one visual or auditory stimulus after another, we never have the chance to sit still. We are so mortified of doing "nothing" we go out of our way to fill every moment with distraction. Why are we so afraid of just being? Because only when you sit still can you feel the profound sadness, the angst that makes up your existence. Only in stillness and silence do you hear the demons in your soul; they rise up to wage battle with you. And that is scary. Let's not romanticize these desert places, these desert moments. In the desert you are stripped naked, and you are vulnerable. You are more susceptible to pain. No one wants to go there.

I am going through a desert this Great Lent. In His wisdom, the Lord has stripped me of almost all the relationships that have sustained me. I have no friends; my marriage is in shambles; my teenaged daughter not only refuses to have a relationship with me, but scorns and abuses me; my spiritual father does not talk to me; my aging mother is becoming senile; my stepson is in jail. Those people I thought were friends have shown a new face (or is it that the mask has come off?) I am utterly alone. But this is perhaps the path I must walk in order to truly know God's will for me. I trust that this is all for my enlightenment. It is vainglory that makes us put our trust in fallible human beings. There is no help: eventually those closest to you, those who you regarded with esteem will let you down. No human is without error or folly. Do not put your trust in princes or in chariots, or in friends or husbands or children, not even in your parish priest. Humans are bound to fail you; they are human after all. Only in God can you trust. He is the source of your sustenance in a place "barren and untrodden and unwatered." As women who put so much stake in "Relationship," this is understandable as we are 'relational beings.' We garner our sense of identity through our relationships. Unraveling relationships is a hard lesson to learn. We are relationship junkies. We tend to every relationship except the two most fundamental: the relationship with ourselves and the relationship with God. It is dangerous to make idols of our relationships—our children, our spouses, our bosses, our friends. They too can become distractions.

For the stubborn soul to change, it has to go through the ringer, an experience of such force that elemental change can take place. It is the desert that provides this again. Only when you are brought to such extremes, at the point of life or death, can the soul truly call out to God for help. It is from the desert that a fountain of prayer sprouts. At the breaking point, you call out to God in humility because you have finally let go of your pride.

I think of Odysseus. Tempest-tossed and exhausted, only when he calls out from the depths of the waves to Poseidon and realizes that he is just a man like everyone else that he is finally saved. It took him ten long years to humble himself. The Desert is the operating table from which pride is extracted. But as anyone who has gone under the knife will tell you, it is very painful.

It is the symbolic significance of the desert that has deeper meaning. I end with an excerpt that came my way, like a crumb in the desert, from a Church bulletin by the Very Reverend Archimandrite Vasilios Bassakyros of St. John the Baptist Church of Gramercy Park. He writes:

> "During Great Lent we experience, if we allow ourselves to, the wealth that the desert has to offer. In this wasteland we grow not only spiritually, but also physically. How can this be you ask, since the desert is a barren place where little or nothing survives? It is in this desert environment that we learn to see through, and cast off, all that we have accumulated, and accomplished in our lifetime. All those attachments weigh upon us, and as a result, they act as a curtain over the true eye of our soul.

> However, in the desert we are stripped of the fortress we built around ourselves so that we can survive any attack or hardship that confronts us in the world. As such, we are left naked to the physical elements, and we become more vulnerable emotionally and spiritually. Only then can we feel the cries and the longings of the soul for God. Just as our stomachs groan with each passing day during Great Lent from the food to which it has become accustomed, so too have our souls begun to feel again, and long for what it was created to feed upon, and savor, the Lord Himself."[1]

We do not have to leave the city to experience what most people have found in the desert. We can search our entire life and never find the gift that awaits us from within. Searching for "the thing" that makes us happy, is only a temporary fix, and when we find it, we think all will be well. On the contrary, it is through the emptiness and desolate landscape of the desert that we begin to find ourselves and there we become what God has created us to be in the beginning.

1. St. John the Baptist Greek Orthodox Church, *Weekly Bulletin* (New York: St John the Baptist GO Church Gramercy, June 20, 2019)

Pentecost

> When the day of Pentecost had come, they were all together in one place. And suddenly a sound came from heaven like the rush of a mighty wind, and it filled all the house where they were sitting. And there appeared to them tongues as of fire, distributed and resting on each one of them. And they were all filled with the Holy Spirit and began to speak in other tongues, as the Spirit gave them utterance. Now there were dwelling in Jerusalem Jews, devout men from every nation under heaven. And at this sound the multitude came together, and they were bewildered, because each one heard them speaking in his own language. And they were amazed and wondered, saying, "Are not all these who are speaking Galileans? And how is it that we hear, each of us in his own native language? Parthians and Medes and Elamites and residents of Mesopotamia, Judea and Cappadocia, Pontos and Asia, Phrygia and Pamphylia, Egypt and the parts of Libya belonging to Cyrene, and visitors from Rome, both Jews and proselytes, Cretans and Arabians, we hear them telling in our own tongues the mighty works of God." (Acts: 2.1–11)

Today is the Day of Pentecost, when the Holy Spirit descended on the apostles gathered together and with a great rush of wind and flame of fire converted them from dumb, uneducated fishermen to eloquent wise servants of the Almighty. I will try to glean from my lowly state some insights into the beauty and importance of this day.

THE POWER OF THE SPIRIT

The Spirit is by far the most mysterious person of the Holy Trinity. It has no face, no corporality, but is nevertheless central to the Triune God. I liken it to the divine energy of God, the Spirit, the Light. It is the Force that moves over the water that makes things happen according to the will of God. The energizer, the creative force. (If I may be so bold, it is the feminine face of God.) That is the energy, the Light, that substance beyond our corporal understanding yet through both our corporal and spiritual understanding able to be sensed. It is the abounding presence of God that can reside from the bodies of mortals to the furthest star in the universe. It is the stuff that I believe brought the universe into creation; that infuses the world as a fifth essence. Saint Seraphim has been quoted countless times, "Acquire the Holy Spirit and thousands will be saved around you."

Without that Spirit, we are not as powerful, not as enlightened, not as holy. Witness the apostles: before the coming of the Holy Spirit--mere ignoramuses bickering amongst themselves, asking dumb questions, vying in their petty foibles. After the Holy Spirit—illumined speakers, casters out of evil, clairvoyants, healers. When the Holy Spirit enters a person, they catch the Divine Energy, the same gem-like flame that burns without burning, that emanates from God. By ourselves, we can do very little; with the spirit, we can move mountains, baptize entire nations, create immortal works of art. It can be seen as the golden halo around the heads of saints in icons. Indeed, this is the goal of our earthly existence—to acquire the Holy Spirit. When we do, we breathe, we beat, we move in God Himself.

THE POWER OF UNITY

The Holy Spirit as it is described in the Scripture comes down as a sort of cloven tongue that flames. The first act of the Holy Spirit is that each of those present were able to speak in other tongues. Why? I conjecture that by speaking in another tongue you are able to understand things you could not on your own. Psychologists say that learning another language is a way to change your brain, to color the way you see the world. It is their ability to speak in other tongues, additionally, that allows the apostles to communicate with those that they could not. The Church maintains that Pentecost is the counterpart of the Tower of Babel; the antithesis of what occurred when the nations tried in their pride to reach God. When the tower of Babel was destroyed scattering all those who had come together for the wrong aim, an act of disunity and dispersal, each of the nations started speaking in their own tongue. Each could not understand the other, thus forcing them into greater confusion, misunderstanding, and distance. Pentecost does the opposite. It brings disparate "Parthians and Medes and Elamites and residents of Mesopotamia, Judea and Cappadocia, Pontos and Asia, Phrygia and Pamphylia, Egypt and the parts of Libya belonging to Cyrene, and visitors from Rome, both Jews and proselytes, Cretans and Arabians" (Acts 2:9-11) and unites them under a single tongue.

The power of language via this Holy Spirit to unite the nations is clearly a takeaway from this holiday. But what language? It is the language of God, that exists not in the mind, but in the nous, the center of the deep heart. It is this energy that allows those who kindle it to feel comfortable and connect to those who due to culture are superficially different from themselves. It makes the Other as one close to one's heart. This power of the Holy Spirit that has initiated the Church, the universal Church. It is why I can attend a liturgy in Japanese and still feel in communion with my home church. The Holy Spirit unites through the power of tongues.

THE PARACLETE

Another name for the Holy Spirit is the "paraclete," in Greek "comforter, counselor, adviser." During Pentecost, we fall down, bending our heads to the ground on bended knee supplicating for this "Paraclete." It is imperative for our souls to pray on this day. With so much turmoil in the last few months, as the faithful people of God wherever we are standing throughout the world, our prayers to the Paraclete are essential. Anarchy has taken over the streets; diseases of soul and body plague the world; economic uncertainty--it is as if the world is hovering on a tipping point that will rush it headlong into the gates of hell. Where do we turn for comfort in these times of woe? Where do we find advice on what to do, where to go? The Paraclete! Whatever problems plague us, whatever internal turmoil robs us of our peace, on this special day dedicated to the Holy Spirit, we bow down to ask for help from this Great Counselor. It is in the language of the heart that the Paraclete will reveal to us what we are seeking, what we truly need, and guide us in all the minute details of our life. It is like getting a counseling session with the most sought-after psychologist in the world, only better, because not only does the Paraclete give us counsel it actually helps us on the road to healing.

For me, who has suffered so much trauma, in so need of healing, I am especially making an effort to call on the Paraclete. It is my life's purpose to attain the grace of this Holy Spirit. May the mercies of our Lord be upon us. May the Paraclete hear our prayers and deem us worthy to find abode in our hearts, transforming us from empty cymbals of the flesh into living temples of light and love, glowing with the flame of the Spirit.

DESCENT OF THE SPIRIT

This week as we commemorate the descent of the Holy Spirit, I muse about the mystery of expression, the capacity for clear thinking, and the limits of human knowledge without this Spirit. I like to think of myself as a writer and a teacher whose livelihood, reputation, and clout depend on words. So much of my struggle has to do with the ability to capture the truth and deliver it in an eloquent, yet straightforward manner so that my readers and my students can grasp the nebulous, inchoate cloud of what I am trying to express.

Many times, I come up awkward, sloppy, klutzy or even empty handed. Sometimes thoughts wring me in a wrestling match where I am unable to disengage and arrange the words from the idea, the essence, the Truth of what I am trying to express. As much as I try sometimes the beauty, the exactness of the thought or feeling, I cannot accurately cloak with words. Words like fabric cut too short cannot cover the immensity of an idea.

The other complication is that the vessel of thinking, our human mind, is also limited. Like a clay pot, it is so many cubits wide and long. While amazingly it can be stuffed with many things, strings of ideas, theories, memories, and even with imaginations that can spiral into entirely new galaxies, the mind has its boundaries. It can know only so much as its sentient powers allow.

I argue with an atheist colleague about this all the time. You cannot know God or any spiritual reality if you rely only on the senses. Faith is a question of epistemology--how we claim to know the things we know. If as a scientist you claim to only know what you can derive from your senses, then it would be hard to make the deductive jump from the physical to the spiritual. The workings of the Spirit can be experienced through the senses but cannot be proven from them. My colleague insists you can only know from the material reality and as such because God cannot be proven from such, no thinking logical person can accept such a claim. God is a delusion, a figment of the mind. Just because you cannot see God who is unknowable with your senses does not mean he doesn't exist. But you can't make the claim that He does either, otherwise you can claim other unknowable beings are possible, beings such as purple fairies that go around painting polka dots.

The issue I have with my colleagues is that they are not willing to admit that the human, material capacity for thought is limited. Believing that the human mind can know everything in and of itself is intellectual pride. It's like believing that the clay pot can fit the entire known universe in itself. How proud to believe that your noggin can contain the Creator? That the oh-so-small container can comprehend the mind of its maker? I saw a bumper sticker on a Nissan parked at a monastery parking lot; it said, "Don't always trust what you think." The Desert Father's and Mothers, wise early chroniclers of human psychology, made the case that our thoughts can be faulty. It is in the realm of thought that the spiritual war between good and evil takes place. The demons are noetic beings and can enter into our thoughts pricking them with dark reasonings. Satan they say is a smooth-talking lawyer able to make a convincing case for evil using the most logical most cogent argument. Human logic, reasoning has provided the rationale for arguments for the Holocaust, war, genocide, and other enlightened acts of reason. Human capacity for reason is tainted by the Fall, not just physically, but ontologically as well.

St Silouan the Athonite said, "The Lord does not show Himself to a proud soul. The proud soul, no matter how many books it reads, will never know God, since by its pride it does not give place for the grace of the Holy Spirit, while God is known only by the humble soul"[1] Intellectuals with many degrees after their names are prime candidates for spiritual pride. Pride keeps the Spirit away so they can never really "see" the spiritual truths that other humbler yet less educated people can. That's because the Spirit acts on a faculty of the human soul that goes beyond the rational thinking brain, that inner part of the soul known as the "nous"

1. St. Silouan the Athonite, Writings, III.11, "Three-Hundred Sayings of the Ascetics of the Orthodox Church," n.d. http://holywisdomorthodox.com/library/ascetics_sayings.html.

that encompasses the thinking part, but is larger and deeper than it as it involves the heart or the emotional and moral part of the psyche.

And here we are this week at Pentecost. The Holy Spirit appears in the icon as swirls of blue waves of wind. Over the Apostles a flame of fire, although the Scriptural term is "tongues of fire." What statement is this icon making on the subject of expression and thought? The truth with a capital T requires divine revelation. Without the Wisdom that comes from the maker the human mind is but a noisy barrel, a broken pot. We cannot know the truth, cannot express the truth without divine intervention. Even with our thinking world we must aim at kenosis at humility of thought. Erasing our own assumptions of what reality is and making room for the Holy Spirit to give us the light and the tongue to express the mysteries that we cannot express with our own mind. The Holy Spirit is like a light that comes on making it easier to use our faculty of light. In other cases it is like eyeglasses or even a microscope. We cannot know the truth let alone express it correctly without the energy and force of this Divine Spirit, the Light whose power gives us the ability to correctly see the spiritual truths we would otherwise miss.

For this reason I have always considered writing a spiritual act. The more I pray and fast, the more the Spirit would guide me. The less "noisy" I am with my own thoughts, the clearer the message from the Word.

May the Holy Spirit give all those who think, who write, who create the Light to express the Truth that transcends words.

Clean Monday: Quarterpounder vs Jesus

It is that time of the year again –the Great and Holy Fast. Yes, that period when we are supposed to abstain from enticements of the flesh. No meat, no diary, no entertainments, no sex (yikes!) St John Chrysostom states that we should not be enslaved to the stomach. But I suspect that Great Lent is more than curbing eating habits, which does take a lot of discipline in any case; it is about realigning the human compass away from the earthly, the fleshy to the spiritual and the godly. It is a turning away from the things that are seen to the things that are not seen, as they are the more important. Of course, we can go into this period begrudgingly and sigh and beat our breast, "Oh what I am giving up! Poor me-oh poor poor me—no cream in my coffee, no "gettin' some" no going to the movies or some fancy party, no shows—for a fortnight. Non-Orthodox friends when they hear all we give up roll their eyes and shake their heads, "Hell no! I couldn't do it for so long."

While that could be the attitude I enter the period with a morose sense of self-pity and self-flagellation, I am challenging myself to enter the season differently. I will go into the Great Lenten period not with the sense of what I am giving up but with what I am to receive (if I am worthy). This is what I forget as a Christian. Yes, there is sacrifice, but with the sacrifice comes love. We are called to give up a lot no doubt, but in return we receive something, or rather someone, much greater. That someone is Christ. The tiny morsels we give up, the blips on the canvas of time or our meager works of charity, are returned in exponential measure by His Grace. You give up a dollop of cream cheese but in return you get Jesus. You give up an afternoon you would have spent at the movies to volunteer in the nursing home, but in return, you get Jesus. You give up sleep during the night, but in the morning you get Jesus. J esus is so worth the tiny inconveniences in our schedule. Great Lent becomes an opportunity to put Christ first by emptying ourselves. By emptying myself, that "kenosis" the Spiritual Fathers talk about, I make more room for Jesus.

So, I have made a pledge with myself during this season to keep the temptations at bay by keeping this mindset. When I am tempted by a quarter pounder as I have not been able to find a snitch of vegan food all day and my stomach sounds like a wounded animal wild with hunger, I will think, "Do I choose a piece of meat or Jesus?" Is not Jesus worth all the Whoppers in the world? I will try to keep in mind, for every chocolate macaroon I give up or every cream cheese bagel, I will get back a little more of Jesus. In this light it is easy to give up what you think you can't do without? And instead of looking at Lent as the cup 40 days empty, it will become at the end "the cup that spilleth over and over."

I hope I will choose the better part because anyone who has tasted Jesus, the real Jesus even in a miniscule drop, knows the sweetness, the joy, the fullness of Christ. Hands down, the choice is simple; it's the choosing that's hard.

Massacre and Martyrdom: The Battle between Light and Dark...

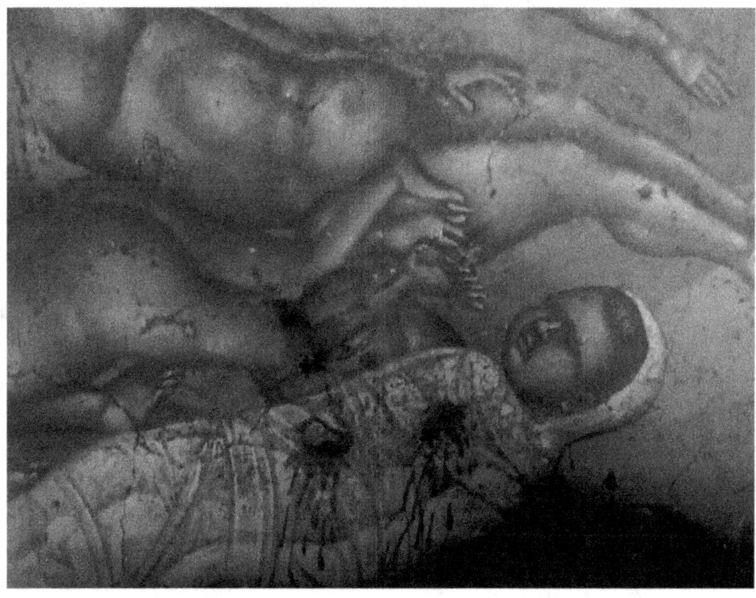

Detail from a fresco of the martyrdom of the Innocents

In this icon fresco the casual observer witnesses a massacre. Mass violence perpetrated by one group of people on another. So many massacres have happened, not only in Church history, but throughout history. A quick turn through every church brings to your eye visions of slaughter, scenes of terrible violence. The slaughter of the 14,000 innocents, the gruesome portrayal of the bloody Persian invasion in Palestine, the 400 martyrs of Sebaste. Icons depicting the gruesome trials and tortures of great martyrs– beheadings, spikes driving through skin, burned alive in vats of boiling oil. These are not pictures you would show to the young and the more sensitive among us. Yet these images fill every place of worship. Most of the saints decorating an Orthodox Church interior hold a cross of martyrdom in their hand.

Icon of the Massacre of the Holy Infants in the narthex of St Barbara Church, Ano Patissia, Athens, Greece

Especially poignant is the icon of St Sofia and her three daughters, Faith, Hope and Agape. The atrocities these little girls were put through even at their mother's encouragement for more agony unsettles my very core. Why? Why must the grand majority of witnesses come to a violent and cruel end? Why do massacres occur again and again throughout each epoch and each culture? Why must we be reminded in a place of sanctuary that such horror is the inevitable step to attain sainthood? That question begs the bigger one, the one humankind has grappled with since the dawn of consciousness, why do the innocent suffer? And not just one but masses and masses of innocents?

I am only a sinful layperson, not a theologian, but I think the answer has to do with the eternal battle between good and evil that takes place in the human heart. The forces of darkness that lay crouching in the jungles of the human heart are unspeakable in their horror. As horrible as the scenes of slaughter that permeate through news reports of terrorist bands, of black and white documentary photos of the Holocaust, the Khyber Rouge, WW1, Sabra and Shantila. (This last reference is to remind those of us good Christians who think that all terrorism comes from radical Islam.) The recurrence of war demonstrates that while humankind has advanced technologically, it has not risen above the primitive ruthless instincts of rival bands of chimpanzees. Evolution has happened on the physical level, not on the spiritual. Those dark primitive forces toward violence, rape, territory are proof that the beast wrestles with the angel on a grand scale. There is an eternal battle waged within each person between these forces, most of the time unconsciously. I think sin might be the dark vestige of a primitive past.

The battle is for each human heart to rid itself of the darkness of these passions. It is God in the person of Christ the God Man that reveals the light. The path of light that develops goodness, mercy, and love, especially love, in the battlefield. It is God who with His Pneuma breathed a new spirit into man. The soul with its potential for eternity.

That darkness is so dark, no horror movie can do it justice. It is hell incarnate. The light stands in such stark contrast to the dark it is a bit blinding, only those used to it can stand to look at it. It is this battle between the light and darkness that each saint, once a regular person like you and me, is celebrated as victor. Those icons of cruel martyrdom show how the saint as a soldier in the battle between good vs evil/light vs darkness succumbs physically to these primitive forces. The good suffer in the world because they refuse to take part in its rules. They follow a higher power. Yet while it might seem as if the forces of violence have won out, a greater law, a more primitive magic that stretches before the dawn of time renders the saint a victor. The saint, even while drenched in her own blood, proves that there is another plane of law that transfigures suffering and cruelty into a triumph of the spirit. Because the saint has been victorious over the passions, the dark drives of the beast, a legacy of our evolution from slime and sludge in a dog-eat-dog environment, he or she is crowned by not reverting to the same.

The Lenticular Jesus During his Passion

When I was a little girl, my pappou and yiayia took me away for a brief vacation on the island of Aegina. (It was really an excuse to wrench me away from the agony of living with the reality that my newly born rival, my sister, that fat red piece of turd, had ripped me from my cherished throne as the center of the universe.) It must have been around Pascha season because I had vivid images of whole carcasses of lamb strung up from hooks in butcher shop windows. You know the image—the bulging black eyes, the mouth pulled back in a sinister smile revealing yellowed square teeth, the fronds of bloody veins running down the pale white skin blotched with skeins of fat like lace; the purple ink circle with certified numbers stamped on its side; its legs straight as bar stools without the hooves. I had a hard time looking at the carcasses of these dead animals—forced upon me in full window display so that I had to shield my face whenever we walked by.

And then there was the little chapel by the port of Aegina. Every afternoon after waking up from the Greek siesta, Pappou would take my hand and we would take a stroll along the aisles of the pier, lined with caiques and yachts bopping up and down in the tide. He'd buy me ice cream religiously. It was pleasant enough walking along hearing the slurping sounds of the waves smashing against the concrete pier, venturing to the edge to watch silver minnows cutting through the cerulean tide like flecks of sun, getting blinded by the scintillating scales of light on the waves, the salty sweetness in the nostrils. At the edge of the pier stood a small, white-domed, one-room chapel dedicated to St. Nicholaos, my Pappou's patron saint.

He would go and light a candle every afternoon with me in tow, my ice cream melting between fingers. I had grown very frightened to enter the chapel because of "The Lamb." You see, contrary to Orthodox tradition, someone had placed one of those lenticular pictures of Jesus crucified next to the candle box. It's one of those cheap cheesy pictures that when you move to one side the image changes a pose, and then when you move to the other it changes again. Standing as high as the candle box, I had the very life-like photo of Jesus right smack in my field of vision. When I moved my head a little to the right, I'd see His outstretched arms bloody with the iron spikes nailed to the Cross, the thorns of His Crown puncturing his forehead exploding into bloody streams, and His face in utter exhaustion and desperation—His eyes looking up to heaven in agony.

When I moved my head to the left, His arm lower, His face would hang down and His eyes would close in resignation. A four-year-old might not have words for life and death, but right there was the iconic realization. All you had to do was make a quick tick of the head, and boom, Life, and the struggle to stay alive in blood, sweat and tears; make a quick tick of the head again and boom, Death and the everlasting sleep. I was terrified. I had a visceral response every time I'd go near that chapel. I walked by the candle box squinting half wanting, half-not wanting to catch a glimpse of the holographic Crucified Christ. Between the cracks in my fingers and the flickering of the beeswax candle, I'd bob back and forth—see the dead man, don't see the dead man. My curious dread intensified walking from the bright white sun of the day into the dark dankness of a cave.

For a little girl, Pascha seemed like participating in a horror show.

Years later, after we had migrated to the US, I remember being off for Holy Week in grade school (lucky for us the Jewish Passover, the basis for the NYC public school calendar, coincided with our spring recess). Religiously, we were watching Franco Zefferelli's "Jesus of Nazareth" on ABC. The moving music, the penetrating blue-eyed stare of the youth that played Jesus, the gruesome realism of the whippings, the spikes, and the blood brought my brother, sister and me to sobs. Gathered as witnesses around the glare of the old mechanical TV with the clothes hanger as antenna, we were a sloppy mob of snots and sorrow until my mother, quote unquote a devout Christian, walked in and turned the knob on the side panel, "That's enough. We have to close it." The excruciating scenes of Christ's Passion were too much. Watching a lamb get slaughtered is not for the sensitive ones.

From childhood to adulthood, from the 1st century to the 21st century, the last week of Pascha climaxes into a pageant of death and suffering, presenting the raw realities of life and death like a butchered lamb on a charger. Holy Week as Passion Week forces us to contemplate the meaning of suffering. Some parts of the answer I understand while others still remain a mystery.

Christ's Passion brings up the biggie: Why? Why is it that the innocent suffer? Why so much suffering?

This part I know: Life without suffering is not life. The late Victor Frankl made that point in *Man's Search for Meaning* after going through the unfathomable suffering of the Holocaust. He says, "If there is a meaning in life at all, then there must be a meaning in suffering. Suffering is an ineradicable part of life, even as fate and death. Without suffering and death human life cannot be complete."[1] It is pain and deep suffering that

1. Frankl, *Man's Search For Meaning*, 2.

deepens the experience of living. It is inevitable and inescapable if you don't suffer you can't make the claim that you are living an authentic life. Frankl says again, "In some way, suffering ceases to be suffering at the moment it finds a meaning . . .The way in which a man accepts his fate and all the suffering it entails, the way in which he takes up his cross, gives him ample opportunity – even under the most difficult circumstances – to add a deeper meaning to his life."[2] Life without suffering paradoxically has no meaning. It is from the darkness that light contracts its power; it is from the bitterness of winter that spring gathers its sweetness. You have to walk through the valley of the shadow of death to get to the Promised Land.

Another part I know: in order for suffering to be meaningful, it has to serve a deeper purpose. Suffering for suffering's sake is little less than self-abuse. Christ took on the Cross willingly out of love for Creation. Yes, I get that part. But what is the fine line between sacrificing for others to the point that you become miserable, bitter and resentful? Shouldn't there be a limit to how much sacrifice someone can muster if it comes at his or her own expense? I know the story about staying away from self centeredness. I know that it is honorable and life-creating to service others, but should you continue sacrificing and serving when you have been run ragged and dry? What about women who have been socially and perhaps genetically wired to give and give and give? That seems more like self-punishment. I have known people, a certain nun as a matter of fact, who has done all the right things—served the poor, chanted the daily cycle of prayers, fasted and given alms, but she was so miserable and resentful—just asking for her to pass the saltshaker during the trapeza meal brought an ice wave of antipathy. "Lord, may I never grow old to be that bitter and resentful," I couldn't help but pray under my breath. Sacrifice, like anything else, should be done voluntarily with sweetness. If it does not come out of a well of overflowing love, it is bitter. Those who are genuinely happy in themselves radiate joy and give those around them permission to find their own. Someone cannot be forced to sacrifice when they do not have the capacity. Sacrifice without joy becomes self-punishment. Can you imagine Christ swearing as He dragged the Cross? Would His sacrifice have been so life-creating if He had done it out of a place of resentment?

2. Frankl, 65.

But there are other parts of this suffering theme that I don't understand—like why do the innocents have to suffer? The Lamb never deserved to die. I have read the memoirs of traumatized youth: girls who have been raped and molested by their fathers; boys who have been wrenched from their mothers juggled from foster home to foster home. So many stories of innocence suffering. It's just so damn unfair. But that is the way it is. Maybe that is the answer. You suffer because you are innocent because you are good. "Yea, and all that will live godly in Christ Jesus shall suffer persecution" (2 Timothy 3:12).

Another part of this story I have trouble understanding is—is it always wise to suffer silently? I think of the story of St. Thomais of Lesvos. She was a pious young woman who obeying the wishes of her parents against her own will married a fisherman named Stefanos. He was what we would call in the modern day an abuser and batterer. He beat her every day for 13 years besides emotionally berating her. Yet she bore this abuse patiently. I think he eventually beat her to death. Many miracles occurred after her death and her relics became myrrh-streaming, so she was pronounced a saint, even a patron saint of marriage. Now I think of all the women I know who have suffered silently in domestic violence, who have had their unborn babies kicked out of their wombs, whipped with leather belts, or even murdered at the hands of their husbands and fathers of their children. I have seen the immeasurable amount of damage done to the children of these unions—damage that can never be "fixed" by however many hours or therapy or drugs. So many of these women suffer silently like the good Saint Thomais. But I wonder whether it would have been better for sweet Thomais to have taken a skillet to her husband's head and climbed up on the rooftop screaming "Murder! Bloody murder!" and denounced the bastard. Would she have been less than holy if she had stood up to injustice and had become a champion of women's rights and worked to stop the needless suffering of so many others? (Another message I can't understand: By touting St. Thomais as a patron of marriage is it condoning silent suffering at the hands of abusers? Is the church marking as a paragon of marriage a battered wife and a class-A abuser who would in our time be jailed for assault and battery?) Not to mock the saint, but my greater question is when is suffering patiently a maladaptive strategy? When should it be replaced by righteous action? Mary Magdalene, St Nino and St Filothei are all good examples. As Hamlet put it, "Whether tis nobler in the mind to suffer the slings and arrows of outrageous fortune or to take arms against a sea of troubles and by defeating end them."[3]

This brings me back to Passion Week. Passion Week–so complex and contradictory. This week we witness the true nature of sacrifice, up close and personal with guts and blood sticking out. The experience of Christ's Passion sensitizes us to the suffering that exists everywhere, across all times and places. We witness the butchering of an innocent lamb. We are reminded that for some paradoxical reason, someone has to die so that others may live. And we are grieved and brought to tears collectively at the sight of the Son of God battered, bloody, and berated by cruel mockers, dragging the weight of the Cross leaving a bloody trail behind as He climbs up Golgotha. We also feel the collective guilt that we too have contributed to this death. During Passion Week we experience the sting of injustice.

Yet it is paradoxically during Passion Week when we vicariously experience death that we feel what it means to be alive. Through Christ, the great role model, we see that it is only through the Cross that we fulfill our purpose here. It is suffering, lovingly, voluntarily, without grudge that gives purpose to life. In this one supreme act of love (as much as our minds can fathom it) we witness how deep and unfathomable the love of God is for His Creation. *Ecce, Homo*—here is love incarnate. A person who is willing to go to hell and back to bring you back to yourself, your true radiant self. To let you know the deeper unknowable core of you that you are worthy, you are beautiful, you are loved.

This is the meaning of Passion Week: that we are made to understand that love is so strong it is willing to die to break the bonds of death. That true love is stronger than death. That ecstasy comes lapping at the bloody heels of grief. This is the meaning of Passion Week: that life and death, joy and pain, suffering and relief are a tightly woven braid. Tick, cock your head a little to the right, and there is the Crucifixion. Tick, cock your head a little to the left, and there is the Resurrection.

3. "Hamlet - Act 3, Scene 2| Folger Shakespeare Library," n.d. https://www.folger.edu/explore/shakespeares-works/hamlet/read/3/2/. lines 64-68.

Monastery St Paissius

Monastery of St Paissius at dawn, 2023

Pico Iyer, the travel writer who has clocked one million sky miles in a year, makes it a point to stay at a Benedictine monastery for at least two weeks. "It is only when you stay still in the same place that you know where you know you are going," he states. I have a similar habit. I make a pilgrimage to a monastery at least once a season. I prefer to stay at a convent as I feel more comfortable among women and do not have to fear showing too much skin under my knees or too much hair under my headscarf. My convent of choice is an obscure one nestled deep in the folds of the deserts of Arizona. To reach it you must hire a car either in Phoenix or in Tucson and meander on lonely freeways that wind through cactus forests for 2 ½ hours at least. The road is long and not well-traveled. After driving for miles without confronting another driver either on my side or on the other side of the thin ribbon of highway, the cloud of "Oh my God! I am all alone!" descends. The isolation of the desert wasteland—no trees, flat red rock, punctuated with saguaro cactus and interrupted by the hyperbolic path of a hawk or a black crow—fills me with dread. Without a tribe, I am vulnerable to the violence of the elements. No internet, no WiFi works on some patches of the highway especially through the mountains. I cannot help but think this is done on purpose; most monasteries have been formed in mountains, deserts, or isolated islands. The physical seclusion acts as a forcefield keeping worldliness out.

Driving alone through deserted God's country, I cannot be distracted by the gyrations of minions going about in their pursuits of greed and glory. The drive to the convent acts like a buffer zone, a vestibule for clearing out the static in my head. In the distance, to the west, the majestic imposing mountain ranges of Mt Graham crowned with a white wedding wreath of cloud above its head and to the east , the Apache and Gila National Forest which is more a desert and less a forest, baked brown and red by the sun that dyes the horizon magenta, coral orange, blood red when it is born and dies day after day. The long desolate road to the monastery absolves the junk and invites my spirit to expand like the wide empty spaces the desert offers as its examination table. This is one reason I keep returning to the monastery; I come to hear the voice of God in the silence; I come to examine my soul and reach down deeper to know who I am truly, to detox from the city and the demands of my social webs. It is easy to understand why so many early Desert Mothers and Fathers flocked to the desert. In the desert you can know God and yourself, one and the same. To get to the gates, gilded in iron with a cross on top, I have to drive through a dirt road unmaintained. During monsoon season, it can be roaring with water making the red mud soft and easy to get trapped in.

The monastery is a closed system. Once the motorized gate opens and I enter, an illustration from my textbook from the graduate seminar in Shakespearean drama pops up: the Great Chain of Being, a Medieval conception of the order of the universe. All the way on top of the pyramid is God, then man, the animals, the plants. It is a system based on order, balance, symmetry, stability, and self-sufficiency. But the focus, the main aim is God: the praising, the singing, the eulogizing, the existing.

The monastery runs like a finely tuned Swiss pocket watch. Matins at 5:30 am, rest/contemplation time to read, write, study, create, trapeza at 11 am, work until vespers at 4 pm, followed by dinner and quiet time. A monastery has etiquette—you ask for a blessing from the Igoumena to be allowed to stay, when you enter the main Catholicon, you bow three times, you kneel and kiss the Igoumeni's hand during matins, you keep your feet covered in socks (that's something I forget often), you do not chit chat but listen to the reading of the saint's lives of the day during trapeza; you wait for the little ring of the bell that signals that you can pour water from the shiny silver pitcher into your silver canteen. There is a strict curfew in place. After 6:30 pm, no guests can walk around the property as the guard dogs are let loose to patrol the six acres.

For an institution based on silence and contemplation, it can be quite busy. The nuns are running around tending the garden, tending the fields, milking goats, scattering chicken feed, making woolen prayer ropes, publishing prayer tracts, answering emails and balancing books, cooking on average from 35-50 people twice a day, tidying up the grounds, cleaning the pilgrim's guesthouse, running the bookstore, monitoring the gates. That's in addition to their own private devotions that take place at midnight.

How can these women go through the cycle of services day after day and not get bored?

"He who can sit and do nothing can do anything," the mystic in *The Cloud of Unknowing* answers.[1] The stability and predictability of the cycles of the day brings a needed rhythm that allows my soul to rest, to find the "still point in the turning world" that T. S. Eliot mentioned. When I first arrive at the monastery, my thoughts jump like clouds of fleas, even my movements judder. Once I lock into the circadian rhythm of its functioning, I slowly begin to let go of my analytical mind and embrace the stillness to feel my heart, or rather, my nous, which is the throne of God in the soul, the center point, the part of the human person that can love and worship Him. This is the greatest gift of the monastery: I stop caring about everything and anything. It lets your soul be. The race of scurrying rats in my brain ends, and my mind finds rest, real rest.

This is done because the monastery strives to live beyond time just as the Holy Liturgy is diachronic. The liturgy chanted in the same way day after day becomes the still point, the omphalos of eternity, the eye of the storm. When I enter the monastery, I step outside the river of time and walk to the foot of the throne where nothing else matters but to lock eyes with the Beloved and become one with Love itself.

Walking from the guesthouse in the dark daybreak, past the gurgling fountain, down the aisle of salmon cobblestones lined with silent cypresses, I enter into the main church, a symmetrical building of one large dome balanced by two smaller ones on both sides. The night is punctured with the light of pulsing stars, so stark and clear, I see the eye of Taurus wink. I gasp in the chilly morning air and pause to take in the awesome heavens: "How magnified are thy works oh Lord." I open the main door flanked with two urns of pine the same height and width and enter the narthex which glows with the golden light of the beeswax candles flickering in the candle stands, one to the right and one to the left. The interior smells of rose-scented beeswax or sweet myrrh. I light a candle and then open the heavy wooden doors into the main church.

1. Wolters, *The Cloud of Unknowing, and Other Works*

I step foot into the river of molten chant, and eternity bathes me in light. Time dissolves and becomes superfluous, like a heavy cloak that you lay on the ground because it weighs you down. The sweet notes of the sisters draped in dark mantles except for the red embroidered cross on their forehead pave a footpath of prayers that transport me beyond this life into a realm where I sense I existed before I was made flesh. Every care and earthly thing melts away. My mind is able to stand still in eternity and it does not mind. It expands like the star-studded Prussian blue sky, the golden sun dawning pink and luminous on my right to the east and the full moon white silver fleeing in flowing chitons of tulle to my left. The whole scroll of human history, like a movie I can rewind and forward-front, flits through my mind, but the prayer is the same: "We hymn thee, we praise thee, we give thanks to thee." It does not matter that the speck that is you is clothed in dust; your soul knows that upon entrance into the river of golden light it has tasted of eternity, even if a drop of a drop, and understands its place there. The other worldliness fills me with longing, and I pray, "Lord, please allow me to stay here forever."

The melodious chanting keeps time beyond time. The service feels long and my mind wanders. Time becomes like the royal runner down the aisle punctuated with repeating motifs. I can see the circles of history, the same red *meandros*. I can see what will come forward and what came behind. It is a carpet wrung by the same weaver. Was it two years ago that I visited the monastery? The episodes match up like the golden crescents on the rug. Will my daughter ever speak to me again? What is one's birth and one's death but one thread in the backbone of the rug? It is my fault that my life is a mess. There will come a day when the rug itself will be rolled out beat up and confiscated into the storage closet. It will not matter anymore. I try hard to remember the mornings of days when I woke up in a railroad apartment and mornings in the central square under the Duomo hearing the peals of the cathedral. Is it monotony or a stubborn virtue, a staple on the rug to keep it from wrinkling, that the sisters keep matins at 5 am and vigil at 5.30 pm day in day out year in year out? Their struggle to keep the isotone, the thin red thread in that river of molten time. Sister Nazaria has not changed her tanned skin, sweet and smooth, even for constant smiling. It is a miracle that a bunch of California girls converted to an ancient faith and sprung up an oasis in the desert matching the monasteries I had seen in the Holy Land.

I took the same pictures of the church with the glowing light emanating from its doors and windows against the dark sky just before daybreak.

I too have repeated the ritual. The stillness of the dawn soothes my analytical mind; I am just being, not doing. I walk outside to catch the pink, rosy dawn splattering the mountains to the east while the snows on the pinnacle of Mt Graham reflect the ruddy glow. The twittering of cactus wrens and the hoo hoo hooing of desert doves sing as if a psalm has come to life. The teddy bear cactus and the pomegranate bushes are still against the rising curtain of dawn. This is the one place I can sit still enough to hear the stream under the stream of my conscious thought. Now I understand why the prophet advises, "Be still and know that I am God" (Ps. 46:10) God speaks through the silence; He nudges you gently and quietly underwater. I wander through the footpaths of the property black olives dawdling from branches, palm fronds and fuzzy blossoms spiny, and shrubs wild and messy like me. The brown dirt under my sandals was once washed with an ancient sea; the rocks hold vestiges of trilobites, mollusks, shells, crinoids, brachiopods from Precambrian, Ordovician even before Adam and Eve. And in the Desert Museum I touched the Allende Meteorite, a rock formed before the earth, even older than the sun. Why is the rock there? On it is God's own fingerprint; the little round grains bits of primordial matter that were once molten droplets formed from the solar system's original dust and gas cloud. In the stillness I can hear the tick of the Watchmaker's watch. Time treacles down enough to taste it.

At vespers, I feel full with the day's unraveling. Like a pair of bookends, the matin and vespers prayers frame the day symmetrically. "The sun knows its going down." It sinks behind the mountain ridge scattering its rosy glow and takes my breath away. Paradoxically, even if it happens every day, it is always miraculous and unique.

When I visit the monastery, I am most myself. I find my *telos*. I return to my everyday life rested and recalibrated with a tanned rosy glow.

Mystic Calling

On the grounds of St Paissius Monastery, Safford, Arizona

I AM THINKING ABOUT dropping out and becoming a mystic. You know like back in the 3rd century Alexandria, Egypt. Men and women newly converted to Christianity, dropped out of the big cities and retreated into the wild abscesses of the desert, disappeared into caves with the aim of becoming one with God.

21st century New York City resembles 3rd century Alexandria. It is the powerhouse of commerce and trade, an island port located on a strategic coast. A center of multiculturalism and knowledge, but also full of corruption, riotous living, and lots of crime and conflict. It is the center of the rat race; a place that can seem cold, uncaring, made for cut throats and hustlers. You can find all manner of sin in its belly. And now with the chances of a humane standard of work for a living wage quickly evaporating, well, it makes one reconsider his or her purpose in life. What's it all for? The mortgage, the climbing up the social ladder to reach a glass ceiling, and after that?

So many of my peers are caught up in what I call the "packaging" of 21st century 1st world living: the cars, the large houses, getting their kids into the best schools, dining in the finest restaurants, paying the 3rd mortgage on the country house. They waste free time and energy filling their houses with Bloomingdale's luxury items: Nespresso makers, Lennox bone china, Manolo Blatniks, Louis Vuitton handbags, the perfect foundation for their skin type, etc. etc. But is this what life is really about? All these things do not make the existential problems that come with living as a human being go away. The more they accumulate, the faster they scramble and try to-do on their long to-do lists, the more crazy, stressed, and unhappy they become.

Back in early Christendom, thousands and thousands heard the call. They literally walked right out of the city into the wilderness. There they practiced extreme forms of asceticism, barely eating or drinking, exposing themselves to the extremes of the desert, staying awake entire nights. Why? Because they were so in love with God, they would go to all lengths to be united with Him. The body and the prison cell of the senses got in the way of this mystical union, so they did everything to tear it away so that the bare soul could connect to the divine Spirit. So enraptured were they, that young women would fling themselves into thorn bushes, or roll about in coils to put the mortal body aside. In hunger, cold, thirst, extreme heat, sleep deprived, they spent hours and hours and days and months on end steadying their mind on the one thing needful, the Jesus Prayer, contemplation of the Scriptures. They were trying to unite with Jesus the mystical bridegroom. They retreated to do battle with the demons who resided in the desert. They prayed especially against the demon of acedia. That cruel demon that is more alive in the streets of Manhattan than in the desert. That demon of depression, of lethargy, that puts into your soul the feeling that nothing matters anyway, who cares? Why should you care about anything? It is this demon that is the driving force of nihilism that has strangled and suffocated the world, sitting on leathery haunches on the city shadowed under its obsidian wings.

Acedia in Greek is less about sloth and more about "weariness of heart" or "listlessness." As described by Evagrius Pontius, a real monastic psychologist, "The demon of acedia, also called the noonday demon is the most oppressive of all the demons. He attacks the monk about the fourth hour (10 am) and besieges his soul until the eighth hour (2 pm). First of all, he makes it appear that the sun moves slowly or not at all, and that the day seems to be fifty hours long. Then he compels the monk to look constantly towards the windows, to jump out of the cell, to watch the sun to see how far it is from the ninth hour (3 pm) to look this way and that lest one of the brothers . .. And further, he instills in him a dislike for the place and for his state of life itself, for manual labour, and also the idea that love has disappeared from among the brothers and there is no one to console him."[1]

Sound familiar? That's you on a typical day at your desk job in Midtown.

No doubt it would be extremely hard for a 21st century educated professional woman to give it all up and settle into a life of apparent boredom. It is hard to get accustomed without the modern conveniences of hot water, microwave, 1500 thread cotton sheets. But what the mystic gives up in material comfort she takes back in spiritual. What is the meaning of 300 pairs of Prado shoes when your soul is tired of it all?

And what about sex and romance? After years even in the most loving of marriages, the glitter glow fades. Things settle into a routine. The good husband strays. The good wife is bored. No mortal man can compare to the Divine Bridegroom. Although human love is fickle, divine love is true. As a nun who gave up a lucrative career in finance to join a convent in Pennsylvania told me, "Christ is the best lover."

Yes, it would be hell to give up everything and retreat to a mountain in the wilderness. But it would be heaven also. What barter we must do to gain the Spirit? Is it worth mutilating the flesh? What profit is all the riches of this world if man loses his soul? Is it worth eliminating the nonsense to gain meaning? I think so. If the soul yearns for the supreme object of its love, that is the purpose of its energy. Can there be any pursuit higher than the love of God?

Historian Ursula King recounts in her book, *Christian Mystics*, this class of women:

> Drawn mainly from the well-to-do, but also from courtesans and dancers. Some have been called "harlots of the desert" since they had pursued the monks to tempt them, but overcome by the men's holiness, they renounced their own way of life and

1. Wadell, Helen, tr. *The Desert Fathers*, 163.

> withdrew into convents or solitude to seek repentance, divine forgiveness and the greater beauty of God. Their stories were told by the ancient monks, then translated into Latin and various vernacular languages. They circulated freely in the medieval world of Western Christianity, illustrating both the power of sexual desire and the insight that such desire can also lead to God. The stories of the "harlots" express both the bondage of desire and the fire of love into which human longing is transformed, once an all-consuming love of the Divine becomes its sole object. [2]

Palladius, a fifth-century historian of monasticism, mentioned almost 3,000 women living in the desert in Egypt. Stories concerning the most famous Desert Mothers, including St. Mary of Egypt, Apollonaria, Athanasia, Hilaria, and Theodora, were popular as early as the sixth century.

It would be rather unlikely that thousands of young, professional women relinquish their careers and their potential in having families and drop out into the desert in 2020. Perhaps what's important is the *tropos* not the *topos*, the *way*, not the *place*, the *how* not the *where*, as the saying goes in Greek. Salvation and the union with God is the goal, no matter in the metropolis or the meadow. Elder Porphyrios says it is possible to become a saint even in the city. Amma Syncletiki says the same thing, "It is possible to be a solitary in one's mind while living in a crowd, and it is possible for one who is a solitary to live in the crowd of his own thoughts."[3]

You just have to cut down on your Starbucks Frappuccinos, Zagat 5-course meals, and instead cater to matters of the spirit. But the ultimate truth is this: life without God even in a luxurious 5th Avenue loft is a spiritual wasteland worse than any desert.

2. King, *Christian Mystics: The Spiritual Heart of the Christian Tradition*,
3. Chryssavgis, *In the Heart of the Desert*.

A Case for Martha

From a sarcophagus in old cemetery of Sleepy Hollow, NY

RECENTLY I HEARD THAT a friend of mine, a fellow parishioner, a beautiful, serious young woman and talented fashion designer, renounced the world and joined a convent. Incidentally we share the same name--for the Great Martyr Irene-- so sometimes we get mixed up in people's conversations. We are both struggling Orthodox Christians who aim above all for our soul's salvation. Yet our lives and circumstances could not be more different. How we go about it remains at the heart of the long-standing debate in theological circles, works or faith; the contemplative life or one of service and action to the other. Our situation is akin to Mary and Martha's, that well-known parable that is preached over and over again as the exemplar of Christian action in the world. Now I know my counterpart has chosen the better part, but somehow I don't think it's fair she gets all the credit. I am just going to take a bit of your time to reflect on the life of the Marthas in the world, to show you that the life of Martha is as hard if not harder than Mary's. And instead of giving all the praise to Mary, forgive me Lord if I seem contrary, you might not just have compassion on Martha and give her some sympathy.

Martha is a servant lest we forget. She is stuck, even if she has an advanced degree, with attending to everyone else's needs except her own. Martha's life is hard because of the myriad of details she must attend to. If Martha is a mother and a wife, not to mention full-time career woman with employees / clients /bosses / co-workers to appease, well, frankly there's mighty little time in the day to devote to praying. I carry a full-time job, care for three very demanding children, two of whom are teens, an ailing mother, a husband prone to moody depression, manage the household finances and its management, while also responsible for mine and my family's spiritual direction. Here's a typical list of some of the responsibilities a typical Martha may be expected to perform throughout her day:

- change the baby diaper as the baby is hollering because of rash while simultaneously making the baby formula
- wake all school age children who grumble are nasty and picky "Oh I don't want to wear that sweater it is too scratchy" "I don't want to wear those pants they don't match." "Where are your socks?" "I can't find them." "Hurry up you will be late." This refrain happens in some variation every morning
- coordinate babysitter's schedule to cover the extra-long management meeting she has tonight
- make lunches and snack packs for brood
- bring coffee to hubby
- make breakfast sandwiches serve cereal

- ”Don’t forget to brush own teeth, Martha, and apply liquid eyeliner” quickly enough to sign permission from that child who forgot to show night before
- pack up kids in car not before a mad search for newly bought alpaca mittens.” Where’s your mittens?” “I don’t know I had them yesterday at cafeteria.” Turns out mittens are lost.
- ”Hurry, hurry!” beat traffic whizzing through double and triple parked caravans of parent cars dropping off their kids before the side door of school to breakfast room. Door slams shut exactly at 8:10 am (Didn’t make it in time; have to get out of car and accompany child into late room; that’s her 15th lateness so far)
- make a mental note to pick up breadcrumbs and pasta sauce for eggplant parm for dinner
- make credit card payment of $300 during lunch break to beat deadline of 5pm
- catch up on emails (have 3456 in my inbox)
- concentrate enough to write report and coordinate with other departments all while constantly interrupted by phone and emails to do this and that; reminders for meetings and cc the hierarchy for any changes
- deal with the pressure of meeting quotas or interacting with clients in a high pressure environment
- eat nuggets at desk for lunch. Getting roll round the middle because there is no time to work out or eat at a decent pace without having to bolt down whatever fast food sustenance one can manage in 15 minutes
- so much whirlwind of activity at work who remembers all that is done during a day?
- after meetings, rush home not without picking up bread crumbs and pasta sauce on the express lane of Pathmark to dethaw cutlets and whip up some lettuce for a salad.
- make sure to pay babysitter and after-school Greek school
- prostrate for the thousandth time to pick up mismatched socks and stray sneakers while folding laundry

- deal with the tantrums of school-aged kids who hate to do math homework and slave patiently while the perfect t is crossed for the sentence beginning with spelling word "there"
- sort and read through the stack of bills and statements that have to be answered
- have a "talk" with the teen who was marked absent/cutting from yesterday's classes;"How are you going to graduate?" I'm so disappointed in you. Why are you a follower?" "It's only one class. I got it under control. I have all the work."
- Set dinner and call camp.
- "Maybe, after dinner table is cleared do I have time to tweeze eyebrows that are becoming box bushes or just breathe" quick thought
- Not before answering the call, "Mom please wipe my butt" because I am the delegated butt- wiper of the house charged with making sure everyone's private parts are sanitary and soft. While in bathroom I notice the mountains of laundry, the assorted socks and t shirts and underwear waging war with dirt and grass and sweat not to mention shit
- While wiping butt, take note to replenish the assortment of household items such as toilet paper, laundry detergent, deodorant, bleach etc etc that are running low or at zero.
- Besides all the physical tasks that Martha must attend to, she is also fraught with playing the life coach/psychologist/advisor of the residence: "Your nose is not too big; you don't need rhinoplasty" a snippet of the longer conversation to one teen followed by a half-ignored talk of the importance of inner beauty.
- Damage control given for "bad score on math test" to the grade schooler who goes into a tantrum that she is a failure at math because "My friend Melia got 100 on the math test while I only got an 83."
- Follow up on the cutting report the other teen must be confronted with.
- Making sure the elderly and crotchety mother's fears are unfounded as Obama Care changed the benefits she was promised on her Medicaid card, "Don't worry Ma, we will go into the office together" next week. "Can't you take me tomorrow?" "I have important conference

tomorrow. Don't worry we will go." "Ah Thee mou, they are going to cut my benefits!" she sighs and becomes anxious unable to sleep

- Prodding a taciturn husband who has been underemployed and whose manhood is threatened because of his inability to provide for his family as a patriarch. "What's the matter honey? It's only a phase." Dancing a dainty tango of not appearing to yank on the male ego and staying within prescribed traditional feminine gender role while at the same time holding back the resentment of being the superwoman having to accomplish everything in the household.

Before the lit vigil lamp in front of the icon of the Theotokos, I barely have energy to say the Lord's Prayer. How do I go have time to reflect on my passions? I can barely keep my eyes open. How do I think about what evil or tempting thoughts I have entertained? I barely have any of my own thoughts; I barely have a brain. I am literally out of my mind. I am lucky I can still keep track of the days on the calendar. I am harried, distracted and exhausted. I hardly have time for a contemplative life. I am a working mother. This is prayer enough. I have lived this grueling form of existence as the meanest basest slave day after day year after year. I don't have time to sin-- I'm too busy running around like a chicken without a head serving everybody making sure the little annoying things in life that no one recognizes as needing attention get done. And what's my reward--the admonition that "Oh Martha, Martha, you are too busy. Slow down." Your sister who is sitting down (ie "doing nothing") contemplating gets the applause. But mind you, if everyone is sitting at the Master's feet, who-who will pick up the table? Who will serve the food and clear up the crumbs? Now wouldn't you, like Martha in the parable, be angry, annoyed and ticked off? You are the one doing all the work and still you get chided for it. If I had been in the parable, I would have clawed at Mary and kicked her behind using a couple of the b words instead of just giving her a mean look. In fact I think Martha handled herself quite nobly in the story given the circumstances. I would have been hysterical.

Let's give Martha the credit that's due. The world needs both a Martha and a Mary to function correctly. In fact, I am sure in her deepest heart Martha really wants to be more like Mary. It would seem like a relief after all to sit down and pray. The prayerful life for Martha seems like a luxury. She yearns for the time she can hang it all up and join a monastery. Is it her fault she must be the "responsible" one? The go-getter, the enabler. The picker-upper of crumbs and boo boos and spirits. S he is the mover in the world. Her sister is the spirit, the wind in the sail, but without the sail pulled taut to the limit of its tenacity, there would be no motion.

I venture to say it is harder to be a Martha than a Mary. The one everyone turns to get things done. Children and families with all their demands can make the most austere of igoumen or Zen masters. Motherhood involves grueling nights without sleep, demands and more demands. Even when I try to be more prayerful, "Go get us breakfast" interrupts my trip to church. Morning prayers are cut short because of demands from empty stomachs. One fellow parishioner, in an effort to console me for falling asleep before my evening prayers were complete said, "a mother's prayer is her labors. God knows that you are meeting everyone else's needs so you are forgiven for not following a prayer rule." It is hard to be true to the Lord and still fill the needs of a human family. You always feel guilty for not properly focusing on the one or the other.

What is a Martha to do then? Should she drop all the dishes, abandon her children and run off to a convent? It would seem that is the answer that gets extolled in the Eastern Orthodox tradition. There has always been a superiority attached to the contemplative tradition to the discouragement if not total disparagement of the matrimonial/ maternal. No doubt to renounce the world is no easy thing. To adhere to the ascetic grueling practice of a monastery, to live in utter solitude is the ultimate test of a human soul for God. But how does Martha become a Mary once she's in the fray of it? Would it be acceptable or even admirable for women to abandon their post as administrators, mothers, wives? Ironically perhaps renouncing our families, the human loves in our lives, is the only sure way to sever all attachments so that we can truly become spiritual beings. Mary has chosen the one thing needful; perhaps she has made the more difficult choice.

So where does that leave Martha? The parable of Mary and Martha has been interpreted as the conflict between faith or prayer and works. They are supposed to be taken together as two necessary sides of the same Christian call. Faith without works is dead and works without faith can be communism or a not for-profit. They are the drive in each person to provide a balance in the spiritual life. No question both Mary and Martha would make it to the kingdom of heaven. And it is not as if Martha will be barred from the heavenly kingdom because she did not make time to pray. Only that Mary chose the better path. But I am sure my counterpart who has donned a cassock and been forced to keep a strict rule of 300 prostrations might be asking the flip side of the same question--"What use am I in the world?" The trick is for Mary to become more like Martha and vice versa.

Next time you read the parable of Mary and Martha, think of poor Martha as she runs around like a chicken without a head. She is tormented by her role as a fixer-upper and eternal go-fer. Take pity on poor Martha, Mary. Pray for her to find the inner and external peace she craves to be more like you as you sit quietly at the Master's feet feeding your soul. She will be too busy feeding the masses, the poor, the snot-sniveling homeless and the cranky elderly at the same time she is changing diapers. Your prayers will have to be enough for her, the same way her labor will feed you.

Dry Bones and Relics

The resting place with remains of St John Maximovitch, Annunciation Cathedral, San Francisco, CA

A Jewish girlfriend of mine, a guest for the summer in Greece, "freaked" when she saw the undecomposed corpse of St. Efraim the "quick to hear" close to the coastal sea town of Rafina. "This is crazy," she protested, "I'm getting out of here." It was bad enough to catch sight of dead bodies under a glass case but worse was to have the living kiss and adore them—that was too much. Indeed, this is a normal reaction. Fear is natural in the face of things we do not understand.

I recently returned from a pilgrimage to San Francisco to the Cathedral of the Holy Virgin. There, perched on a dais to the far right of the open space of the beautifully adorned church stood the coffin of St John Maximovitch of Shanghai and San Francisco. The top of the coffin too was covered by a thick glass so that you could peer into his reposing corpse. His body lay in full view—regaled in his richly decorated archbishop's robes, his pointy bejeweled slippers, looking like they should belong to some Chinese princess instead of an old wise man. At his head lay his Archmandrite's crown with the central icon of Christ in majesty circled in a frame of gold. His face was covered by an *epitrechelion*, also richly embroidered with religious scenes and symbolism. But at his bosom were his hands, holding a wooden cross. His hands were dark mahogany brown, the flesh of which was clearly visible to curious peepers.

Now to the uninitiated, gazing into an open casket of someone who's been deceased for over 48 years could be spooky. In fact, a mother with two grade-school boys visiting the church was taken aback. When the smaller of the brother's (the one with the black eye) curiously peered into a golden reliquary box lined with neat rows vertically and horizontally of tiny pieces of relics staged on neat cushions around symmetrically circular mounts, he fingered each edge desperately trying to make sense of it, "Mom, what is this?" Even she couldn't really answer.

Some in the West might be scandalized to see so many body parts, from chips of elbows, to dislocated mandibles, pieces of nail, sometimes entire skulls or hands, exhibited under plain sight. How then do we explain the Orthodox (and Catholic) fascination for the dead? As DH Lawrence once remonstrated, "Christianity is a religion of dust and death." There are several reasons for deconstructing this Christian fascination with the dead.

First, unlike the West which tries to bury death with the dead, that tries so hard to anaesthetize all traces of it by neat glossy cellophane packaging of animal parts, Father Paissios the Athonite recounts an anecdote in a 3rd century coenobic monastery of a monk whose job was to go around to all the other monks of the community and to remind them on a daily basis, "Father, you are going to die."[1] East exhorts its faithful to stare death in the face, to keep the remembrance of death daily. Remembering the truth that all flesh is born to die, to the contrary of making us morbidly depressed and desperately mournful, has the opposite effect. It imbues our day with the weight and significance that living under a carefree delusional aura of safety cannot. Every act, every choice, every word becomes precious if one keeps the forethought that this day you too might die. Remembrance of death, which the relics spewn all over the

1. St Paisios the Athonite, *Spiritual Counsels*, 237.

sanctuary do so nicely, is actually a blessing. It helps you to savor the day and give thanks for the joy of living. Only when you are intensely aware of death can you appreciate life, ironically.

Secondly, the bodies of these dead are brought to view not by human will, but via the divine. Those are not just any dead people, these are saints. They are the sacred dead; our heroes. Their bodies are not to be discarded but revered as vessels of the Holy Spirit. These people in life struggled to gain the likeness of the Holy and in so doing they channeled the Holy Spirit into their very flesh. This is fundamental to our Church's understanding of the Incarnation. The Spirit not only acts on the spirit but on the body. Indeed, Orthodoxy consecrates each of us as a living icon of the Holy, holding the potential to carry the sacred even in our deepest bones and to the tips of our fingers. It was Christ's unparalleled act of the Incarnation when God chose to become Man and the Spirit entered physical time and the material universe that allows for this similar mystery—an ordinary person was so pleasing to God that the Grace of the Holy Spirit infused every part of their body and soul. It's the vestige of this holiness that we revere—whether a particle of their bone or a tattered piece of their vestment. The stuff of the material world can carry the holiness of the Spirit so that we can see, taste, feel, hear, smell the sacred, as anyone who has experienced the Divine Liturgy can attest to its appeal to all five senses.

Thirdly, taking apart of the body of the saints decries the sacrificial and sacramental function of the living martyrs of the Faith even after, or rather especially after, death. The sanctity of some saints and martyrs is manifest after their death. In their physical bodies they reenact the act of the Eucharist as Christ the paragon. Their bodies are broken and scattered in a thousand pieces, some winding their way to opposite sides of the globe, yet uniting and drawing disparate members unto a whole and the One. It seems that what the Eucharist is all about, the One breaking apart into many to be dispersed to many so that they may become One again. It is an eternal energy loop—the One source breaking into many only to return back to the One. A great mystery this is spoken of by Christ Himself. That in order to live one must die, that by breaking the one fruit into its many seeds can the many flourish and become one again. The saints have the honor of expressing this mystery through their flesh and bones, especially since any church cannot be consecrated without the existence of relics, the saints leave their shells behind like so many peanuts, but their spirit, released from its physical cage, is free to be everywhere.

Perhaps this is the greatest reason we as Orthodox like to showcase the bodies of the dead—they are a reminder of the truth of the Resurrection. That your body might lie asleep in the grave, like an old man's suit as Elder Porphyrios used to say, but your spirit, your spirit is what is eternal. It's the spirit of St. John that is closer to us now than ever when he was alive, because now he is free to be everywhere. I think it's the same with our deceased relatives. I am closer to my father (God rest his soul) now than ever I was when he was alive. The bodies of dead saints bring the comfort and the joy of the Resurrection that we too might be heirs to. And not just the resurrection, but the Second Coming where our bodies will be mystically and mysteriously refashioned with our souls to enter the New Creation. The relics of saints even at their bare bones' minimum demonstrate that goodness, love, piety—they last forever, especially in death, saints manifest the power of love to surpass the grave. Because as everyone knows, love is more powerful than death. Unlike the poets and painters whose legacy lives on in their work, the saints live on in their whole selves as they gave their entire selves to Christ and not just the work of their hands or minds.

For those who don't understand the symbols of Orthodoxy, its transference of that symbolism onto physical reality, what translates to the eye as a lot of heavy-draped pilgrims trekking miles to bow to a dead body, might seem like "spookism" as an unwitting onlooker remarked. "Spookism" just might be holiness and when a secular person comes into the presence of the holy, it might give them "the creeps" but for a faithful pilgrim, the bodies of the dead become like seeds waiting to germinate into eternal life. When you understand the what and why of what you see and do and come to terms with the symbols, what scared you becomes your comfort.

Indeed, I spent many hours by the open casket of St. John Maximovitch. Here before my eyes lay his body but when I looked up into the famous icon painted of Him over his coffin, I felt the truth of the Resurrection. Those who die, our loved ones, those loved of God, they might act like the glue of the One Church. I am sure I can visit the Church of Shanghai dedicated to St. John Maximovitch and find affinity with his presence and with my fellow brethren as I do in the church in America.

So here lies the mystery of death in the bones of our saintly dead, that death serves as a reminder for our own striving toward holiness, that it serves as a reminder for appreciating the days we have in the land of the living, that it serves as a peephole into the unfolding greater mysteries of eternal life to come.

On the Dormition of the Theotokos

For all of Greece, and in fact for all Orthodoxy, this feast is considered a second Christmas. It always gives me a pause to reflect on this looming figure in our culture—the Theotokos, the God-bearer. Walk into most traditional Byzantine churches and there she looms, the center point above the sanctuary, the Queen of Heaven sitting on a jewel-studded throne, sweeping red and lapis lazuli robes open in a giant act of embrace, the Infant Christ on her lap He himself in a serene pose of benediction upon the congregation. For someone who is barely mentioned a handful of times in the Scriptures even less by name and only once or twice gives direct testimony ("The Song of Mary" upon the meeting with her cousin Elizabeth), she is an over towering figure.

The reverence we hold for the Virgin Mary in our Church gives me much to ponder. Paradoxically she seems to be who does the most by "doing" least. When we are introduced to Mary in the Bible as narrative, she is a young maiden at prayer. The Desert Fathers believe Mary never held an impure thought, not even once. Grace had been perpetually with her and that is why she was deemed worthy to be the God-bearer, not an easy task as the vessel that carries fire must be of sturdy mettle to bear its potency. There was even one apostle who upon meeting the Virgin in Jerusalem admitted that had he not known about Christ, he would have believed she was God. So holy did he feel in her presence.

The Theotokos stands like an anti-role model in certain ways. She never gave a long speech, never gave witness to Christ in a forceful way as the other apostles and martyrs, she never founded a church or a charitable institution. You can see her as a highly passive figure, even secondary in her closet role. But paradoxically, it is her reticence, her solitude, her reclusiveness, her absence that makes the most impact. Her work was focused on the internal landscape. Generating a quiet prayerful life of inner stillness, focusing mental and emotional energies on God, turning introspectively instead of outwardly is one of the toughest jobs there is. And there is not much you can show for it on the outside, not much you can see or put your finger on as a point of pride or achievement. Had she not cultivated that inner heart, if she had not put so much emphasis on keeping her spiritual center centered on Christ and God the Father, she would not have been deemed able to bear the Holy Spirit in the form of the God Man. If one can stop and think of this for a minute, one will come to understand the incredible miracle, a miracle that our bounded minds cannot really fathom, that of being so pure she could bear God. No man was ever worthy of that honor—only a woman could be so pure.

So many times, the belligerent feminist in me fights against the poetic allusions to the Theotokos as "the ladder" "the bridge" "the throne" "the vessel." In my mind, she is depicted as this passive object whose only use is to make room for the Masculine. But with age and spiritual maturity, even against my most forceful feminist arguments pointing their many fists in a corona around my head, I have come to see that the Feminine, in the guise of vessel, is of the utmost importance. We as a society downgrade the Feminine, the bearer, but in her metaphysical truth, she is above the saints and is on the same pedestal as Christ and the Father. Her worth is taken for granted just as the foundation underneath the most awe-inspiring architectural marvels is. How can you have a feast without a banquet table? Where do you put the dough if not for the pan? By focusing on the things that are invisible, the things we take for granted, is what the example of the Theotokos tries to do. To lead a blessed spiritual life is harder than erecting a skyscraper. Look how many times a day you judge, or grumble or swear or worse. To control the mind and heart and keep it in a state of blessedness so that by your very being you bring about the greatest miracle, the salvation of humanity—that is truly remarkable. She reminds me that it is the acts of unseen benevolence, the quiet prayers, the repetitive routine, what could be described as "boring" of faithful routines, what has been eternally described as "woman's work" that is most worthy of admiration. Her very essence, the mystery of mysteries of the heart and soul, is what we revere—not her physical works. The greatest miracles I think have been created invisibly and imperceptibly. They hide their power until they are revealed and recognized mystically.

So, with all the faithful the whole world, visible and invisible, let us cry out:

> Hail Mary full of Grace,The Lord is with thee. Blessed art Thee among women, And blessed is the fruit of thy womb, For thou hast borne the savior of our souls. It is truly meet to call thee blessed oh Theotokos, ever blessed and most pure and the mother of our God, more honorable than the Cherubim and beyond compare more glorious than the Seraphim who without corruption gavest birth to God the Word. Truly oh Theotokos do we magnify.

June 4th: Mary of Bethany, Radical Feminist of Passive Resistance

THIS MONTH ON JUNE 4th, we commemorate the feast of St Mary, one of the many Marys in the Bible and Orthodox Church tradition (so many they are often confused one for the other). But this Mary was the sister of Martha and Lazarus who all lived together in a stone house in Bethany that Jesus would often visit. We all should know the parable by now, of how on one of Jesus' visits to their house, Martha and Mary were getting things ready for the table, but Mary chose to stop and listen to Jesus preach sitting down at his feet, while Martha, stressed out with so much to do, turned to the Lord to rebuke her for not helping out. Instead of criticizing Mary as Martha thought He would, He turned the tables and castigated Martha for being busy about so many things and reminding her that her sister Mary had taken the better part. Now most explications of this story see it as a parable between work and faith, embodied in the two sisters Martha and Mary respectively, but thanks to Eva Catafygiotu Topping in the chapter devoted to the saint in her book *Saints and Sisterhood*, we have arrived at a different feminist reading of the story.

Mary was both younger and lesser in status than her hyper older sister. According to the tradition of those times, it was Mary's lot to serve and act as hostess for guests who came to the house. So in that episode when Jesus comes over and she sits at his feet and listens to what he was saying, she was engaged in an act of radical defiance. First, the phrase "to sit at someone's feet" means "to study with that person." So basically, Mary had dropped what she was doing, the conventional role allotted to her as a woman by her society and her sister, so that she could become a disciple, so that she could get an education at the feet of the greatest teacher of all time.[1] It was unheard of for a woman to become a disciple of any religion let alone get a basic education. Jewish rabbis did not have female disciples as their customs forbade it. For a humble girl from a village to claim a male privilege for herself was radical.

In addition, Mary's gesture serves as a radical step of personal defiance. It was her sister, another woman, who was putting the pressure on her to conform to the norms set out for her—the kitchen and the table. She viewed Mary, her little sister, as a deserter, someone who was skipping out of her responsibilities with the pots and pans. Martha had the conventions of female domesticity more firmly implanted in her head and was trying to enforce them on Mary. But what a surprise! The radical teacher turned the tables and rebuked her for fussing over unimportant things. He praised Mary for having chosen the better part and "it shall not be taken away from her." With these words Jesus rejected the stereotype accepted by Martha. The domestic sphere was not the only "place" for women; he accepted her into his circle asserting that the intellectual and spiritual life was even more proper a place for women as it was for men. (Ahhh! Don't you just love Jesus! He too was a feminist.)

I read this story as depicting the choices women have and take. Women have the right to make choices first of all. That Jesus affirmed Mary's right to choose for herself shows how pro-woman He was. That two sisters chose two different lines of work, so to speak, one by sitting down and the other by running around serving and cleaning up, shows that in life we can choose to serve the body and the other physical needs people have or to the soul, our own and others. Ultimately, whoever chooses spirit over body will be the one with greater rewards. And in this choice, one sister, the older with more power, pressures the other into doing what society expects of her, limiting her potential. (It is sad that sometimes our so-called sisters, those closest to us, put the most restrictions on us and keep us from making our own decisions.) In the end, both sisters get into heaven; both lines of work can bring fulfillment.

Mary's simple act of sitting down and listening, far from being passive and unproductive, served as a radical call to action. In her passive sitting down, she signaled women's spiritual and legal right to gain an education and defied the strict standards of domesticity relegated to women.

1. Catafygioyu, *Saints and Sisterhood*, 165.

St Irene the Great Martyr (May 5th)

The story of St. Irene is so extreme her life takes on mythic superstar status. By some accounts she was born in Persia; by others she was born in Thessalonika or even further higher in Macedonia in the 2nd century or the 4th century. There are several differing accounts of her life and the many tortures she endured so that her escapades make her a legend among saints. And as with many other heroes and legends, her struggles and labors are multiplied and magnified to appear mythic.

In fact, her story has elements that make it seem like it comes out of a book of Greek mythology. She was born to wealthy pagan parents who named her after the faithful wife of Homer's epics, Penelope. Her father, wanting to "protect" her from the wiles of the world as she was exceedingly beautiful and gifted, had her imprisoned in a high tower with lavish comforts and a retinue of ladies-in-waiting. (Sure, like that tactic worked in all the other myths and fairytales.) The only person from the outside world allowed to come in was an old tutor who taught her classics. During a critical point in her development, she had a vision or actually saw a succession of birds come through the one window of her tower. First, a dove entered carrying an olive branch; next an eagle flew in carrying a crown of woven flowers, and lastly a crow entered carrying a serpent. When she asked her teacher what it all meant, he interpreted them as signs. The first for her conversion and cultivation of mind; the second for the many triumphs she would gain and lastly, the crow with serpent represented the pain and martyrdom she would receive.

After this the princess in the ivory tower was visited by an angel who renamed her "Eirini" or "peace." Some accounts say she was converted to Christianity via her tutor; others say she was instructed into the faith by an angel himself who prophesied that she would save hundreds of thousands of souls.

When her father found out that she was not Daddy's little girl anymore as she had disobeyed his commands and gone against her family's faith (not to mention the fact that she had gone on a rampaged and smashed a few of the family's very valuable marble statues of the gods), he ordered that she be tied and trampled by horses. At least this got her out of the tower and into the light of day even if for a really bad reason. Once the horses were released, instead of trampling on Irene, attacked her father who was killed instead. She prayed for him, and he was brought back to life. On the spot in one shot, three thousand people who had witnessed the miracle became believers. Her father then repented for his mistreatment of his daughter, abdicated his throne, and chose to live in the tower he had imprisoned her in.

The new king, King Sedekias, did not really take a liking to Irene's new-found faith either. Like her father before him, he forced her to worship the old pagan gods. When she refused, he threw her in a ditch crawling with poisonous snakes. That angel again protected her against all harm and when she emerged 14 days later without a bruise or bite, he put her through another series of tortures. She survived them all causing another eight to ten thousand people to convert on the spot.

Now a third king came into power, Sabor, who had usurped Sedekias' throne. She met the rebel army outside the city and with her prayers she defeated the tyrant. The earth split into two swallowing ten thousand soldiers. All at once another 40,000 converts.

This was the pattern; she would go preaching, performing miracles, and converting thousands in her wake. Her fame brought her to the attention of the King of the Persians, Saborios, the very emperor himself. He decided he and the kingdom had had enough. He had her beheaded and buried. Now you'd think that would put an end to her career. But yet again, that angel came to her rescue and resurrected her.

Not ready to end her winning streak against a row of powerful kings and tyrants who tried to curb her zeal by a variety of tortures, Irene went against yet another. This time when she entered the city and presented herself to the king as a Christian holding an olive branch in her hand, her presence was enough to convert him without all the mess that continual torture required. From then on, her power to convert became invincible. In her wake hundreds of thousands of people converted to Christianity.

In fact, so great was the power of St Irene that the only way she could be eliminated was if she would do it herself. She got swept up in a cloud and transported to Ephesus where she met up with her old teacher. She instructed him to find a new tomb and to roll a huge stone to cover the entrance once she entered. She instructed him not to remove the stone until four days had passed. When he did this, he found, as you would expect if you knew the ending of another greater story, that she was gone. What can you say? Some saints are saints and others are super saints.[1]

1. Summary of the saint's life from St. Nikolai Velimirovic, The Prologue of Ohrid – Volume One

The Ungraspable Miracle: St. Katherine's Monastery, Mt. Sinai

"My soul has thristed for Thee; how often hath my flesh longed after Thee in a land that is barren and untrodden and unwatered" –Psalm 62

THE DESERT IS AN overwhelming place. Miles of miles of nothingness. It is in the empty lonely spaces that one feels the presence of God. I am overwhelmed by my own precariousness. Clutching a copy of the Quran and the Bible in my lap, dressed in a black traditional Palestinian dress, I mutter the Jesus prayer "Lord Jesus Christ have mercy on me" while glancing now and then from the corner of my eye at the middle-aged taxi driver to my left dressed in all-white jilbab and then to the right at the golden-brown hills and . The taxi is at least 15 years old. The passenger door does not open from the inside. The glove compartment snatch unhitches every time we go over a pot hole. Ibrahim, the cab driver, has brown teeth but he smiles incessantly. Luckily, he perceives me as a "hajina" I am on a pilgrimage to St. Katherine's monastery, the first monastic community to be founded in the world 17 centuries ago (and still in operation), so he does not try to flirt or ask me to marry him. "Santa Katerina," Ibrahim says with his emphatic English, "number one in Sinai." He keeps repeating this mantra pointing his index finger in the air and smiling. He plays the same bedouin song with wild flutes in the background, a love song between an *adrous* and a *dreez,* (a bride and groom) for the entire two-and-a-half-hour journey to the monastery.

There is no emergency service in the Sinai desert; if the dilapidated taxi has an engine malfunction, no AAA, no emergency phone at the side of the road, no ambulance, no gas station. I found the hard way– there is no ATM either. I had less than $70 on me. It has to last me until tomorrow and cover my accommodations at the monastery and the long cab ride back to Taba, the Egyptian-Israeli border.

In the desert, one relies entirely on the mercy of God. The stretch of overwhelming desert that threatens to engulf us, the heat radiates from every direction, from the car engine, from the sweltering sun, from the ground, from the mountains. In the black gold-embroidered dress, I feel the trickles of sweat channeling down the ditch of my spine. I think of Hagar. When Sarah gave her a couple of loaves and a jug of water and sent her on her way, she was really giving her a death sentence. And she was carrying a baby in her belly or leading a young boy, depending on the version. From experiencing this desert, Sarah was a cruel, cruel mistress. But Hagar relied on the mercy of God, and she became the mother of many (she is still breeding given that on average one Arab woman has eight children.

My only prayer is to arrive at the doors of St. Katherine's, nothing else. I swear to myself I will prostrate at its doors. I know it has to be a sanctuary. One day fits just enough worry for its fullness. Saint Katherine's is part of a National Parks protectorate as I have to pay 11 Egyptian dollars to enter into the village of St. Katherine's. I have to flash my passport at least ten times by the time we reach the village while Ibrahim explains that I am a hajina to Santa Katerina. The village is little more than two or three central streets horseshoed around the security/customs booth. Three thousand Bedouins of the Jebeliya tribe make up the majority of the inhabitants of Saint Katherine's village. Shimmering sequined silks wallpaper the suqs advertising bedouin jewelry, guidebooks about the monastery in five different languages, alabaster stones, wooden crosses, and incense. Busloads of Coptic Egyptians from Cairo hustle to remove suitcases from the hood of the bus that looks like a throwback to Lawrence of Arabia times. They are gaggling in frenetic Arabic as they flock in tens to pass through the customs doorway.

I feel sorry for Ibrahim. He will have to drive back two and a half hours to Taba and drive back the next day to pick me up. I tell him to stay the night, and he can take me tomorrow. He smiles, his olive-brown skin glistening against the white of his Egyptian cotton tunic, and says, "OK, OK, tomorrow here. 12 o'clock."

I cannot prostrate in front of the gates of the monastery as there are none. St. Katherine's is surrounded by a large fortification wall of orange clay. It reminds me of a medieval castle with Bedouin servants bustling about. A row of low-lying rooms to the right house a few old "haj". One is sitting on a wooden chair, hanging on to a walking stick, and staring with that dumb-wise stare the extremely elderly have. To the left is a hand-made sign in blue lettering, "Coffee Shop, Reception, Book Store" with an arrow pointing to a walkway with stairs that leads to another level. It is a busy place St. Katherine's is. It is a miraculous place. It has remained unchanged for close to 17 centuries.

The woman responsible for the largest sacred construction project in history, St. Helena in 330 BC had the first finger in the birth of this holy place. St. Helen dedicated the first monastery on those grounds to The Transfiguration. From the remains of that monastery, another monastery dedicated to the Holy Bush of the Virgin was built. However, the church and the familiar monastery radiating around it that we see today were built during the reign of Emperor Justinian (527-565 AD), who expanded in glory and beauty what St. Helena had started. In the 11th century the monastery was dedicated to St. Katherine of Alexandria, who had died in 310 AD. Her remains, reportedly found by monks on a mountain peak next to Mt Sinai, are buried in the monastery's Basilica. Ironically, St. Katherine had little to do with the original site but disputes between rival churches forced the early Fathers to move the remains to the highest peak in Egypt to put an end to the bickering.[1] The church lies at the foot of the *Gabal Muses* or Mt. Moses, the site where Moses received the Ten Commandments.

I am shocked that it took the World Heritage Site committee until 1985 to recognize the value of this treasure house of sacredness and exquisite beauty. Ducking through a low doorway, I am led through a walled concave passage that explodes into a wall icon of the Mother of God of the Burning Bush. The colors of the fire, ochre, vivid red and yellow contrast with the brown of the Virgin's gown. The Messiah sits delicately on her lap and greets the pilgrim with the sign of benediction. Moses, in the act of removing his sandals, stands to the left while St. Katherine, her head lowered in humble reverence, stands to the right.

The interior grounds of the monastery, spotted with cypress trees, fragrant jasmine juggling over walls, ceramic oversized planters with lemon tree plants, remind me of Greece. This could be Mt. Athos. Descending a series of steps on both sides of the central church, the thick wooden carved doors stand ajar. Father Nektarios, one of two monks that stand as security in the central church making sure visitors do not touch the exquisite 6th century icons or use flash photography, tells me the Emperor Justinian commissioned craftsmen to carve them from two cedars of Lebanon that he had specially shipped here. "Everything you see in this church," he explains, "comes from somewhere else. There are no materials in the desert, no wood, just granite and rocks." The walls of the church are adorned with precious examples of Byzantine iconography. This is one of the finest collections of iconography the world will witness.

Father and I embark on a theo-philosophical discussion about iconography and capturing reality. "It is very clear to see from the object of creation the way this particular human being or this procession of human beings imagined a face which evidently wanders from a realistic rendering," he explains. "In an icon, light comes from within. It breaks with reality because what you perceive as reality can only go so far. The 'realism' the Europeans talk about is a myth. It is only a partial perspective. The icon attempts to take away the *chondroidi superfice* which obstructs our

1. https://www.mountsinaimonastery.org/holy-summit

ability to see from the inside. There is a subtraction of the external details so that the essence, the truth of the image, can be revealed.

There are dusty perimeters on the walls of the church where icons have been removed for shipment, conservation, or safe keeping. I ask Father Nektarios' opinion, what is his favorite piece. He points to the tholos over the altar of the church. It is a mosaic from the 11th century of Christ in the Transfiguration. The Emperor Justinian was responsible for that one as well. It is unique first because it is a mosaic, second because of its depiction of the Transfiguration as opposed to the Virgin and Child in glory, and third, because its placement on a curved dome surface of a wall makes its very existence ethereal. "Do you know what the Apostles saw when they gazed on Christ during the Transfiguration?" he asks me. "Bright white light," I answer. "A glow." "Yes," he corrects me, "but behind that light they saw the ancient 'kalos.' They saw an icon of how God had formed our body. They saw the body as it had been created in full glory, not in its corrupted form as it appears now, the body which is subject to pain, hunger, sickness, death. This is not the body God had originally fashioned for man, but a consequence of the Fall which alienated the body from its former glory. An icon is a way of revisiting the untarnished image of man, of returning to the garden.

He shows me two marble carved sarcophaguses dating from the 1st century, curiously unique because of the images of the shepherd with grapevines, early Christian semiotics. The narthex of the church originally was not elevated from the nave as it is now. Father Nektarios gives a sweeping description of the treasures in the church: two oversized coffins made of silver, a gift from the tzars of Russia, a Psalter in gilded cover studded with jewels, mosaics around the perimeter of the church dating back to St. Helen's craftsmen. Twelve Corinthian-topped columns made of granite commemorate the twelve apostles, the pillars of the early church. Each column bears an antique icon of the apostle and the name of the month of the year with images of three categories of saints–those recognized in the Bible, those by Church tradition, and those known locally. The dry heat of the desert has preserved these treasures for millennia. "Please, do not touch the icons," Father the everlasting watchdog yells to the back of the church at some tourists with curiously wandering children. The heat does more than just preserve the icons. Father tells me how the early Desert Fathers would search for caves to live in ascetic isolation but would find other monastics who had died kneeling or standing up in prayer. The living monks could not move the dead monks who were left to pray for eternity

Without warning, he leads me to a chamber beyond that reveals another small chapel, an iconostasis with two golden candleholders. Before I know it, he is telling me to take off my sandals; he draws back heavy red velvet drapes, and we enter a hidden chamber. Its marble floors are covered by red flokati rugs. Here it is, the site of the Burning Bush. I am taken completely off-guard. I bow in front of the sacred space; it is a room perhaps 22′ x 16′. The site of the Burning Bush is commemorated by a marble half-moon on the ground with a chasm that leads deep into the earth. Here is where Moses heard the voice of God; here is where he was handed the Law; here is where he received his calling to lead his people to the promised land. I prostrate fully with my forehead smashed against the *flokati* rug. It is not what I had expected. I do not know what I expected. It seems too humble a site to be where God revealed His presence. Father explains the second holy site of the Burning Bush is at the pinnacle of Mt. Sinai where there is a church. Pilgrims start the journey up the mountain at 2 a.m. and walk up for 2 and a half hours to reach the top in time for the sunrise.

I thank Father Nektarios with his sharp, dry wit and go outside. Flocks of tourists surround an overgrown bush that grows from within a chasm in the ground. It is a remnant of the original Burning Bush supposedly. It scrambles over the wall and the plot of ground the monks have created for it. Its trunk is surrounded by a metal grate through which pilgrims push pieces of paper scribbled with prayers and the names of loved ones. There is a stray photo of a child, a young man or woman, or even a middle-aged man around the base of the bush. The noonday sun is so bright and scorching I can see the veins of each waxy leaf of the bush and even the crumbs within the cracks of the earthly-clay wall. Tourist guides profess the wonders of the Bush to tourists absorbed by their telling in English, French, German, Spanish, Arabic. Even if it is not in flames, it is a miracle enough that such an overpowering bush is growing in such a dry desert.

I need to meet with the Igoumen of the monastery, Father Damianos, for a blessing and for some answers. I saunter back to the pilgrims' hotel, a recent addition to the monastery grounds, having been built just 30 years ago to meet the demands of the constantly appearing faithful. The rooms, although sparse, are clean and tidy. Individualized water heaters grace each white marbled bathroom. There is centralized heating, and a mahogany closet filled neatly with hand-woven woolen blankets by the women in the village to counter the cold desert nights when temperatures drop to less than 40 degrees Fahrenheit. Musa , the manager of the hotel, tells me that currently on any given day the monastery averages 1,000 to 1,500 visitors. Most come here as a day trip from Sharm El Sheik or Cairo. However, before the turbulence it was customary to have over 3,000 people visit the monastery on any one day. The monastery employs 90 full-time workers mostly as porters, kitchen staff, cleaners, who live in the town of St. Katherine's. Most are Bedouins from the Jebeliya tribe. "The Bedouins love St. Katherine's," Musa explains, "They have grown up together for over a thousand years." He himself is half-Greek: his father was a merchant from Thessaloniki and half-Egyptian, his mother was an Arab from Cairo.

By grace, I couldn't have met with the Igoumen of the monastery more easily than had I made an appointment with him. There on one of the sofas of the reception hall of the Pilgrims hotel was a benevolent-looking, hearty gentleman with thin grey hair tied back in a bun. His ruby-studded oversized Crucifix protruded conspicuously from the bulge in his belly. Throughout our conversation, a busy line of Arab Christians from Cairo would approach him and ask for his blessing. He had by now become a master at kissing and crossing all sizes and levels of pilgrims.

"There is nothing better than faith to a human being," he tells me in Greek, "Faith proceeds from the respect of love." He is a wise man, of course, and deeply spiritual so he tells me things such as , "Everything is Christ" and "Repentance is necessary every moment." He also tells me about the long-standing relationship between Christians and Muslims at St. Katherine's. Although he warns against the times we find ourselves, it is very important to keep close "our own" without diluting them with other faiths, but we cannot not say "Kalimera" to our neighbors even if they are of a different faith. Many Muslims, Father Damianos remembers, have had their health restored by praying to St. Katherine. Many Muslims pray at the monastery as they acknowledge the saving power of our saints. Muslims and Christians have co-inhabited at Sinai for thousands of years, he says. Even though the concept of the Holy Trinity is hard for a Muslim to understand, there have been some conversions, not many as it is a crime punishable by death to convert to Christianity from Islam. During the time of the Desert Fathers in the 1st century, when St. Katherine's was founded, many Christian Arabs were at the vanguard of asceticism and monasticism. He lists St. Anthony the Great, St. John the Damascene, St. George of Damascus, St. Paranius, St. Macarius, St. Cyprian of Carthage. But the one true faith is Orthodoxy.

"Go talk to Father Justinian," he directed me. "He's an American convert. He works in the library."

I walked around the horseshoe shaped monastic cell quarters, climbed to the second story, wound my way around the wooden balcony, and walked into the manuscript library, the world's second most important after the Vatican for sacred manuscripts, especially in the Greek. A tall lanky monk, soft-spoken but exuding with scholarly erudition, greeted me at the door. He is in the middle of overseeing a digital reproduction project. Each and every one of the library's 3,300 manuscripts will be digitally copied, page by page, and made available to scholars and faithful via the virtual galaxy. This particular manuscript is a service to the Holy Archangels, a special request from Dochario monastery on Mount Athos, dedicated to the Holy Archangels. It is one of four important but unpublished manuscripts of the service dating from the 14th century. The monastery on Mt. Athos wants a copy to make a service book. The methods of duplication might have changed but the fundamental job of copiously copying sacred texts has not for over 19 centuries. Father Justinos' assistant is a young Bedouin with a stubby beard and glasses; he is also a computer scientist. Hamid Sobhy is the first university graduate of the entire Jebeliya tribe, considered the oldest tribe in the South Sinai area whose ancestors were the guards stationed there by Emperor Justinian in the 6th century.

The manuscript to the Holy Archangels is held in a cradle of canvas under the eye of a big dig camera. Each page is turned gingerly for a digishot. The entire apparatus is behind a glass enclosure.

Father Justinos leads me into the inner confines of the library. Two digital experts from Greece, funded by a large grant from the Flora Family Foundation, are busy transferring jpeg files to a virtual manuscript library on a server. The library is small, too small, for one to understand the significance of its holdings. Wooden bookcases wedge themselves in "L" formations. A second story balcony harvests another layer of manuscripts. Hippocrates' "*Medicus Appendicus*" in gilded letters is sandwiched between slowly unraveling leather spines of *The Iliad*. In order of volume, the manuscripts are written in ancient Greek, Arabic, Syriac, Georgian, and early Russian Slavonic. There is an ocean of information here, no one librarian monk can sort through it all. Father

Justinos relies on scholar-researchers to shift through the collection and uncover nuggets. "Two weeks ago," Father recounts, "a visiting scholar let me know we had the oldest Gospel printed in Arabic dating from 846 AD." Apart from manuscripts, the library holds codexes and incunabula (books printed up to 1500).

The monastery has a close connection with Crete, he explains. St. Katherine's shares a metochion in Crete. Crete was under Venetian domination in the Renaissance, and the first Greek printer was located in Venice in 1472, it was very easy to transfer books from Crete to Sinai. As a result, the library after the church, became the spiritual center for the monastery as it contained spiritual writings, homilies, scriptures, scriptural commentaries, saints' lives, and the like.

"Can you show me a secret treasure, Father?" I ask him. He walks over to a metal office filing cabinet and pulls out a heavy bulky golden-carved Gospel. He places it lovingly on a wooden table whose legs end in a lion's claw and says, "Look" (like Gandolf revealing a secret passage in the mountain side). I catch my breath. On the first page after turning over the membrane of tissue as protection–Christ the Pantocrator standing in robes of royal purple, a golden halo framed in an intricate brocade of sinuous inks, stands with the Book of Life in one hand, his other in the gesture of blessing. It is not a Gospel, but a Lectionary, a collection of the Scripture readings for the church year. This one is one of the three or four that still survive in the world, a work of the Imperial Scriptoria of Constantinople. It includes seven stunning illuminations and each and every page is written in gold letters. It is magnificent! A masterpiece of the Macedonian Renaissance which was the classicizing of the art of Constantinople that flourished at the end of Iconoclasm.

Father is writing the introductory essay for the catalogue of the first ever exhibit dedicated exclusively to the iconography and manuscripts of St. Katherine's monastery at Mt. Sinai. The exhibit will open at the Getty Museum in Los Angeles this coming November 4th. Certain other manuscripts will be featured in the Smithsonian Institute's exhibit, "In the Beginning: Bibles Before the Year 1000" starting from October 17th ending January 7th.[2]

"The daily cycle of the way of life in the monastery," Father Justinos reminds me, "has been preserved for 19 centuries. We can take a 10th

2. This essay is a reprint of an article that dates to January 2007. The Getty Museum featured "Holy Image: Hallowed Ground, Icons from Sinai" November 14, 2006 - March 4, 2007

century lectionary from the manuscript library, take it down to the service, and follow it word for word. It's an astonishing continuity. As much as the outside of the monastery has changed, the inside has preserved the traditions of early Christendom."

From Justinian's time, the monastery has remained a still point in the turning world, especially the turbulently gyrating world of the Middle East. The waves of change have pounded through its valley–the Mohamedian caravans, the Persian invasions, the charge of the Crusaders, the galloping of Marmulkes, Ottomans, Germans. However, its remoteness and the gruesome trek it took to arrive to it have provided it with sanctuary from the shifting sands of time. It would have taken a pilgrim ten whole days to come from Suez on camel back with a driver, and even then he/she would have to face the austerity of the desert, wild animals, marauding Bedouin thieves and robbers before arrival. It was inaccessible to pilgrims up to 50 years ago; motorized transport only started in the 1970s. As a result, its remoteness imbues it with a holy air. St. Katherine's has remained an oasis of unchange, a still point in a turbulent world due to its inexorable isolation. Even today with a car, the ruggedness of the desert, the emptiness of the mountains wells a soul with piety and awe, all-consuming awe of the place. As Father Nektarios notes, "This here that you see is so great that your mind cannot grasp it, cannot fit around it. It is so big of a miracle that we cannot understand what it is."

The Church and Convent of St. Lazarus, Bethany

Procession on St Lazarus Saturday in Bethany, West Bank, Palestine

St. Lazarus Church and convent in Bethany has only five sisters, including the Igoumena Efraxia. On Sunday, Father Ioachim from the Ascension Church in Gethsemane serves liturgy to a total of six or seven people. "We used to be ten sisters in total, but now we have dwindled to five," Sister Mitrodona says as she greets me and a small group of Cypriot pilgrims who have come to pay their respects to the patron saint of Cyprus, St. Lazarus. "One sister is 96, how long will we last? We are over 70, I am 60," she confesses, "Sister Makaria is 70. What are we going to do? We need at least two more sisters to call ourselves a community." The Church lies in the Dead Zone, the area occupied by Israel, ten minutes outside of Jerusalem. It is here under an icon of Christ resurrecting Lazarus that a stone dating from the 5th century purports to be the one Jesus sat on outside Bethany when Martha spotted him and ran to give him her complaint. He had come too late; Lazarus was dead already three days in the grave and his body had started to stink. The town once only 10 minutes from Jerusalem has seen a dramatic drop in tourists as a result of the Wall constructed by the Israeli government to enhance security. It takes twice the time to come from, an arduous ordeal that entails backtracking on a circuitous path around Jerusalem, passing through a checkpoint. And that is if one has the proper pass to enter into the town.

The original church was founded by St. Helena in the first century but was destroyed and fell into disuse. It was not till 1879 that a new church was constructed over the original foundation. Father Theodosios, Igoumena Efraxia, and two sisters, including the 96-year-old one Sister Agathoniki still living in the convent[1], started the convent in the 1960s. "Even up to twenty years ago, this was all a desert. All that existed was a solitary police station," recounts Sister Makaria, hailing from a small village outside of Limassol. The Church has a distinctly Cypriot flavor, as Cyprus shares a unique bond to St. Lazarus, who after fleeing persecution in the Holy Land settled in Cyprus and became Bishop in Larnaca.

The community suffers from several problems. The most serious is the decrease in the number of Christians living in the town and attending church. "In the old times, we would have eighty Christian children attending liturgy," remembers the Igoumena. "There were 12 or 13 nuns, very austere, that took care of the grounds. It was beautiful." Currently, only two families come to church on Sundays now and then. Bethany is now a predominantly Muslim town with perhaps two or three Christian Arab families.

Additionally there are occasional skirmishes with the Muslim and Israeli factions. "There are over 50,000 Israeli settlers who took our monastery of St. Martirios and they made it into an archeological site," she says. "Now we have to pay to get into what was once our property." The Israeli settlers have not been the only threat. Two weeks ago thieves from the town broke into one of the side windows of the church and stole the cash from candle offerings and silver religious articles. "They took everything, but they are just thieves," Sister Mitrodona continues, "Palestinians are good neighbors. We have good relations with our Muslim neighbors."

1. Since writing this article, Sister Agathoniki fell asleep in the Lord.

The convent has experienced other incidents where thieves cut off electrical and telephone lines to break in undetected at night when the convent is the most vulnerable. The most serious event occurred in 1983 when an Israeli terrorist organization, Terror Against Terror, dropped a bomb the type used by the Israeli military wrapped in a carpet in the garden of the convent. The Igoumena accidentally nudged it and it exploded sending shrapnel into her legs from which she had to undergo numerous surgeries. The same group set off a similar bomb at the Bethany Mosque seriously injuring the 26-year-old Imam. Since then, however, the town and the Church have managed to exist in relative calm and tranquility.

"When the bells of St. Lazarus ring," Sister Makaria recounts, "they can be heard all the way to Jerusalem. When the bells did not ring for one month, the neighbors who had been hearing their peals since they were children started asking questions, "What's wrong? Why aren't the bells ringing?"

To the group of rapt young Cypriot pilgrims, Sister Mitrodona warns, "Be careful, my children. Here in the Holy Land, Satan does not walk on the ground as he does in other places. In every other place on earth, Satan walks the earth and wreaks havoc with temptations and scandals. But here in the Holy Land because Jesus walked on the ground, he is burned. Instead he sits on our shoulders, and for the priests he perches on the top of their heads."

The Tomb of Lazarus proper lies in Muslim hands on the grounds of the central Bethany Mosque halfway to the top of a steep hill. Judging from the steep and slippery steps a pilgrim has to descend to get to it; Lazarus had to do a lot of climbing when he heard his name. During Jesus' time, the tomb and the house of Martha and Mary a few feet next to it over which a Catholic Church has been built, were the same level. The tomb carved from rock is at least 10 feet deep. Pilgrims have graffitied the walls of stone, sweating from the accumulated humidity at such depths, in white and black markers to commemorate their passing through. "Jose Ramos, Republica Dominicana, 03/96" or "Ebenezer Tours, Dallas, TX." Scraps of shriveled papers list the names of "The Living" and "The Dead" in shaky letters of Greek, English, Arabic, Russian. The papers are stuffed in the crevices at the rounded corners of the tomb.

To end their visit, Sister Makaria offers visitors homemade *chalepi*, a tapioca pudding, chilled to combat the dry, hot Palestinian summer. She drowns the gooey white masses of chalepi in a dark burgundy syrup made of sour cherries or *bysino*. Even with only five sisters and even less

Christians than before, Sister Mitrodona does not despair. "At the end of times when we will not have priests to commune us, the Lord will send an angel to give us Holy Communion." The Igoumaena echoes her sentiments, "The Palestinians will leave first before we do."

St Chariton en Farah

The cave church of St Chariton's en Farah in Judean Desert, Israel

St. Chariton's Monastery is located inside the natural park and reserve of En Peralt (Farah in Arabic) in the heart of the expansive Judean desert. It was built in the 4th Century by a mild mannered monk, one of the earliest Desert Fathers, in face one of the first monasteries in the desert. As the story goes, St. Chariton was on his way to the Judean Desert to pray in order to establish a coenobium and monastery. He was assaulted and kidnapped by a band of thieves on the way. They gagged him and tied him up and took him to their desert hideout. They were going to kill him, but were called away to another big heist. In their absence, the holy man prayed for their souls and his. It so happened that a viper, a black one with a green understripe on its belly, one of the current poisonous species of desert snake native to the region, entered into the vat where they kept their wine. Upon their return and full of thirst, they fell to drinking the wine without hesitation. The monk being gagged made motions to them to be careful that the wine might be dangerous to drink to no avail. It was the will of God that in the morning, following Father Chariton's night of vigil, the entire band of thieves slept dead never to rob again. Attributing this to God's providence, Father Chariton buried the dead men and in the process uncovered the cave where they kept their loot. With this money, he proceeded to build the monastery. He had so much left over that he erected several hospitals, senior citizen centers, and orphanages in the city of Jerusalem.[1]

The monastery lies 800 feet above a ravine resplendent with wild tulips, purple heather, majestic pines, and overbearing sweet eucalyptus trees. Two or three natural springs gush through the cracks of the mountains of rock to supply the area with cool sparkling waters and serenely break the silence of the place with its soothing gurgling down the steep ravine. Black desert birds squawk like parrots as they zigzag their way into the crevices in the boulders high above where they tend their nests. In the early morning and early evening, mountain gazelles shy but sure of themselves scale the rockface to drink by the spring pools. Hyraxes, those strange little varmints with furry spiky bodies and long teeth, even stranger considering they are in the same family as the elephants, scurry under the shadows of rock. The mountains of the Judean desert are dry rock. They roll gently over the landscape; the winds have carved narrow terraces into their sides sloping in sinuous trails around their circumference. It is a place of awesome beauty.

It is hard enough to climb in the scorching sun and heat up to the top of the rock that leads into the cave which served as Saint Chariton's cell. A mild-mannered monk, thin with piercing blue eyes, a pilgrim from Munich serves as the interpreter for the stouter Russian monk also named Father Chariton. "Attention here," he says as he leads me up the iron ladder bolted into the sides of the rock mountain, completely straight up for 25 to 30 feet. How did these monks manage to climb to their cave cells back in the day where there were no ladders, at least not iron ones? "It is very slippery when the rain comes," he says. I am out of breath after the first flight of "stairs," terraced footholds carved from

1. "VENERABLE CHARITON THE CONFESSOR THE ABBOT OF PALESTINE" https://pravoslavie.ru/97728.html

the jutting rocks. "Go slowly. We must pause more and more," the monk stops on a landing. "This is the first lesson I learn in the desert. You must to go slowly." This is perhaps the first law of the desert: Go slowly so that you might go quickly. There is no rushing time, wind, or God here.

As I hold my hand to my chest to catch my breath another mountain of rock serves as the view directly in front of us. It is crème golden with a few patches of thistle bush spotted with the dark spots of caves throughout its surface. "In the 4th century there were thousands of monks here," the monk explains. Back in the 4th century, this was the place to come if you wanted to become a monk, to become closer to God, to live ascetically, reclusively, to listen to the wise counsel of "Geronta Chariton," the spiritual center of the monastery that also housed a school and library of ancient sacred texts.

Father Chariton was the first to build a coenobium in the desert. In fact, he started three *lavras*, two in the desert and the one that is now at the top of Temptation Mountain in Jericho, the place where Satan tempted the Lord after He had fasted for 40 days and nights. Apparently Saint Chariton loved high, daredevil places, mountains high over valleys and unexplored caves, because all three of his monasteries have these same features. After the death of their beloved spiritual father, the monks of the three monasteries bickered about the proper burial place for him. After meeting in a synod, they decided the first where he was called and served would be his last, and so conjoined the three monastic communities into the one here.

Out of the thousand or so monks who chose to live the ascetic life in the hills of the Judean Desert, 700 followed in the example of their spiritual father and did not have their bodies rot after death. This is a sign of sainthood, if not heavenly grace. "Where are their bodies or the texts they left behind?" I ask. In 641 the Persians invaded and slaughtered all the monks who had continued the ascetic tradition; they burned their sacred manuscripts, they toppled the church and looted it of any valuable objects. Then the Crusaders arrived in the following century to take any of the bodies, including Saint Chariton's, and transport them to Rome and scatter them into little pieces of relics throughout the European continent. All that remains of Saint Chariton now is a fragment of a piece of his relics, framed in a round golden glass bubble embedded in the central icon of the cave church dedicated to his memory.

The monastery fell into disuse for a long while afterwards until at the beginning of the 20th century, 15 monks from Mt. Athos came to the Holy Land, discovered the desert monastery, purchased the land and tried to revive the monastic tradition by settling on it. As one by one each succumbed to his death, the monastery remained without a master until the establishment of the state of Israel in 1948 when it was purchased by the Russian Church Outside of Russia and where today a single, solitary monk bearing the name of its founder treats pilgrims to cool water, homemade iced tea, and different types of chocolate bonbons wrapped in different kinds of shiny red, green, and silver papers while recounting the history of the monastery. A cistern and water pump connected to ground water keeps the place alive with verdant plants, a vegetable garden and a collection of multi-colored flowering pots. Canaries in delicate wooden cages hang from the beams of the covered thatched roof underneath which lie long refractory tables with even longer benches. A female German shepherd, the hostess of the monastery, sleeps lazily under one unless a pilgrim haplessly drops a morsel of the cookies or chocolates brought out by the monk. A band of striped gray cats circulate under the tables and along the rocky ledges. The place breathes "Welcome" without a word. In such an unwelcome, harsh place, the welcome of hospitality is a relief as is the shade of the grape vine in the sweltering heat.

The mount up the steep iron ladder is dizzying. One slip and a body falls heavy onto uncushioned rock beds. How did the monks do this way back in the 4th century I wonder. How did they get their bread? Emerging from the ladder, we reach another rocky landing. Iron doors with bolts hide the entrance to three caves. "This is my cell," the pilgrim monk says pointing to one of them. The view from here is spectacular. It is so high I see the tops of the open wings of the squawking desert birds under me. There is a wooden door hiding the entrance into the central cave church, the cell of Saint Chariton. The gentle monk opens the door revealing lace-embroidered curtains and woolen red Persian rugs covering the floor of the cave this way and that. The roof of the cave is covered in black smoke, probably from the smoke of the candles and oil lamps burning for centuries during late night vigils. The cave is wide but it is short. A tall person must huddle or at least bow on his or her knees to fit. It is serene. You feel a wave of serenity and peace settle over you. Your soul, whatever murmurings it has, breathes silently. The stubby iconostasis has the four traditional icons, Christ and the Mother of God holding Christ to the left, Saint Chariton to the right. Four gold-filigree vigil oil lamps hang lovingly in between the spaces of the four icons. The monk lovingly snips the black mangled tops of their wicks with a short scissor expressly for this purpose. A "window," an open space overlooking the side of the opposite mountain, provides the only natural light. The walls of the cave-church are decorated with icons of this saint and that, some in the traditional Byzantine way, others in the neo-Classical Romanticized Russian way, the way that depicts the Virgin in pale white skin and turquoise blue eyes like a Russian tsarina.

I scribble the names of my relatives on two sheets of paper, one in red letters the other in black, signifying the living and the dead. They will be commemorated here I am sure more than other places of worship in the Holy Land. The monastery in En Peralt is not overrun with pilgrims and tourists as the other churches are in Jerusalem. It is hard to get to, not many know about it, and plus, there is an entrance fee one must pay to enter the nature reserve in order to come, perhaps the greatest deterrent to visitors. This way I know, the names of my relatives will have first dibs on the lips of the reclusive monks.

Architectural drawing of the cave of St Chariton, Ritmeyer Archaeological Design

In the center of the cave, on a wooden podium is the central icon of Saint Chariton, the one bearing the fragment of his relic. He is serene but austere, holding a book in his one hand, the other outstretched with the fore and middle fingers upright and the other three hugged together, a traditional gesture of benediction in the Orthodox tradition. Cyrillic inscriptions fill the empty spaces of the icon. "Love God above all else so that you will receive His glory," the Russian monk translates.

The Persian and Crusader invasions left nothing of the sayings of this holy man save for this short but simple edict. St. Chariton placed the love of God above everything else. Loving God, the first and eternal commandment, becomes the penumbra under which all the rest of the laws of God and moral conduct follow. This should be our soul's first priority. This is the purpose of our earthly journey—to become places of hospitality in a brutal unrelenting environment. For our earthly bodies to become pillars of heavenly grace so that the corruption of death will not eat them. For our deserts to become oases of love and verdant splendor—all in the love of God. So that our natural tendencies for anger, revenge, ill-will, greed, lust for power and for flesh be changed. So that instead of wanting our murderers dead, we would petition for their salvation. So that what we gain illegally we could offer as tokens of charity. All through the love of God.

Isn't this just how the spirit of God works? I meditate. He forces the soul to drive down deep into its depths and emerge with water. In a place of utter desolation, to batter the soul to wrench out of it life, and not just life but a life of beauty and serenity, order and goodness. In the secret place of my heart, I utter a prayer, "Lord, I am a desert, a lifeless, barren, dry nothingness on the surface. Help me to struggle, to struggle with the demons in me. Give me your grace, give me the spirit to love you and to pray to you."

By giving full reign to the God-force in us, we will be led to a place of cool waters. A desert will be transformed into a life-giving sanctuary. But how deep we must drive ourselves to unearth the love that must be born from way beneath our depths. How deep we must dig to find the love that must be there in order for us to be transformed into the beings of beauty we must become in the name of God and through His love. If I could have just a crumb or a crumbling of that crumb of love for God that Saint Chariton did, I would be transformed. Love is the most transformational force in the universe. More than the harsh abrasive winds that relentlessly carve lines into the sides of soldering rock; more than the gushing waters that erode and crack solid ground into pebbles, rubble, and then sands. Love is what can turn a marauder into a saint. I think of the love I do not have that keeps me a dry dry barren place. How deep I must dig to find the place of living waters that can gush forth and show forth the beauty of a once unwelcome place.

Bibliography

Alfeyev, Hilarion. *St Symeon the New Theologian and Orthodox Tradition*. Oxford: Oxford University Press, 2000.

Archos, Irene. "Monkey Man vs. Christ: A Reconciliation of Science and Faith in One Woman's Coming of Age by Irene Archos." Orthodoxy in Dialogue, November 17, 2019. https://orthodoxyindialogue.com/2019/11/16/monkey-man-vs-christ-a-reconciliation-of-science-and-faith-in-one-womans-coming-of-age-by-irene-archos/.

Baggot , Jim . "The Cat that Wouldn't Die." Aeon. April 28, 2025. https://aeon.co/essays/no-schrodingers-cat-is-not-alive-and-dead-at-the-same-time.

Booth, Graham, dir. *GASP: One Strange Rock*, 2018. National Geographic. Prime Video.

Brunell, Laura, and Elinor Burkett. "Feminism." In *Encyclopaedia Britannica*. 2024. https://www.britannica.com/topic/feminism.

Cacciottolo, Mario. "Nick Yarris: 'How I Survived 22 Years on Death Row.'" BBC News, November 16, 2016. https://www.bbc.com/news/world-us-canada-37974904.

Capra, Frank, dir. *It's a Wonderful Life*. Edited by William Hornbeck. Los Angeles, CA: RKO Radio Pictures, 1946.

Carroll, Rory. "Haiti: Mud Cakes Become Staple Diet as Cost of Food Soars Beyond a Family's Reach." *The Guardian*, October 19, 2022. https://www.theguardian.com/world/2008/jul/29/food.internationalaidanddevelopment.

Catafygioyu, Eva Topping. *Saints and Sisterhood*. Minneapolis: Light And Life, 1990.

Chryssavgis, John. *In the Heart of the Desert*. Bloomington: World Wisdom, 2003.

———. *The Monk and the Demon: A Study of the Ladder of Saint John Climacus*. New York: Harper & Brothers, 1986.

Damascus, Saint John of. *An Exact Exposition of the Orthodox Faith*. N.p.: E-artnow, 2021.

De Saint-Exupéry, Antoine. *The Little Prince*. Ware, UK: Wordsworth Editions, 1995.

Double, Isabella, and Smith College. "Women and Their Roles in Early Christianity." https://sites.smith.edu/dies-legibiles/wp-content/uploads/sites/602/2022/05/DLVOLUME2-Women-and-their-Roles-in-Early-Christianity.docx.pdf.

Dunbar, William. Academy of American Poets. "Lament for the Makaris." Poets.org. https://poets.org/poem/lament-makaris.

Elder Paisios of Mount Athos. *With Pain and Love for Contemporary Man*. Monastery of St. John the Theologian, Vasilika, Thessaloniki: 1996.

"Excerpts from the Soul after Death." 2026. Orthodoxinfo.com. 2026. http://orthodoxinfo.com/death/excerpts_death.aspx.

Fortune Business Insights. "Pet Care Market Size, Share, Growth & Industry Trends [2028]." July 28, 2025. https://www.fortunebusinessinsights.com/pet-care-market-104749.

Frankl, Viktor E. *Man's Search for Meaning*. Boston: Beacon, 2006.

Freud, Sigmund, and W. J. H. Sprott. *New Introductory Lectures on Psycho-Analysis*. Mansfield Centre, Ct: Martino, 2013.

Friends of Mount Sinai Monastery. "Holy Summit." Accessed January 20, 2026. https://www.mountsinaimonastery.org/holy-summit.

Gavrilia, Gerontissa. *The Ascetic of Love*, Athens: Eptalofos, 1999.

Goussetis, Alex. "Considering Marital Separation & Divorce." Ancient Faith Ministries, podcast, December 14, 2022. https://www.ancientfaith.com/podcasts/familymatters/considering_marital_separation_divorce/.

Hansen, Bert. "Hennig Brandt and the Discovery of Phosphorus." ScienceHistory.Org. July 30, 2019. https://www.sciencehistory.org/stories/magazine/hennig-brandt-and-the-discovery-of-phosphorus/.

Henson, Jim, dir. *Labyrinth*. Edited by John Grover. Culver City, CA: TriStar Pictures, 1986.

Hoff, Benjamin. *Tao of Pooh*. New York: Dutton, 2019.

Holy Wisdom Orthodox Mission. "Three-Hundred Sayings of the Ascetics of the Orthodox Church," n.d. http://holywisdomorthodox.com/library/ascetics_sayings.html.

Hopkins, Gerard Manley. "God's Grandeur." Poetry Foundation, April 22, 2024. https://www.poetryfoundation.org/poems/44395/gods-grandeur.

International Labour Organization. "Global Estimates of Modern Slavery: Forced Labour and Forced Marriage." Geneva: International Labour Organization and Walk Free Foundation, 2017. https://webapps.ilo.org/wcmsp5/groups/public/---dgreports/---dcomm/documents/publication/wcms_575540.pdf.

Isaac the Syrian. *The Ascetical Homilies of Isaac the Syrian*. Translated by Dana Miller. Boston: Holy Transfiguration Monastery, 1984.

Ivereigh, Austen. "Architect Gaudi the Blessed." *Godspy Magazine*, 2026. https://oldarchive.godspy.com/culture/Architect-Gaudi-the-Blessed-by-Austen-Ivereigh.cfm.htm.

James George Frazer. *The Golden Bough*. New York: Simon and Schuster, 1995.

Julian of Norwich. *Revelations of Divine Love*. Garden City, NY: Dover, 1911.

Jung, C. G. *The Collected Works of C. G. Jung, Volume 9 (Part 1): Archetypes and the Collective Unconscious*. Princeton: Princeton University Press, 2014.

Kempis, Thomas à. *The Imitation of Christ*. Translated by Leo Sherley-Price. London: Penguin Classics, 1952.

King, Ursula. *Christian Mystics : Their Lives and Legacies throughout the Ages*. Mahwah, NJ: Hiddenspring, 2001.

———. *Christian Mystics: The Spiritual Heart of the Christian Tradition*. New York: Simon & Schuster Editions, 1998.

Kitsantonis, Niki. "Greek Orthodox Church Faces Criticism as Virus Hits Its Ranks." *The New York Times*, December 5, 2020. https://www.nytimes.com/2020/12/05/world/greece-orthodox-church-coronavirus.html.

Lewis, C. S., and Walter Hooper. *Christian Reflections*. Grand Rapids: William B. Eerdmans, 2014.

Malaty, Tadros Yacoub. "Desert Fathers on Fasting." St Shenouda Monastery (website), March 10, 2022. https://stshenoudamonastery.org.au/desert-fathers-on-fasting/.

Mccaughrean, Geraldine, and David Parkins. *The Epic of Gilgamesh*. Grand Rapids: Eerdmans Books For Young Readers, 2003.

McEvoy, Sean. *William Shakespeare's Hamlet: A Routledge Study Guide and Sourcebook*. London: Taylor & Francis, 2023.

Montgomery, R A, Laurence Peguy, Sittisan Sundaravej, V Pornkerd, S Yaweera, J Donploypetch, T Kornmaneeroj, et al. *Choose Your Own Adventure*. Waitsfield, VT: Chooseco, 2006.

National Domestic Violence Hotline. "Domestic Violence Statistics." 2025. https://www.thehotline.org/stakeholders/domestic-violence-statistics/.

Nietzsche, Friedrich. *Thus Spoke Zarathustra*. N.p.: Lulu Press, 2013.

Palamas, Gregory, and John Meyendorff. 1983. *The Triads*. New York: Paulist Press.

Patristic Nectar. "The Mother of God Destroys Secularism and Feminism." YouTube, August 14, 2020. https://www.youtube.com/watch?v=J7X1TwsaIN8.

Perimeter Institute for Theoretical Physics. "Superposition Explained (Schrödinger's Cat)." 2023. https://www.youtube.com/watch?v=IHDMJqJHCQg

PetExec. "Pet Industry Trends: Pet Spending Statistics in 2024." August 12, 2024. https://www.petexec.net/resources/marketing/pet-spending-statistics.

Pravoslavie.ru. "Venerable Chariton the Confessor the Abbot of Palestine." May 10, 2010. https://pravoslavie.ru/97728.html

Quotefancy. "Top 40 Don Herold Quotes (2026 Update)." https://quotefancy.com/don-herold-quotes.

Ramis, Harold, dir. *Groundhog Day*. Edited by Pembroke J. Herring. Culver City, CA: Columbia Pictures, 1993.

Rohr, Richard. *Everything Belongs: The Gift of Contemplative Prayer*. New York: The Crossroad Publishing Company, 2014.

Rose, Fr. Seraphim. *The Soul after Death*. Platina, CA: St. Herman Press, 1982.

Shakespeare, William. "Hamlet - Act 2, Scene 2." Folger Shakespeare Library. https://www.folger.edu/explore/shakespeares-works/hamlet/read/2/2/.

Spielberg, Steven, dir. *Indiana Jones and the Raiders of the Lost Ark*. Edited by Michael Kahn. Los Angeles, CA: Paramount Pictures, 1981.

St. Augustine of Hippo. "*Confessions* 1, 1.5." www.vatican.va. https://www.vatican.va/spirit/documents/spirit_20020821_agostino_en.html

Saint Paisios the Athonite, *Spiritual Counsels*. Vasilika: Thessaloniki: Holy Hesychasterion of the Evangelist John the Theologian, 2018.

Steindl-Rast, David. *Gratefulness, the Heart of Prayer: An Approach to Life in Fullness*. New Jersey: Paulist Press, 1984.

St. John the Baptist Greek Orthodox Church. *Weekly Bulletin*. New York: St. John the Baptist Greek Orthodox Church, 2019.

Stuart, R. "Entheogenic Sects and Psychedelic Religions." Maps.org, 2025. https://maps.org/news-letters/v12n1/12117stu.html.

Tadej, Otac, and Herman Of. *Our Thoughts Determine Our Lives : The Life and Teachings of Elder Thaddeus of Vitovnica*. Platina, CA: Saint Herman Of Alaska Brotherhood, 2009.

"Timor Mortis Conturbat Me." In *The Norton Anthology of English Literature*, 10th ed., edited by Stephen Greenblatt. New York: W. W. Norton, 2018. 1234.

United Nations. “One Woman Killed Every 10 Minutes: The Harrowing Global Reality of Femicide.” UN News, November 25, 2024. https://news.un.org/en/story/2024/11/1157386.

U.S. Customs and Border Protection. “Human Trafficking.” Cbp.gov, April 3, 2024. https://www.cbp.gov/border-security/human-trafficking.

Waddell, Helen. *The Desert Fathers : Translations from the Latin.* Ann Arbor: University of Michigan, 1981.

Ward, Benedicta. *The Sayings of the Desert Fathers: The Alphabetical Collection.* 1975.

Williamson, Marianne. *A Return to Love:Reflections on the Principles of A Course in Miracles.* 1. ed., 9. Print. New York: HarperCollins, 1993.

Wolters, Clifton (ed.) *The Cloud of Unknowing and Other Works: by an English Mystic of the 14th Century.* New York: Penguin Classics, 1978.

World Health Organization. “Child Maltreatment.” November 5, 2024. https://www.who.int/news-room/fact-sheets/detail/child-maltreatment.

Zukav, Gary. *The Dancing Wu Li Masters : An Overview of the New Physics.* New York: Harperone, 2009.